a beginner's guide to short-term trading

a beginner's guide to short-term trading

TONI TURNER

Adams Media Corporation
Avon, Massachusetts

Published by
Adams Media, an F+W Publications Company
57 Littlefield Street, Avon, MA 02322. U.S.A.
www.adamsmedia.com

ISBN: 1-58062-570-3

Printed in Canada.

J I H G F

Library of Congress Cataloging-in-Publication Data
Turner, Toni.
A beginner's guide to short-term trading / by Toni Turner.
p.   cm.
Includes index.
ISBN 1-58062-570-3
1. Speculation. 2. Stocks--Charts, diagrams, etc.
3. Stock price forecasting. 4. Investment analysis. I. Title.
HG6041 .T87   2001
332.63'228--dc21   2001046345

This publication is designed to provide accurate and authoritative information with regard to the sub-ject matter covered. It is sold with the understanding that the publisher is not engaged in rendering legal, accounting, or other professional advice. If legal advice or other expert assistance is required, the services of a competent professional person should be sought.
  —From a *Declaration of Principles* jointly adopted by a Committee of the American Bar
Association and a Committee of Publishers and Associations

RealTick® is a registered trademark of Townsend Analytics, Ltd. ©1986–2002. All rights reserved. Any unauthorized reproduction, alteration, or use of RealTick is strictly prohibited. Authorized use of RealTick does not constitute an endorsement by Townsend Analytics of this book. Townsend Analytics does not guarantee the accuracy of or warrant any representations made in this book.

Many of the designations used by manufacturers and sellers to distinguish their products are claimed as trademarks. Where those designations appear in this book and Adams Media was aware of a trade-mark claim, the designations have been printed in initial capital letters.

This book is available at quantity discounts for bulk purchases.
For information, call 1-800-872-5627.

I dedicate this book to my students, worldwide. You have become my teachers and my friends. Thank you for your unending gifts of support and encouragement, laughter, and inspiration!

Contents

ACKNOWLEDGMENTS . . . . **xi**

FOREWORD BY STEVE NISON . . . . **xiii**

INTRODUCTION . . . . **xv**

America's Love Affair; How the Romance Began; The Internet Played Cupid; Enter the Day Traders; My Relationship with the Stock Market; Why I Wrote This Book; Strategy Overview; What You'll Need to Succeed; Short-Term Trading: The Good News; The Flip Side; The Journey . . . ; It's Showtime!

CHAPTER 1—WALL STREET:
THE GREATEST GAME ON EARTH **1**

Where It All Started; Out of Chaos Comes Order: The Crash of 1929; The Crash of 1987: More Chaos and the Resulting Order; The New York Stock Exchange: How It Works; The Nasdaq Stock Market: How It Works; The American Stock Exchange LLC: How It Works; Let's Dissect the Indexes; Wall Street as "The Animal House": The Bulls and the Bears, the Sheep and the Hogs; Two Emotions That Rule the Markets (and Most of the Rest of the World); Supply and Demand; Check Your Understanding; What Is "Center Point"?; Center Point: You . . . A Golden Buddha

CHAPTER 2—OFF TO A RUNNING START:
SETTING UP YOUR BUSINESS. **17**

Map Your Business Plan; What's Your Time Commitment? Your Most Important Commitment: Money; Quick Asset Allocation Plan; Selecting/Updating Your Office Equipment; Choosing a Broker; The Commission Maze; Slippage: What It Means; Margin Accounts: How They Work; You Gotta Have Goals; Check Your Understanding; Center Point: Commit: Transform Your Dreams into Goals

CHAPTER 3—MASTER A MONEY-MAKING MINDSET. 33

The Market as an Unstructured Entity; The Stock Market Is Always Right; Meet Your Emotions—Up Close and Personal; The Winning Mindset—Train Your Brain; The End Result: What It Looks Like; R & R: Don't Go Shopping Without It; Self-Respect and Deservability; Check Your Understanding; Center Point: Make Your Circle Bigger

CHAPTER 4—MARKET MACHINATIONS 101:
THE FUEL THAT SPARKS THE ENERGY. 45

The Buck Stops Here; Fundamental Analysis vs. Technical Analysis: The Tug O'War; Fundamental Analysis, Quick Yet Thorough Sources; IBD Proprietary Corporate Ratings; More Instant Info, CNBC, CNN, and Bloomberg; Wonderful Web Sites to Wander Through; Magazines; Check Your Understanding; Center Point: Invite Spontaneity into Your Life

CHAPTER 5—MARKET MACHINATIONS 102:
BASIC CHARTING TECHNIQUES THAT MAKE YOU MONEY. . . . 55

Cycles: The World's Operating System; Let's Draw the Curtain on Stage Analysis; Different Stages Call for Different Reactions; Additional Cycle Components; Support and Resistance, or Action and Reaction; Quiz; Center Point: Develop a Prosperity Mindset

CHAPTER 6—JUMP-START ON CHARTING BASICS 73

Charting Essentials: Line Charts and Bar Charts; Candlestick Charting Basics; Quiz; Center Point: Reach for Your Highest Potential

CHAPTER 7—CHARTING CLOSE-UPS:
THE PIECES OF THE PUZZLE 93

Anatomy of Your Friend: The Uptrend; Buy Signals: What to Look For; How to Draw an Uptrend Line; Trading in a Range, Congestion, and Consolidation; Anatomy of a Downtrend; Overview of Sell Signals: What to Look For; How to Draw a Downtrend Line; Quiz; Center Point: The Power of Synchronicity

CHAPTER 8—PUTTING THE PUZZLE TOGETHER 119

Volume: A Mega-Important Indicator; Moving Averages: What They Are, How to Use Them; Quiz; Center Point: Thoughts Are "Things"

CHAPTER 9—THE BELLS AND WHISTLES: HOW THEY CHIME AND TWEET 135

Oscillators: What They Are; The RSI, What It Is, How to Use It; Stochastic Oscillator: What It Is, How to Use It; The MACD: What It Is, How It Works; On-Balance Volume: What It Is, How to Read It; Bollinger Bands: What They Are, How to Read Them; Fibonacci Retracements: What They Are, How You Read Them; Gaps: A Trader's Black Hole; Quiz; Center Point: You Are Perfect Right Now!

CHAPTER 10—IT'S SHOWTIME! 157

Continuation and Reversal Patterns: What They Are; Reversal Patterns: What They Look Like; Let's Take It from the Top!; Big Picture Dynamics; Choose a Leading Stock in a Leading Industry, Check Out the Fundamentals; The Industry Group or Sector Shows Immediate Strength; Indicators: All Systems Are Go!; The Urge to Fudge; Get Ready to Pull the Trigger: The Buy Setup; Buy Trigger List; Quiz; Center Point: Awaken to Forgiveness

CHAPTER 11—WHERE THE RUBBER MEETS THE ROAD: MONEY-MANAGEMENT TECHNIQUES 183

Plan Your Trade and Trade Your Plan; Piece of the Pie; Risk/Reward Ratio: What It Means, How to Calculate It; Where to Place Your Stop-Loss Orders; Now That You've Got It, What Do You Do with It?; Intra-day Reversal Periods: What They Are, What They Mean to You; Market Orders, Limit Orders, and More; Quiz; Center Point: The Circle of Giving

CHAPTER 12—WINNING STRATEGIES FOR SELLING SHORT 199

Overcoming Mental and Emotional Roadblocks to Selling Short; Selling Short: The Rules; Here's the Process; What Makes Your Shorts Fall Down; Fundamentals: What to Look For; Chart Patterns and Setups: What to Look For; Shorting Indicators: Ugly Is Good!; How to Place Your Order; Shorting Strategy: The Overextended Stock; Shorting Strategy: The Overextended Double Top; Sell Short Trigger List; Shorting Tips: FAQs (Frequently Asked Questions); Quiz; Center Point: Banish Fear and Let Your Light Shine

CHAPTER 13—ANATOMY OF A TRADE **219**

Find an Industry Group or Sector to Target; The Preparation; The Journey; The Rest of the Story . . .; A Quick Look at Intra-day Charts; Center Point: Detachment Brings New Possibilities

CHAPTER 14—YOU, THE WIZARD OF ODDS **237**

Back up and Look at the Big Picture; The "If, Then" Mindset; Analyze the Broader Markets; Learn to Assess the Trading Environment; The Advance/Decline Line: Market Narrator in a Capsule; A "Heads Up" on Economic and Earnings Reports; Options Expiration Day—You're Outta' Here!; FOMC Reports; Mother Market's Contrarian Indicators; Stay Tuned to Changing Conditions; A Word about Losses; The Best Gift to Give Yourself: A Trading Journal; Level-II Trading: Is It for You?; Quiz; Center Point: Come Back to Center

GLOSSARY OF TRADING AND FINANCIAL TERMS **253**

RECOMMENDED READING **273**

INDEX **275**

Acknowledgments

If ever a book was created out of patience and love, this is the one!

I consider myself blessed to have been surrounded by so many people who gave of their encouragement and support while I wrote this manuscript. My thanks and gratitude to . . .

First and always, my daughter Adrienne, who is the light of my life and my best friend.

My agent, Deidre Knight, the best ally an author could have, along with being a business partner, friend, and mother of another beautiful soul, Tyler.

My editor, Gary Krebs, who helped shape and mold this book into final form, editorial assistant Elizabeth Gilbert, whose patience shall endear her to me forever, business editor Jill Alexander, and another patient soul, Copy Chief Laura MacLaughlin.

Harold Kornhaus, who offered constant support and lots of hugs.

Best friends Dan Gibby, David Kohn, and Vince Shorb, who gave wise advice, along with gentle, much-needed prods when I slowed down.

Mark Frauman, mentor and friend, as well as Mike McMahon, Cathy Vlad, Jennifer Perrier, Claud "OEX" Staples, and Chris Dover.

Dr. Dale Townsend of Tesserack, along with my wonderful friends, the "Hot Dogs," who motivated me and pushed me to the outside of my personal envelope.

My Internet group, who gather each day for "Toni on Trading." They have become like family.

Again, thank you all, and God bless!

Foreword

I had the pleasure of first meeting Toni when she introduced herself to me after I gave an online trading seminar. Toni told me how important candle charts are to her. Immediately, I knew she was intelligent, perceptive, generous, and with excellent taste. But then again, I might be biased.

All kidding aside, I have to be honest and say that when I first met her, I was outside of the public speaking circuit (all my seminars previously had only been for financial institutions). I did not recognize her name, nor know how popular she was.

Her name, though, did sound familiar for some reason. I soon realized why. I had purchased her online trading book, *A Beginner's Guide to Day Trading Online,* a few months previously. Toni flattered me by asking for a foreword to this book. I can think of no better testimonial than saying that before I knew who she was, I had gone to many bookstores to find just the right online trading book, and ultimately chose hers above all the others.

The reason I selected that book is the same reason I recommend this one: It has the perfect blend of the tools and psychological components needed to win your daily trading battles.

Toni has a sentence in this book: "I traveled a challenging road to learn this business, and now you can profit from my mistakes." This brings to mind a Japanese proverb, "If you wish to know the road, inquire of those who have traveled it." I can recommend no better guide than Toni to lead you down the road to successful online trading.

—STEVE NISON
PRESIDENT OF CANDLECHARTS.COM
AUTHOR OF *JAPANESE CANDLESTICK CHARTING TECHNIQUES* AND *BEYOND CANDLESTICKS*

Introduction

AMERICA'S LOVE AFFAIR

America's having a love affair with the stock market—a big, juicy love affair! Oh, to be sure, this affair has its ups and downs, and our emotions run the gamut from rosy to rocky, but it's a love affair, pure and simple!

And what a wild and fickle lover our temptress is. She's gentle and considerate one minute, then witchy and irritable the next. She's apt to treat good news like poison, and wave off bad news like no news at all. A mere word (read: inflation) sends her to the depths of despair, while the rumor of war may turn her giddy with delight. She's rude and bossy, genteel and loving. Her moods ricochet between selfish and generous, hostile and benign, pessimistic and euphoric.

Did she give you a present? Or take away more than you wanted to give? Your gratitude or groans are equally ignored. She laughs when you cry, and smirks at your happiness.

When at last you stalk off in anger, she waits for the right moment, then lures you back into her arms, whispering sweet promises you can't refuse.

HOW THE ROMANCE BEGAN

America's infatuation with the stock market started with the inception of the "great bull market" that has stretched over the last decade. During this time, stock market returns have exceeded most investments in alternative financial instruments, such as bonds and real estate.

Increased volatility, or price swings, are the order of the day. In the early to mid-1990s, if the Dow Jones Industrial Average fluctuated 100 points or more, we watched in amazement. Today, 100-point swings for this venerable index is the norm.

As we catapult into the twenty-first century, those who have learned how to capitalize on the market's volatile price swings are pocketing hefty profits. With some stocks rising multiple points a day, then plummeting as quickly, nimble players have learned to capitalize on both upward and downward movements by buying during the dips and selling during the rallies.

THE INTERNET PLAYED CUPID

The advent of the Internet contributed greatly to our infatuation with the stock market. Suddenly, we Americans were spending more time in front of our computer monitors than in front of our television sets.

The mighty Web transformed global communications, and in doing so, liberated us to think and act for ourselves with regard to our financial affairs. No longer did we have to rely on financial advisors to mail us an analyst's report about a company. All the financial data we could ever hope to digest lay right at our fingertips. Stock research reports, detailing news, fundamentals, institutional holdings, and proprietary rankings, were ours for the price of a mouse click.

As more and more of us decided to take control of our portfolios, brokerage houses soon got the picture by offering us the opportunity to purchase and sell equities online. Since we were conducting our own research, we had no intention of paying big commissions to have the trade made. Discount brokers offered slashed commissions, and many large brokerage houses followed their lead. Except for those traders/investors who are still willing to pay for the luxury of a full-service broker, three-digit commission schedules have dissolved. Today's commissions average $12 per transaction, down from $48 in 1996.

As of this writing, online brokerages now manage 18 million accounts, with 1.06 million transactions conducted daily via the Internet. Estimates predict the total number of online accounts will double by 2003. Retail trades placed online (as opposed to orders placed via telephone) grew from 17 percent in 1997 to 43 percent in 1999. By the end of 2000, that number topped 50 percent.

ENTER THE DAY TRADERS

Toward the end of the decade, day traders flocked to the market in droves, attracted by narrower spreads (the difference between a stock's purchase and selling price), ECNs (electronic communications networks, think "stock swaps"), and the availability of sophisticated order-entry systems that give direct access to exchange floors. Some of those traders took home big bucks. Others crashed and burned! These hopefuls were sure they'd be rich overnight, so they jumped headfirst into the most challenging arena on earth, with little knowledge, less discipline, and no experience.

They blew out their accounts faster than you can say "buy high, sell low."

The stock market saw them coming. She bided her time, then laughed, and ate them for breakfast. Just as quickly, she spit them out, minus their money and self-esteem.

Fortunately, a group of us who decided to buy and sell stocks on an active basis did so with a bit more caution and a lot more work. We survived the training period and emerged as self-reliant traders who consistently take money out of the markets.

MY RELATIONSHIP WITH THE STOCK MARKET

I started investing more than thirteen years ago, and quickly decided that if I were going to support myself from my investments, I would have to know as much as my stockbroker. Most brokers haven't the time to dote on our portfolios the way we do—or, rather, should.

Five years ago, I became an active trader. For the next year and a half, I made tons of mistakes. The market slapped me around, big time!

Although I kept losing money, I white-knuckled it, refusing to give up. I watched CNBC until my eyes crossed. At night, I studied charts until I toppled out of my chair. I read every book about trading I could get my hands on. I traveled to New York, studied under top traders who became my mentors, and asked so many questions I drove those around me bananas. Finally, I crawled out of the learning curve—victorious. I knew how to take consistent profits out of the market.

My friends, relieved that I survived the fiery trial, suggested that I could help others who wanted to learn how to trade. I agreed, and combining my writing background (I had been a professional writer for fourteen years) with my trading skills, I wrote *A Beginner's Guide to Day Trading Online*. Published by Adams Media in March 2000, the book became a bestseller in the day trading field.

Now, when I speak in public, I tell my audiences that I hold stocks from "two minutes to two years," and I do. My favorite time frames, however, are those that target swing trading and position trading, the subjects of this book. When properly executed, these two styles of trading put you in the market when the "getting's good," and keep you on the sidelines when the market corrects.

WHY I WROTE THIS BOOK

Once you learn the principles of short-term trading, defined in this book as swing and position trading, you can make the most amount of money with the least amount of time and risk!

+ If you day trade, you can make quick profits; however, during market hours, you have to stay glued to your computer screen. You must cultivate the concentration level of a rocket scientist, and the bladder of a camel.

+ The traditional investing stance of "buy-and-hold" has lost much of its sanctity. With a few exceptions, gone are the days when you could buy a national icon of American industry and rest secure in the knowledge that it would pay for your offspring's college education, or your retirement condo in Florida.

+ When executed properly, the styles known as swing trading (intended hold, two to five days) and position trading (intended hold, four to eight weeks) can deliver the juiciest gains with the least amount of risk.

STRATEGY OVERVIEW

Here's the strategy: Just like everything else on this planet, stock prices move in cycles. You'll learn about these in detail later, but for now, know that four stages make up a cycle.

In your mind, picture a valley, then a hill that rises and falls down into another valley. Now, overlay a stock price pattern onto the topography. The stock bases in the valley, then breaks into an uptrend (side of the hill) that may last from weeks to months. After the uptrend exhausts itself, the price action moves sideways, usually for a shorter time period (top of the hill). When buyers refuse to purchase the stock at higher prices, the stock "rolls over" into a downtrend (other side of the hill). When the downtrend finally ends, usually near the previous valley price, the cycle is complete and a new cycle begins.

As relatively short-term traders, our money-making goal will be to grab the middle—or "sweet spot"—of a stock's uptrend (or downtrend). We'll know when to enter a stock, when to exit, and when to stand on the sidelines. Since you can apply these principles to any style of trading, that's priceless knowledge no matter what time frame you play!

WHAT YOU'LL NEED TO SUCCEED

Office requirements for trading are basic, and you probably have most of it in place. Plan to equip a quiet corner or office with an up-to-date computer (including a fast, reliable connection to the Internet) and a television.

Perhaps the biggest requirement is that you must commit a chunk of your most precious commodity—*time*. Learning how to pull consistent proceeds from the toughest playing field in the world takes dedication and persistence. But it's worth it!

SHORT-TERM TRADING: THE GOOD NEWS

Maybe you're a professional in your field, an entrepreneur, a retiree, a student, or a homemaker. You've probably observed the stock market and realized tidy profits can be made from the market's current volatility. Whether you plan to trade on a full-time or part-time basis, the benefits of trading are fantastic.

If you make trading your full-time occupation, you can choose *when, where,* and *if* you choose to work. You can trade from any location, as long as your computer is hooked up to the Internet. Office politics? There are none. A persnickety boss? You're the boss! Want to wear your bunny slippers to work? Do it! Catch the flu? Pull the covers over your head and stay in bed for as long as you want. Got the time and money to take a week off? Have fun!

If you'd rather trade part-time, harmonize it with your regular job and add "luxury" money to your wallet.

When you learn how to trade cautiously and wisely, your earnings may transform dreams into real rewards, such as the sailboat you always wanted, the vacation cottage in the mountains, or a college education for your children.

Here's a benefit some folks don't think of: When executed properly, short-term trading can have lower risk than long-term investing. Many traditional buy-and-holders ride out bear markets fully invested, gritting their teeth while they watch their capital shrivel in value.

Now you will know when to go "flat," or close all of your positions. You'll calmly put your holdings in cash during corrections and/or bear markets. And, you'll have lots of money to shop with, when the bulls once again take control.

THE FLIP SIDE

The stock market is the most challenging arena on earth. It takes no prisoners. It's a dog-eat-dog world, and only the fittest survive. Those who jump in without adequate knowledge or discipline usually get their heads handed to them in a hurry!

To compete in this field, you have to be willing to persist and study *hard*. You have to cultivate the nerves of a bomb-detonator and develop the discipline of a marine corps drill sergeant.

Short-term trading is riskier than socking your money into fixed income returns, such as Treasury bonds or money market funds. And the truth is, you *will*—especially at the beginning of the learning curve—experience losses. (The size of the losses are within your control.) Are you highly risk-averse? Does the thought of losing money send you running for the Maalox bottle? If so, you may want to choose a different investing avenue.

Are you naturally a disciplined person? Can you control your emotions, or do you let your impulses run away with you? Market players who rake in the big bucks trade like steely-eyed robots, *sans* emotions. Can you develop that attitude?

When you first step into trading, remember the adage "Speed kills." Are you willing to enter the market at a turtle's pace and take small profits while you learn how the game is played? As a wise trader, are you primed to observe, apply your knowledge, plan your next step, and then take that step while adhering strictly to your plan? That's how the pros fatten their wallets, and if you follow in their footsteps, you can join them at the top.

Short-term trading isn't for everyone. So, ask yourself the preceding questions before you plunk your money into the pot. Self-examination isn't always the easiest thing to do, but it rewards us by keeping us on a path that best suits our individual needs.

THE JOURNEY . . .

In the pages that follow, I'll give you an overview of the most exciting street on earth—Wall Street. Then, we'll talk about setting up your trading business, delve into winning market psychology, and discuss fundamental and technical analyses. You'll learn how to read chart patterns, how to choose stocks, and how to play them. You'll also master money-management techniques. (It's easy to *buy* a stock—the skill comes in knowing when to sell it.) We'll also discuss news and recurring market events, and how to interpret them. Most importantly, we're going to have fun along the way.

I'm going to talk to you as one friend talks to another—as though we're good buddies chatting over a cup of coffee. I promise you this: Every sentence in this book comes from my heart. I traveled a challenging road to learn this business, and now you can profit from my mistakes. In the following pages, you'll learn how to dodge market potholes and seize gains by using wisdom and common sense. Believe me, if I can do it—you can do it.

IT'S SHOWTIME!

Okay, guys and girlfriends, here's where the rubber meets the road. It's time for you to decide whether or not short-term trading is for you. Only *you* can make this decision.

Again, you're going to need a firm commitment—*from* yourself, *to* yourself—of time and money. If you decide to join me on this journey, *let's get going*. Hang on tight, 'cause it's going to be the most exciting ride of your life.

Good luck and good trading!

MEET JESSE LIVERMORE . . .

If ever a book has been recognized as the "bible" of this industry, it's *Reminiscences of a Stock Operator*. Originally published in 1923, it is the classic story of Jesse Livermore, a legendary, turn-of-the-century trader.

The author, Edwin Lefevre, interviewed Livermore for several weeks. Then, giving Livermore the pseudonym of Larry Livingston, Lefevre did a masterful job of capturing Livermore's thoughts and recollections of his trading career.

Now, more than seventy years after Livermore made and lost fortunes trading commodities and stocks in rowdy bucket shops, his observations ring true and accurate. You'll find one at the beginning of each chapter. Enjoy them, reflect upon them, and integrate them into your trading career.

CHAPTER 1

Wall Street: The Greatest Game on Earth

The game taught me the game.

—JESSE LIVERMORE

Wall Street and the financial markets represent a global tournament played with heart-stopping stakes, in which people from the world over come together to trade money for dreams.

Will humans ever stop trading? Doubtful. No matter whether the assets involved are tangible or intangible, the act of trading seems inherent to our very souls.

WHERE IT ALL STARTED

Mankind's love of trading—or swapping items of equal value—started with our earliest ancestors, Oorg and Grok, who decided to swap meat for fish and furs. As Oorg and Grok's thought processes evolved into more complex frames of reference, their trading systems evolved along with them. Now, we, as contemporary men and women, have transformed the exchange of goods of perceived equal value into a sophisticated art form that involves all sorts of maneuvering.

The first actual stock exchange opened its doors in 1602 in Amsterdam, Holland. It was called the Dutch Bourse (bourse means moneybag), and it was backed by the Dutch East India Company.

The U.S. financial center, Wall Street, literally has its roots in an earthen embankment, erected in 1644 to keep the cows from wandering around the southern tip of the farmland now known as Manhattan. In 1663, Governor Peter Stuyvesant of New York (then called New Amsterdam) ordered that the embankment be raised and fortified with logs to protect colonists from the British, whom he suspected would attack New York by land. The British, however, arrived in 1644 by sea. They captured the settlement without firing a shot. Later, the British burned the ramshackle wall. The street that ran alongside survived, though, and retained its name: Wall Street.

The securities markets in the United States began with speculative trading in the debts of the new colonies and government. When the first Congress met in New York's Federal Hall in 1789, it issued roughly $80 million in government notes, creating an exciting new market in securities. These securities, along with additional stocks, bonds, orders for commodities, and warehouse receipts were put up for sale to the public.

To participate in these markets, investors funded American companies by buying shares of ownership. In this way, common citizens had "equity" and could prove so by the "certificates of stock" issued by the company in exchange for capital given by the investor. The stock proved the investor's participation, and so secured the debt. That's why shares of stock are alternately called stocks, equities, *and* securities.

In 1791, the first U.S. stock exchange was established in Philadelphia. At the same time, New York City's exchange was more informal; traders gathered each day under the sycamore tree at 68 Wall Street to buy and sell.

The New York Exchange began trading formally in 1792, when two dozen brokers formed a club. Competition was fierce. The brokers focused on padding their own profits and commissions, rather than on their customers. When the public rebelled, the brokers regrouped and instituted brokerage houses that offered stocks to the public at fair prices.

In 1827, the new Merchants Exchange building, erected at Wall and Hanover streets, housed the New York Stock and Exchange Board. By 1842, the American Stock Exchange opened its doors, and the New York Stock Exchange (NYSE) adopted its present name. Both exchanges enforced strict rules governing the sale of stocks.

In the early 1900s, leading up to the Crash of 1929, "bucket shops" flourished. These independent businesses provided opportunities for individual traders and investors to speculate on the price of securities by tossing money into a bucket carried around by a clerk.

The action in these shops—most of which were unlicensed and illegal—ran fast and furious. One clerk read the ticker tape while another jotted prices on a chalkboard. The speculators bought and sold the stocks as clerks called out prices from the "ticker," a nonstop telegram.

The honesty of the shop operators determined how much money the traders won or lost, and honesty was a rare commodity. As "Larry Livingston," the character who represents the turn-of-the-century trader Jesse Livermore in Edwin Lefevre's *Reminiscences of a Stock Operator*, lamented, "There are no bucket shops here [in New York] that a fellow could trust."[1]

---

[1] Lefevre, Edwin. *Reminiscences of a Stock Operator*, p. 22 (NY: John Wiley & Sons, Inc. 1994).

In the 1930s, the exchanges became strictly regulated and evolved into premier financial centers: the New York Stock Exchange (NYSE, or the Big Board), the Nasdaq Stock Exchange, and the American Stock Exchange LLC (now part of the Nasdaq). Regional exchanges include the Pacific Stock Exchange (PSE), the Boston Stock Exchange (BOS), the Philadelphia Stock Exchange (PHLX), Chicago Board of Trade (CBOT, which trades commodities), and Chicago Board Options Exchange (CBOE, which trades options).

As previously mentioned, the floors of the New York Stock Exchange and the American Stock Exchange are located in New York City. The Nasdaq Stock Exchange doesn't have an actual trading "floor"; rather, it's an electronic market housed in a computer network in Trumbull, Connecticut.

OUT OF CHAOS COMES ORDER: THE CRASH OF 1929

The Crash of 1929, and the Great Depression that followed it, transformed America's way of transacting business. In 1934, Congress established the U.S. regulatory commission, the Securities and Exchange Commission (SEC), after the Senate Committee on Banking and Currency looked into the New York Stock Exchange's operations.

The NYSE's business conduct had been a bit dicey, to say the least. To ensure that another market crash would not take place, the newly formed SEC instituted sweeping regulations. Its mission was to restore investor confidence by ending misleading sales practices and stock manipulations that fueled the collapse of the 1929 crash.

Once in gear, the SEC established regulations that prohibited the purchasing of equities without having adequate funds to cover the transaction. Next, it provided for the registration and supervision of all U.S. securities markets and stockbrokers, wrote rules for solicitation of proxies, and prevented unfair use of nonpublic information in stock trading. The organization stipulated that a company offering securities make full public disclosure of all relevant data. Finally, the commission decided to act as advisor to the court in corporate bankruptcy cases.

The most recent ruling by the SEC is Regulation FD. It stipulates that if a publicly traded company discloses material nonpublic information to securities professionals, such as fund managers, it must also make public disclosure. Translation: Great Big Company Inc. can't slip privileged information about a new product to its favorite fund manager, unless it first broadcasts that same information to the public via a Web cast, conference call, or other public announcement.

Okay, back to the calendar. In 1971, the National Association of Securities Dealers (NASD) created a fully integrated, computerized trading system called the NASDAQ, or National Association of Securities Dealers Automated

Quotation. Its purpose was to automate and trade over-the-counter securities, and it linked the terminals of more than 500 market makers to its automated system in Connecticut. By the 1990s, the Nasdaq grew into the second-largest securities market in the United States, and the third largest in the world.

THE CRASH OF 1987: MORE CHAOS AND THE RESULTING ORDER

During the 1970s and 1980s, the exchanges rotated between bull and bear markets until the collapse of October 19, 1987. The "crash" caused America's investing public to panic. Frightened customers overwhelmed their stockbrokers with sell orders, yelling, "Just get me out." Stockbrokers flooded specialists and market makers with these frantic orders. At one point, some market makers stopped answering their phones—which caused frustrated stockbrokers to stop answering *their* phones, in turn causing some investors to ride it out.

After the panic subsided, the SEC once again executed new regulations to protect the individual investor. The organization ruled that when individual investors wanted to sell, Nasdaq market makers had to buy a specified amount of stock from them. Later, additional regulations allowed investors to participate in the market by connecting them directly *to* the market via their computers and the Internet, and market makers were required to handle the transactions. Just like specialists on the NYSE, market makers were responsible for conducting "fair and orderly" markets.

THE NEW YORK STOCK EXCHANGE: HOW IT WORKS

In terms of market capitalization, the New York Stock Exchange (*www.nyse.com*) is the largest stock market in the world. That's why it's also termed "the Big Board." Located at Broad and Wall Streets, it is called the "Sunshine Market" because the public can always view its trading floor through gallery windows. CNBC and other financial television networks televise the busy floor each morning.

The NYSE lists more than 3,000 companies, representing in excess of 253 billion shares of stock, valued at over $11 trillion. These equities are referred to as "listed stocks" and most have large market capitalizations. "Market cap" is measured by an equity's number of shares outstanding (shares available to the public not held by corporate insiders) multiplied by the price of a single share of stock. For example, as of this writing, industry titan General Electric (GE) has 9,908 million shares outstanding. The price per share is approximately $50. So GE's market cap is a whopping $495,400,000,000!

You may have heard GE referred to as "the bluest of the blue chips." Trivia lovers take note: The term "blue chip," a moniker applied to the thirty stocks that make up the Dow Jones Industrial Average, comes from the game of poker. Of the chips used to represent dollar valuations, the blue chip has the highest value of all: $500.

Within the New York Stock Exchange, a number of major indices give us daily clues as to the inner workings of the market. The most famous, of course, is the one just mentioned, the Dow Jones Industrial Average.

The 105-year-old "Dow," as we call it in Street short-speak, started with twelve stocks and now consists of thirty reigning icons of American industry. Traditionally, only NYSE stocks were appointed to the Dow. In the last couple of years, however, Intel (INTC) and Microsoft (MSFT), two of the 800-pound tech gorillas that led the Nasdaq to dizzying heights in the late 1990s, were appointed to the index.

Other important indices within the NYSE are the Dow Jones Transportation Index, consisting of twenty leading transportation stocks, and the Dow Jones Utility Index, comprised of fifteen utility stocks.

The NYSE operates on a centralized auction system. Different "posts," each representing a different stock, pepper the floor of the exchange. At each post, a specialist (read "auctioneer") conducts a two-way auction between buyers and sellers and provides a market for that stock. Only one specialist represents each stock; for example, GE has only one specialist. Specialists, however, can represent more than one stock.

Where You Come In

Say you want to buy 100 shares of Citicorp, Inc. (C). Basically, your order can be filled one of three ways:

1. You call your broker or you place the order through your online broker. The broker sends your order to the floor of the NYSE. A floor-broker representing your broker takes your order to the post where Citicorp is traded and asks the Citicorp specialist for a market. The specialist announces the "size" of the market, or the number of Citicorp shares offered for sale at the best price, and the number wanted to buy at that best price. Your order is filled, and your broker confirms the price to you

2. You give your broker the order by phone or Internet, and he or she enters it onto a SuperDOT (designated order turnaround) machine, an electronic system that routes your order to the specialist. (SuperDOT handles about 80 percent of all orders entered on the NYSE.) The specialist fills it and shoots it back to the clerk. The clerk informs your broker of the "fill" (the number of shares and the price at which your order was filled), and your broker informs you.

3. You execute the order yourself on your direct-access trading (DAT) software system (described in the next chapter). This zaps the order from you to the specialist, and you usually receive the fill information in less than a minute.

When we say the specialist announces the "market" in Citicorp, an example would be "48.88 x 49, size 5,000 x 10,000" (the "x" meaning "by"). Translation: A buyer, or buyers, is waiting to buy a total of 5,000 shares of Citicorp and is willing to pay $48.95 per share. A seller, or sellers, currently offers (wants to sell) a total of 10,000 shares at $49 per share.

The price difference between the best (lowest) price you can purchase the stock for and the best (highest) price you will receive if you sell it is called the "spread." In the previous example, it would come to five cents per share.

If stocks were people, NYSE stocks would bear the reputation of being haughty statesmen and dignitaries. Perhaps, because their specialists are charged with keeping "a fair and orderly market," listed stocks may have rapid price changes, but most tend to step up and down their price ranges in a mannerly fashion.

If you're new to the stock market, I recommend you target NYSE issues for your first trades. You'll be less prone to the eye-bugging, stomach-clutching attacks that can be brought on by Nasdaq high-flyers.

THE NASDAQ STOCK MARKET: HOW IT WORKS

The Nasdaq Stock Market (*www.nasdaq.com*) is a shareholder-owned, for-profit company consisting of two distinct and separate markets: the Nasdaq National Market and the Nasdaq SmallCap Market.

The Nasdaq National Market is the one we usually refer to when we say, "the Nasdaq." It currently lists nearly 5,000 companies with a combined market capitalization of nearly $6 trillion. Average daily share volume runs at about 1.7 billion, which occurs in nearly 10 million transactions per day!

The Nasdaq SmallCap Market is the smaller capitalization tier of the Nasdaq. Companies that apply to be listed on this exchange must have a market cap of at least $50 million.

By now, you've heard the Nasdaq referred to as "the tech-heavy Nasdaq." Although Nasdaq companies cover the entire spectrum of the U.S. economy—from banks to biotechnology to transportation—its staples are technology stocks. These sectors include wireless telephone, software, computers, semi-conductors, and broadband companies. Surely, you recognize some of the Nasdaq tech icons, such as Cisco Systems (CSCO), Microsoft (MSFT), and Intel Corp. (INTC).

Nasdaq stocks are the NYSE's rowdy cousins. As I said earlier, most NYSE stocks tend to be purchased and sold in a somewhat genteel and dignified manner. Rambunctious Nasdaq stocks, however, can trade like a raucous free-for-all. No doubt it's due to the way shares exchange hands. In comparison to having a single specialist orchestrating every trade for a listed stock, a Nasdaq stock may have as many as fifty or sixty market makers (think middlemen) and ten ECNs (electronic communications networks, or trader "stock swaps") bidding on and offering it at any given moment. Prices can soar, then tumble, at mind-numbing speed!

When you call your broker or go online and ask for a quote for Dell (DELL), for instance, your answer might be "30.25 by 30.26." This means that 30.25 is the "inside bid" or the highest price you can demand if you want to sell Dell as a market order. Thirty dollars and 26 cents is the "inside offer" or the "ask." ("Offer" and "ask" are interchangeable terms.) They represent the lowest price for which you can buy Dell if you want to buy at the market price. Remember, when you get a quote from any exchange, whether verbal or written, the bid is always announced first, the offer second.

If you're new at this game, please avoid trading explosive Nasdaq stocks until you've got some experience under your belt. Believe me, these roller coasters can give you—and your account—a white-knuckle ride you'll never forget!

THE AMERICAN STOCK EXCHANGE LLC: HOW IT WORKS

As the nation's second largest floor-based exchange and third most active exchange, the American Stock Exchange LLC (*www.amex.com*) lists more than 800 common stocks, index shares, and equity derivative securities. Located at 86 Trinity Place (adjacent to Wall Street), Amex has buyers and sellers who compete in a centralized auction marketplace similar to the NYSE. Stocks listed on the Amex usually represent younger companies, and their prices are less volatile than their NYSE and Nasdaq counterparts.

LET'S DISSECT THE INDEXES

As a savvy market participant, it's important that you get up to speed with the indexes used by the financial markets as benchmarks.

The Dow Jones Industrial Average

The Dow Jones Industrial Average (DJIA) is a price-weighted index of thirty giants of American industry. Price-weighted means that higher-priced stocks receive more weighting than their lower-priced companions. Often called "Blue Chips," the companies of the DJIA include Microsoft, Intel, IBM, General Electric, and General Motors, among other big names. Prepared and published by Dow Jones & Co., "the Dow," as we call it, is the oldest and most quoted of all market indices. The average is calculated by adding the closing prices of the component stocks and using a divisor adjusted for splits and dividends equal to 10 percent or more of the market value of an issue. Just as with all of the averages discussed here, it's quoted in points (not dollars).

The NYSE Composite Index

The NYSE Composite Index is a market value-weighted index made up of all NYSE issues. Market value weighted equals price weighted. Like the Dow, each company's security affects the index in proportion to its market value, or price per share.

Standard & Poor's 500 Index

Standard & Poor's 500 Index (SPX), commonly called the "S&P 500," and "the broader market," is a market capitalization-weighted index (shares outstanding multiplied by stock price per share). Because this comprehensive index currently tracks 400 industrial stocks, twenty transportation stocks, forty financial stocks, and forty public utilities issues—representing stocks from the NYSE, Amex, and Nasdaq—it's a terrific benchmark of the American economy. Standard and Poor's Corporation, a division of McGraw-Hill, maintains this index.

The Nasdaq 100 Index

The Nasdaq 100 Index includes 100 of the largest non-financial domestic companies listed on the Nasdaq National Market. Launched in January 1985, each security in the index is represented by its market capitalization in relation to the total market value of the index. The index reflects the Nasdaq's largest growth companies across major industry groups. All index components have a minimum market cap of $500 million and an average daily trading volume of at least 100,000 shares.

The Nasdaq Composite Index

The Nasdaq Composite Index is a statistical measure that indicates changes in the Nasdaq Stock Market by measuring all Nasdaq common stocks. It is market-value weighted; the more expensive equities are given more weight than lower-priced issues.

The Wilshire Total Market Index

The Wilshire Total Market is the broadest of indexes. It's a market value-weighted index of all U.S.–headquartered companies (currently about 6,800) listed on the NYSE, Amex, and Nasdaq.

The Russell 2000 Index

The Russell 2000 represents the small-capitalization stock index. Some gurus insist that the small caps lead us into—and out of—bear markets. So, it's worth keeping an eye on this index. You can also compare your small-cap holdings, if any, to its trending action.

WALL STREET AS "THE ANIMAL HOUSE":
THE BULLS AND THE BEARS, THE SHEEP AND THE HOGS

Perhaps because the island of Manhattan previously served as farmland, Wall Street's prominent players are still referred to with animal names. These "party animals" have clear-cut characteristics.

Bulls fight by striking *up* with their horns. Therefore, stock market "bulls" make money from advancing prices. During soaring markets, they profit from the uptrend. When the market corrects or drops, bulls are the optimists who roar that, "It will turn around soon."

Bears fight by striking *down* with their claws. Market "bears" make money when the market falls. Many bears are short-sellers who profit from ugly downtrends by selling falling stocks and buying them back at an even lower price (you'll learn how to sell short in Chapter 12). Whenever the market surges skyward, the pessimistic bears crawl out of their caves to growl that the good times will be over soon.

Sheep follow anybody with a tambourine. Too lazy to learn for themselves, they rush in and out of stock positions on the advice given by the guru *du jour*. Listen to them bleating as their portfolios take a beating.

One of the oldest sayings on Wall Street goes, "The bulls make money, and the bears make money, but the hogs get slaughtered." Count on it. Hogs always get sliced into bacon. When piggies go to market, they load up on high-flying issues that many times flop faster than they fly. Greedy gluttons also "bet the ranch" on risky issues, or hold on when they could take reasonable gains. Listen to their squeals as the market chews up their account!

TWO EMOTIONS THAT RULE THE MARKETS
(AND MOST OF THE REST OF THE WORLD)

Two polar opposites reign side by side over the world's financial markets: *greed* and *fear*. Faster and faster, this ruling duo passes the scepter back and forth, inciting the volatility we witness—and participate in—each day.

To be sure, greed operates up and down the scale from mild optimism to euphoria. Fear ranges from apprehension to outright panic. The degree to which these two emotions exert power propels stock prices upward or downward. These emotions are never spent, never exhausted. As timeless as the markets they rule, they reign supreme, fueled by their own energy.

Want to see them in action? You can watch them command stock prices any time during the trading day. For example, on a volatile morning, check the price of a liquid (high-volume) stock from one hour to the next. Let's say we're watching Peoplesoft (PSFT), the software giant. When the market opens, the stock is priced at 38. By mid-day, the price has risen to 42.

Now, did Peoplesoft's fundamentals (i.e. quarterly earnings, products, or sales volume) change significantly during that time period? Probably not. Greed pushed the price up. Greed and the resulting demand created by buyers who decided to "pay up" for the stock. When the price falls—and it will at some point—fear will be the culprit. Much of the time, these two emotions rule according to perception, not logic.

What's this got to do with you? Everything!

Are you greedy? Sure! Are you fearful? I'd bet my new duck slippers on it. "Yeah?" you reply, crossing your arms over your chest and squinting at me through narrowed eyes. "What about you? Are you ever greedy or scared?"

Absolutely. Although experience (and hard knocks) has tempered these two emotions in me, there was a time very early in my trading career when I'd happily gorge my account with high-flying stocks. If (when) they tanked, I'd get scared spitless and sell out as fast as I could, usually at big losses. Was I a horrible person? No. I was human. And so are you.

When you first venture into the stock market, unless you are different from everyone else in the world, greed and fear will be your constant companions. They're part of human nature. Trouble is, in large doses they color your perception of the market and urge you to make choices you wouldn't make in more rational moments. Some of those choices may be harmful to your wealth.

Greed causes us to chase stocks, or in other words to buy into the euphoria of the moment by agreeing to pay higher and higher prices for a rocketing stock. By the time our order is filled, the buying frenzy has nearly dissipated. The stock usually staggers south, taking our money with it.

When everyone around us screams that a stock is going to the moon, greed urges us to "load the truck"! As our good sense dissolves, we max out our accounts with this dream baby that will surely send our kids to college and us on a luxury vacation. *Not.* The dream shrinks faster than we can yell, "Sell!" and our would-be profits shrivel with our bottom line. Rats. Double rats.

Greed convinces us to hold oversized positions in rocky markets. It spurs us to grab IPOs (initial public offerings) on the first day they trade. It drives us to gobble up market laggards "because they're cheap."

Greed's ruling partner, fear, on the other hand, motivates us to action even more quickly. The fear of losing money reigns uppermost in our minds. Fear causes us to sell a winning position too quickly, and interestingly enough it also causes us to hang on to a losing position too long. When the market slaps us hard, fear stops us from capitalizing on the next good opportunity, because we're afraid to "get burned" again.

How do you eliminate these unsavory feelings from your trading and investing decisions? By learning how to replace them with positive ones. Read this book and others on the subject. Learn how to read market actions and reactions. Move slowly, study hard, and apply what you've learned in a disciplined, cool-headed fashion. If you can accomplish that, you'll have the edge over 99 percent of all market players!

SUPPLY AND DEMAND

Fear and greed act as trailblazers for those age-old economic factors of supply and demand. Many market advisors talk about fear/greed and supply/demand as if they are separate entities. They are not. They are intertwined and perpetuate one another into action.

So, now that you understand how greed and fear operate, let's focus on *supply* and *demand*. These two factors move world markets—from rocket ships to jelly beans—around the clock!

The concept is simple: We want what we can't have.

Pretend it's your birthday, and you're so-ooo excited. Over the last six months you've been saving your money for the biggest, most expensive present you've ever given to yourself. Heck, you've worked hard. You deserve it.

Now, you're on the way to the showroom floor to plunk down your money on the sleekest, fanciest sports car ever to spin off of an assembly line. Your heart starts to race. An afternoon spent on the telephone and researching the Internet affirmed this was the only one in the area. It's the perfect color—a deep, brilliant red—with buttery, camel-colored leather seats. In a previous test drive, it purred down the highway as if it had found its home.

Once you reach the dealership, you park and start walking toward the showroom. What if it's not there? What if someone else feels the same way you do? No, it couldn't be. That glorious hunk of precision has got your name on it.

You enter the showroom and the car fills your vision. Sparkling in the lights, feverish in brilliant red, it seems to whisper your name. You move toward the car as nonchalantly as your shaking legs will let you. You reach out and touch its cool, gleaming metal. Yessss!!!!! This baby is yours. It was created for you. Only you.

You lift the door handle, then slip into the driver's side. Sinking into the seat, you breathe in the scent of polished leather. The satin-like wooden steering wheel nestles into the palm of your left hand. Your right foot touches the silent gas pedal, a perfect fit. Your fingers wrap around the gearshift knob, ready to take control of the gutsiest hunk of machinery this side of heaven.

"Here again?" The salesman's voice jolts you out of your reverie.

You take a deep breath and find your voice. "What's the best bottom line you can give me on this baby?"

"The bottom line is gone." The salesman smirks. "I just sold it."

"What? No!" You jerk your body out of the seat and jam your feet onto the cold, hard floor. Your stomach flips upside down. "You couldn't have."

"Sorry, buddy. This sweet little baby is going home with its new papa."

"Wait. Hold it." You put your hand on the salesman's arm, as he slaps a "Sold" sticker under the windshield wiper. "I'll pay you more for it. More than the other guy. A LOT MORE."

The salesman lifts your hand off his arm. His eyes glitter behind his glasses. "No can do. Got me a signed contract. A deal's a deal."

Frantically, you clutch your checkbook. "When is the next one coming in?"

The salesman sighs and rolls his eyes. "We're not getting anymore in. Rumor is, it's being discontinued."

"Discontinued?" Your pulse pounds in your head.

"Hey," he leers. "This isn't the only car in the showroom. Couldn't I interest you in another model? Why, I've got a sweet—"

"No. No, thank you." With your heart crushing your chest, you turn and trudge out of the showroom.

A few days later, you're driving through the other side of town. Suddenly, you spot a large automobile dealer and your gaze travels down the line of cars at the front of the lot. You blink in disbelief. Are you seeing things? An entire line of the car you wanted, sitting idle in the sunlight with flags waving on their antennas. You slow and park.

Before you can get out of your car, a salesman approaches. "Wanna take one of these babies home? Just park it in your driveway and watch your neighbors drool."

You stand and squint at the lot, shading your eyes from the sun. "How many of that particular model do you have? I heard it was discontinued."

"Discontinued?" He chuckles. "Not this creampuff. I've got a dozen on the front lot and more out back. That's why I can give you such a terrific deal on one of them."

You eye him warily. "How much?"

He spews out the same sticker price displayed by the other dealer.

You shrug, waving him off. "You gotta do better than that. I'll check back with you later."

As you drive away, you think *that guy must be nuts if he thinks I'm paying sticker price, when he's got a lot crammed with the same model. I love that car, but I'm not going to get suckered!*

Get the picture?

When only a limited amount of a quality item exists at a certain price—remember the Harley-Davidson craze—we are willing to pay retail prices, and sometimes higher, to own it (demand). But if a huge quantity (supply) of that same item floods the market, the owner typically has to lower his price to sell it.

Prices in the commodities markets reflect supply and demand in a big way. If severe winter weather causes the orange trees in Florida to freeze, the reduced orange crop causes the cost of orange juice to rise in the grocery stores (demand).

Likewise, say you're monitoring your target stock, Bossy Banks, Inc., and it soars to a new fifty-two-week high of 50. You quickly buy 200 shares at that price. The next day, Bossy tanks and heads for the low 40s. "That stupid stock," you mutter, watching in dismay. "If it ever gets back to 50, I'm going to sell and get out even!"

During the following week, Bossy sinks to 35. After moving sideways in the mid-30s for a few days, Bossy perks up and climbs to 40 (demand—buyers are willing to pay a higher price). Within another two weeks, fueled by more demand, the stock struggles back to 50.

You breathe a sigh of relief, then shoot your "limit sell" order to the market: Sell 200 Bossy at 50. Bossy falls to 48.75. Huh? There were too many shares (supply) to be absorbed at 50 by too few buyers. Your order is left hanging. You cancel and lower your price to 48.75. Too late. The stock sinks to 48.65.

Frantically, you cancel your order again, and throw in a market order (sell at current inside bid). A moment later, your order is filled at 48.50. By the way, this is called "chasing a stock down."

Here's where fear and greed, the motivating factors, come in. When you originally purchased Bossy Banks at 50 and it immediately sold off, the fear shown by other buyers that they would pay no more than $50 per share drove the price down. That created supply. The continued supply drove the price down even lower, down to the mid-30s. When supply dried up as new buyers came in, the stock moved sideways (indecision). As buyers committed to higher prices (demand created by greed) at each level, the price rose higher.

When it reached the previous high of 50, fear of getting burned again caused you to throw in your sell order. Others felt the same way, and together you flooded the market with supply, once again forcing the stock down. Lowered prices, sustained by fear, pushed the stock back down to 48.50. Eventually, greed steps back in and creates demand and the cycle repeats itself.

So, remember, greed and fear act as the immediate trailblazers for demand and supply. Later, we're going to add *support* and *resistance* to the equation.

CHECK YOUR UNDERSTANDING

Now that we've covered the basics on the markets, here's a quick review:

1. The securities markets in the United States began with speculative trading in the debts of the new colonies and government. When the first Congress met in New York's Federal Hall in 1789, it issued about $80 million in government notes, creating a market in securities.
2. Congress established the U.S. regulatory commission, the Securities and Exchange Commission (SEC), in 1934.
3. The NYSE lists more than 3,000 companies; their equities are referred to as "listed stocks" and most have large market capitalizations.
4. "Market cap" equals number of shares outstanding (shares available to the public not held by corporate insiders) multiplied by the price of a single share of stock.
5. On the NYSE, shares are traded via a centralized auction system. Each stock has a "specialist," who facilitates the trades and is charged with conducting "a fair and orderly market" in that stock.
6. The price difference between the best (lowest) price you can purchase the stock for, and the best (highest) price you will receive if you sell it, is called the "spread."
7. The Nasdaq National Market lists nearly 5,000 companies with a combined market capitalization of nearly $6 trillion. Although Nasdaq companies cover the entire spectrum of the U.S. economy, its staples are technology stocks.
8. Shares on the Nasdaq trade hands via broker/dealers represented by market makers who act as middlemen. Many market makers may participate in a stock at one time. Traders and institutions can also place orders with electronic communications networks (ECNs).
9. "Bulls" make money from the rising stock prices. "Bears" profit from falling stock prices.
10. Greed and fear rule the financial markets. They are the precursors to demand and supply.
11. Limited quantities of a high-quality item create demand. Sellers can raise their prices as long as greed goads buyers to continue to "pay up."
12. When large quantities of an item flood the market, this creates supply. As fearful buyers flee, sellers must lower their prices to unload the product.

✦ ✦ ✦

WHAT IS "CENTER POINT"?

Many of us who live and breathe the financial markets tend to get caught up in the dizzying pace of this ever-changing arena. Inadvertently, we forget that we are "whole people" who need balance in our lives to thrive. This linear world of numbers, charts, and technical rhetoric swallows us, and we're too busy calculating to look up and take notice.

If the market moves fast, it also moves roughly. Fortunes are won and lost in a heartbeat and only the fittest survive.

When I was new to this field, I spent many a day feeling battered and beaten. I often wondered if I would ever escape in one piece, mentally and monetarily. Only my stubborn resolve to emerge victorious, coupled with my strong belief system, kept me in the game.

In my previous book, *A Beginner's Guide to Day Trading Online*, I shared balancing reinforcement concepts at the completion of each chapter in a one-page discussion called "Center Point." The positive feedback I received on these Center Points encouraged me to continue them in this book.

Through the years, these concepts have encouraged me to keep reaching for my dreams, both financial and non-financial.

May they also inspire you as you move forward on the pathway to success!

✦ ✦ ✦

✦ ✦ ✦

CENTER POINT

Come to the edge, he said. They said: We are afraid. Come to the edge, he said. They came. He pushed them . . . and they flew.

—GUILLAUME APOLLINAIRE

You . . . A Golden Buddha

It was 1957 in Thailand. In the process of relocating a Buddhist monastery, a group of monks were appointed to move the giant clay Buddha that resided within. The monks started to push the huge statue, but soon noticed a crack down one side. They decided to wait until the next day to continue with the job. By then, maybe they could figure how to move the precious cargo without damaging it.

That night, however, a curious monk returned to examine the clay Buddha. He shined a light close to the crack. To his astonishment, he saw something glitter!

Quickly, the monk grabbed a hammer and chisel and chipped away at the clay. Hours later, he finished his chipping and stood back in awe. He could hardly believe his eyes. Standing before him was a huge, solid gold Buddha!

It was later discovered that several centuries before, while the Burmese army was advancing on the area, Thai monks had concealed the Buddha in clay to keep it from being stolen. During the attack, however, all the monks were killed, so the true nature of the treasure lay in secret until 1957.

You and I resemble the golden Buddha. We often conceal our true brilliance with protective clay shells. We use social masks, boisterous masks, impatient masks, tough masks, insensitive masks, even masks of false humor and enthusiasm, to hide who we really are. Disguising our feelings of inadequacy, these masks also shield us from the outside world—a world we may perceive as overwhelming, uncomfortable, or simply tiresome.

Once we become aware of these masks, we can chip away at the clay and toss the pieces behind us. Only then can we reveal who we really are: shining, loving, successful beings on the road to fulfilling our dreams and visions!

✦ ✦ ✦

CHAPTER 2

Off to a Running Start: Setting Up Your Business

A man must believe in himself and his judgment if he expects to make a living at this game.

—JESSE LIVERMORE

Short-term trading is a business like any other. You'll want to formulate a plan and set goals so that you have a clear-cut sense of direction.

First, you need to establish how much time and money you can realistically dedicate to your trading business. Then, you can choose your equipment or update existing equipment. Finally, you'll decide what kind of order-entry system best suits you and open an account with a broker.

MAP YOUR BUSINESS PLAN

When you set out to drive somewhere you've never been before, you check out a map and ask for directions from someone who's been there before. Otherwise, odds are you'll get lost and have a much longer trip than you anticipated—if you get there at all.

Your journey into the financial markets as a trader is much the same. Unless you've traveled this road before, you'll succeed far more quickly and easily if you have a map or plan.

The optimal plan is a written one. It's a fact: People who write down their plans on paper usually achieve their goals. People who merely hold their plans in mind as vague generalities achieve a lot less. If you'd like to meet your objectives more quickly, consider jotting down your trading business plan as we outline the basic concepts in the next few pages.

WHAT'S YOUR TIME COMMITMENT?

First, do you intend to be a full-time or part-time player? If you intend to tackle the market full-time, you may have a large portfolio. Possibly you've been trading part-time and want to become fully involved. Or, maybe you want to study hard and fast. You realize that by watching market action as much as possible, you'll absorb the most knowledge at the fastest possible rate. You got that right!

A benefit of swing and position trading, holding positions from two to five days, or four to six weeks, is that the longer-term time frames (as opposed to day trading) lend themselves to part-time participation. Most part-time traders fall into one of three categories:

1. *Closet traders.* These are, for example, dentists, physicians, attorneys, office managers, and assistants who keep an eye on their stock positions between drilling teeth, removing appendixes, taking phone calls, and attending meetings.
2. *First-and-last-hour traders.* They pinpoint the stock that they want to enter the night before, then depending on market conditions at the open the next morning, they make their move. Before the market closes, they check out their positions again for exit/entry decisions.
3. *Laid-back traders.* They enter one or two positions a week, max. Once in, they set automatic stop-loss orders with their brokers. They keep an ear to overall market action, and every few days peruse their portfolio for possible profit-taking opportunities.

Do you see yourself in any of the previous examples? All of the options are valid and have high potential for success. Please remember that in the beginning, though, whether you commit to being a full-time or part-time trader, you'll need to allocate extra time for study and research, over and above time set aside for actual trading.

And while we're on the subject, keep in mind that you'll never know everything there is to know about this business. If you're still trading years from now, you'll still be studying years from now.

YOUR MOST IMPORTANT COMMITMENT: MONEY

Next, let's look at the capital you've earmarked for your trading account. First, size *does* count. You're better off knowing the truth up front: that you *must* start with a large enough amount of money to get you through the learning curve. Unfortunately, an account funded with a few hundred dollars won't make the cut. You'll also find that some online and all direct-access brokers require minimum amounts for opening accounts.

Next, the money you're targeting is now labeled "high risk." This capital *has* to be money you can afford to lose. This point is not negotiable—for many reasons. When you enter the stock market as a newcomer and make your initial trades, you're going to make mistakes. Result? You're going to lose money. Count on it.

If you follow the money-management techniques you learn in this book, you'll minimize your losses. Still, initially you *will* incur losses. So, please don't use money intended for your children's college education or the down payment on a new house. Simply put, don't fund your trading account with money that, if lost, will alter your lifestyle in any way!

If you trade with money that isn't disposable, it will be "scared money." Trading with scared money colors your perception of the market. Your common sense flees under these conditions. Greed and fear mushroom out of control. Controlled losses are no longer a cost of doing business—they balloon into catastrophes. At the least, your fear of losing money will stop you from entering proper setups that have a great chance of profitability.

Finally, if you've thought of borrowing the money to fund your trading account, please don't. That's considered instant "scared money." Instead, sock away a percentage of your income over time until you have enough to start with.

The flip side of all of these cautionary notes: If you have a clear mind because you're trading with money you've set aside for just this purpose, you will approach the market with a calm and confident mindset that is conducive to reaping profits!

QUICK ASSET ALLOCATION PLAN

For those who have large portfolios, consider this method of asset allocation: Subtract your age from 100. If you're fifty-one, that leaves forty-nine. Fifty-one percent of your portfolio should be in safe investments, such as bonds, annuities, and money market funds. Forty-nine percent may be invested in higher-risk instruments, such as large-cap stocks. Finally, allocate 5 percent of the 49 percent for your trading account.

SELECTING/UPDATING YOUR OFFICE EQUIPMENT

One of the great perks of trading is that setting it up requires far fewer expenditures than for a traditional start-up business.

Identify your office space first—whether it's a grand, mahogany-paneled suite, a corner in a spare bedroom, or somewhere in between. Of mega-importance, no matter where you set up to trade, is that your environment supports your ability to focus. Make sure you have a quiet, private place from which you can study, research, and place your trades.

Got zero equipment with which to start? For starters, beg, borrow, or buy a no-frills television. Tune it to CNBC. Got that done!

Next, you'll need an up-to-date personal computer with a good monitor—the bigger the monitor screen, the better. Get at least a seventeen-inch screen and upgrade to a larger model as soon as you can. The more generous the screen, the more grateful your eyes. Trust me. Analyzing charts on a laptop-sized screen for any length of time stresses your vision.

If you trade more than occasionally, you will want to add extra monitors to your PC so you can keep research and extra charting capabilities at an arm's length.

In terms of money, plan to spend in the ballpark of $2,000 to $4,000 for a PC, large monitor(s), and software. You may also want to add a high-quality surge protector or two. Nothing spells "gut-grinder" like discovering a high-voltage storm fried your PC internals, and your only connection to your broker is via telephone!

One of the most important components to your system is your Internet connection. The minimum connection you'll want to use is a 56K modem and an ISP (Internet service provider), available for a monthly cost of roughly $15 to $30 a month. The downside to opting for a regular ISP is a frequent inability to get online during heavy traffic.

ISDN (Integrated Services Digital Network) lines are more expensive ($40 to $100 a month) but faster, although frequent disconnections are also possible.

Even better, cable modems offer a reliable, higher-speed option at a reasonable price, $40 to $50 per month. The downside is that cable bandwidth is limited. The more people who use the service, the slower it will operate. If you live in an area where cable is new, chances are you will encounter lightning speed. As more customers jump onboard, the speed may lag.

Depending on your level of service, DSL (Digital Subscriber Line) can cost from $40 to $190 per month. It offers good connection speed, but the speed relies on your distance from the Telco vendor. DSL may not be available in all areas.

If you intend to trade more than occasionally, you'll want to think about having a backup Internet connection, just in case your primary one goes down. Why? Because the trading god has a perverse sense of humor. When Alan Analyst decides to downgrade the entire biotech industry, we're usually maxed out in biotech stocks. As we frantically push the "sell" button to escape with at least some of our profits, our Internet connection will inevitably crash. Unless a backup connection is available allowing us to jump on the Net and sell, we can end up taking nasty losses. Or, we end up morphing from a short-term trader into a disgruntled long-term investor. So, consider backing up your Internet connection with a second alternative (perhaps an inexpensive ISP). One saved trade, or in other words rescued profits, will probably pay for the entire year's service.

Aside from your Internet connection, you'll encounter other monthly expenses. When you start, you can use free charting services posted on the Internet (see Chapter 4). As you progress, however, you'll want more sophisticated charts. When you purchase a software-charting package, you'll need a data feed for quotes. (Software-charting companies will provide data feed information to you.)

Finally, budget for recurring expenses, like newspaper and magazine subscriptions.

CHOOSING A BROKER

There are three basic ways to buy and sell stocks: through a full-service broker, an online broker, or a direct-access broker.

The "Old-Fashioned" Way

The first method, now known as "old-fashioned," is to pick up the telephone and call your full-service broker. In this world of high-speed Internet connections, it's the most inefficient and costly way, but if you're comfortable with your broker and want to continue this way, by all means do so. Just be aware that you pay the highest commission rate of all order-entry methods, and those commissions shave a hefty chunk off of your profits.

Selecting an Online Broker

The next method is to open an account with an online broker and place your orders over the Internet. Find one that offers:

+ Access to real-time quotes, which means stock prices are current when displayed. For precise entry points, real-time quotes are a must. Some companies still give "delayed" quotes, which are fifteen or twenty minutes old.
+ A Web site that is accessible and easy to navigate, with graphics that snap on the screen rapidly; also, pages that appear quickly when you move from screen to screen.
+ A well-organized order-entry screen built to guard against data entry errors. For example, are the "buy" and "sell" buttons far enough away from each other? I know lots of traders (I've done it) who, in a panic to sell a tanking stock, have accidentally *doubled up on it* instead of selling the original shares. That particular episode always adds excitement to the day!
+ A quick confirmation system, account balances, and portfolio updates.
+ Alternative ways of reaching the broker. What happens when the market plunges? Are orders accepted and filled, or does their system jam? If the Web site crashes from heavy traffic, can a broker be reached by phone, and fast?

✦ Low margin rates; you'll be surprised at how they differ.

✦ A reasonable minimum dollar amount to open an account, if any.

✦ Automatic buy- or sell-stops. Make sure they will set them on Nasdaq stocks. All brokers will set stops on NYSE stocks (that service originates at the NYSE, the Nasdaq doesn't furnish it at this time). Most brokers will offer this on Nasdaq issues as a customer service benefit. Ask if the buy- and sell-stops are "day" orders or if they can be "good-till-canceled" (GTC). GTC sell-stops are particularly useful if you want to keep a core holding in your account while you go on vacation. (If the designated price hits your sell-stop, it triggers a market order and the position is automatically sold.)

One great source of information about online brokers is Gomez Advisers (*www.gomez.com*). The site reviews and rates online brokers according to variables such as ease of use and consumer confidence. Sometimes, it also offers cash rebates if you sign up for a participating brokerage.

You can also peruse the National Association of Securities Dealers (*www.investor.nasd.com*) if you want to find out if charges or complaints have been charged against your broker in the Individual Investors Services' Public Disclosure section.

Also check out GetSmart.com (*www.getsmart.com*), which shows you the costs, benefits, and features of online brokers before you open an account with them.

Finally, ask other traders with online accounts what Internet brokers they use, and whether the brokers are reliable and efficient. Take your time and do as much research as possible. Here is a selection of popular online brokers:

A.B. Watley	*www.abwatley.com*	(888) 229-2853
Ameritrade	*www.ameritrade.com*	(800) 454-9272
Brown & Co.	*www.brownco.com*	(800) 822-2021
CSFBdirect	*www.csfbdirect.com*	(800) 825-3723
Datek	*www.datek.com*	(888) 463-2835
E*Trade	*www.etrade.com*	(800) 387-2331
Muriel Siebert	*www.msiebert.com*	(800) 872-0444
Quick & Reilly	*www.quickway.com*	(800) 837-7220
Schwab	*www.schwab.com*	(800) 435-4000
Suretrade	*www.suretrade.com*	(800) 793-8050
T.D.Waterhouse	*www.tdwaterhouse.com*	(800) 934-4410

Some investors start with an Internet broker and later transfer to the direct-access trading method we'll talk about next.

Opening an Account with a Direct-Access Broker

The third way of placing a buy/sell order is through a direct-access broker. Before we venture into a quick overview of direct-access trading, let's define the quote systems.

Three types of quote systems are used in trading:

1. *Level I.* Real-time quotes given to you by your broker. (We talked about these quotes in Chapter 1.) The quotes represent the best price for which you can buy, or sell, at that moment.
2. *Level II.* Continually updated quotes displayed on a level-II screen. Besides the best (inside) bid and ask (offer) quoted to you on level I, on an actively traded stock there may be many more participants waiting in line, hoping to buy or sell the same stock at an even lower or higher price, respectively.
3. *Level III.* Quote systems used by specialists and market makers to refresh their positions; they are generally unavailable to the public.

A direct-access order-entry system, using level-II screens, is the fastest way to send your order to an exchange. While we swing-and-position traders aren't as adamant about speed of execution as day traders are, it's a nice feeling to know we're in control of our orders when they're placed.

Level-II screens let us see "inside the markets" on the NYSE, Amex, and Nasdaq, so it's often said that a level-II screen gives a stock "transparency." When you place your order, it bypasses all intermediaries and goes straight to the designated exchange.

A level-II quote screen for an active stock moves and changes rapidly, as it is constantly being updated. Most traders add a "time and sales" screen to their level II. Time and sales displays the actual "prints," meaning the trades that are taking place and the time that they were executed. We'll talk later about how to use this screen, but in the meantime, Figures 2-1(a) and 2-1(b) displays level-II screens of General Electric (GE, a NYSE stock) and Sun Microsystems (SUNW, a Nasdaq stock). The level-II screens are slightly different because they originate from two different markets. We'll get into the variances later in the book. If you intend to make short-term trading your full-time occupation, consider opening an account with a broker who offers a level-II order-entry system. Because they cater to traders, brokers who offer direct-access trading with level II usually include comprehensive packages with customizable charts and watch lists with streaming quotes, ticker tapes, and up-to-the-minute news.

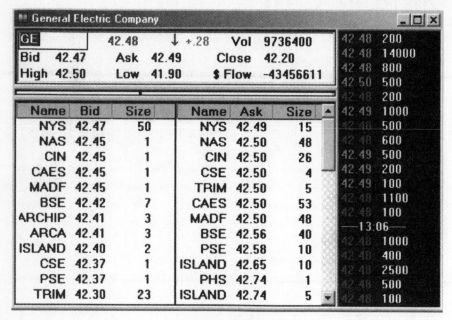

Figure 2-1 (a).

Level-II screen of General Electric (GE).

The downside: You may have to place a minimum number of trades per month, or else pay a fee.

Here is a partial list of direct-access software companies. Their Web sites list participating brokers. More software comes onto the market regularly, so check financial Web sites and magazines for new additions.

CyberTrader	*www.cybercorp.com*
RealTick	*www.realtick.com*
RediPlus	*www.onsitetrading.com*
Tradeportal	*www.tradeportal.com*
Tradescape	*www.tradescape.com*

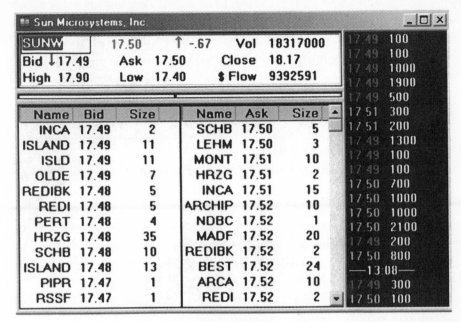

Figure 2-1 (b).

Level-II screen of Sun Microsystems (SUNW).

A few online brokers now offer direct-access trading or a hybrid of level I and level II systems, sometimes referred to as "level 1½." You'll see their ads in trade magazines and newspapers.

Once you've selected a few direct-access sources, you may want to call the companies and ask a customer service representative the following questions:

- Do they require a minimum opening balance?
- Is there a monthly charge for the system? Do you have to make a minimum number of trades per month? Does the number of executions you make affect the monthly charge?
- Is the system reliable? How often does it go down? (If the company representative chokes before answering these questions, politely end the conversation and go on to the next company.)
- Can the charting program access weekly charts? (This is important—some trading software doesn't include weekly charts.)
- Does it use candlestick charts? (You'll learn about candlesticks in Chapter 6.)
- Does it include a full menu of indicators, such as moving averages, MACD, Commodity Channel Index, Stochastics, Relative Strength Index, and

Fibonacci retracements? (You'll learn about these indicators/oscillators later as well.) For now, just inquire about the system's charting capabilities.

✦ Can you overlay one chart on top of another? This is useful when comparing a stock's price action to the S&P Index, for example.

✦ What's their commission structure? Do charges differ depending on whether it's a listed or Nasdaq stock?

✦ What are the margin rates? Do they pay interest on credit balances?

✦ Does the system offer alarms? If so, you can set them to sound off when specified stocks hit a certain price.

✦ Does the system offer news? What's the extra charge?

I encourage you to research at least three systems before you choose one. Ask each company to send you information, then note how fast they respond. Their attitude right out of the gate will tell you something. When you call them on the phone, how fast do they answer? Does a canned voice ask you to leave a message? Are their customer representatives friendly and knowledgeable?

Finally, talk to others who have direct-access systems. Even in this electronic age, word of mouth can be the most reliable reference.

THE COMMISSION MAZE

Commissions are a necessary business expense since, by law, your trades have to go through a registered broker. The rates vary from broker to broker.

To make sense of the maze of commissions, remember that the most important service a broker can give you is to fill your orders—quickly and accurately. Generally speaking, the faster your order is filled, the better price you will receive.

The higher the commission you pay to online brokers, the more "bells and whistles" you have access to, meaning charts, real-time quotes, fundamental analysis, and news. One option is to pay high commission prices (assuming they fill your orders rapidly and efficiently) and use their charts and research.

The bad news: Many brokers' charts aren't detailed enough; they don't have the indicators and oscillators you need as a short-term trader for decision support. The good news: Many fine charting software packages exist in the marketplace. As I mentioned earlier, some reasonably good Web sites offer real-time charts and updated news. If you don't mind wading through their advertisements, some give you the information at no charge. So, an alternative is to open an account with a plain vanilla broker and obtain your charts and news from another source.

Direct-access brokers also offer a range of commission structures. They are usually more intricate than online brokers, so if you want to open an account with one of these brokers, make sure to request a detailed list of charges.

On balance, direct-access software usually provides high-quality, intra-day charts and streaming news, so you don't have to go elsewhere for these tools.

Okay, are you out of breath yet?

Let's sort this stuff out:

+ *Option*: If you intend to jump into short-term trading with both feet and make it a big part of your life, consider opening your account with a direct-access firm that offers level II order-entry capabilities.
+ *Option*: If you intend to wander into trading at a slower pace and trade on a part-time basis, an account with an online broker should be sufficient.
+ *Option*: You may want to venture into the market with an online broker, then transfer to a fancier direct-access system when you feel comfortable.

Know this: The least effective way to learn how to trade is to take on too much at once, then crash and burn because of information overload. Develop your own style that parallels your personality. Comfort is key to successful trading choices.

SLIPPAGE: WHAT IT MEANS

Slippage occurs when you put in your market order to buy or sell, and your order gets filled at a different price than the quote at that moment—higher if you're buying and lower if you're selling. A high degree of slippage can take place when you throw a market order to buy a stock that's "running," or rocketing up in price.

Slippage also chews into your profits when you place a market order to buy a "thinly traded" stock, which means a stock that trades on low volume (less than 300,000 to 500,000 shares per day). The market maker will see your lone order to buy at the market floating in, and he or she will "adjust" the price a bit to suit his or her needs. He or she will drool a little, then raise the price a fraction of a point, and fill your order. (To date, this practice has become more prevalent on the Nasdaq than the NYSE, but I've seen it happen on both exchanges.)

The cure for slippage is to issue limit orders (your order will be filled at a specified price or not at all), or place your orders on a level-II screen through a direct-access broker.

To excel in short-term trading, you must learn the challenges involved. After all, the stakes are your hard-earned money. So, here's a reality lesson: The moment you enter a position, or purchase a stock, you're already "in the hole." Your broker's commission is added onto the price of the purchase. That could total anywhere from $5 to $25 or more. If you add ten cents a share slippage, you're a bit deeper in the hole. On 500 shares, that equals $50. So, if you paid a commission of $15 and add that to slippage of $50, you've already got a drawdown (paper loss) of $65. In order to climb out and profit, the stock has to rise at least eleven to twelve cents a share for you arrive at the even money point, and move even higher for you to profit. When you exit the trade, you again pay commissions and experience possible slippage.

MARGIN ACCOUNTS: HOW THEY WORK

When you open your account, your broker will ask if you want to designate it a standard "margin account." The standard margin is called a "50-percent margin account." (Day trading accounts have different procedures.) That means whatever amount in dollars you deposit into the account, your broker will match your deposit with a loan of equal value. So, if you open an account with $50,000, your broker will automatically loan you another $50,000. Suddenly, you have $100,000 at your fingertips! Isn't that sweet?

But, wait. It's not time to start shopping just yet. As with any bank, your broker charges interest on the loan. The rate is usually low, and no interest is charged unless you actually use the money.

There are two reasons to open a margin account. First, as you become more experienced, the margin gives you extra buying power. Thus, you're "leveraging" your money, or making more money (we hope) than the interest on the loan costs you. Second, the only way you can sell stocks short is to open a margin account. And believe me, in this volatile market, selling short can reap big profits.

If you're an old pro in the stock market, you may already have a margin account. If you're new to this game, your best strategy is to open a margin account, then immediately forget you have the extra buying power.

One of the riskiest things you can do as a new trader is max out your entire account, margin and all. Please understand—when a stock you are holding on margin falls, you lose *twice* as much money as you would if you were playing with just your own cash. Gulp!

As a safety measure, when you first begin trading, forget you have a margin account and use only your original equity to trade with. Keep a portion of your account in cash at all times. Sound boring? Don't worry. The market will provide plenty of entertainment and excitement along the way!

YOU GOTTA HAVE GOALS

Okay, we've discussed your investment in your trading business, as it relates to time and money. You're probably well on your way to furnishing your trading space, and you may have your account paperwork in the mail.

Now for the fun part of the trip.

Studies show that a delicious "carrot" (make mine chocolate!) dangling in front of our nose urges us to work harder and smarter. Let's identify some carrots, or goals, to use as signposts and an ultimate destination: *success*.

In the Short Term

First, let's define short-term goals. Time frame? Six months to a year.

This is the part where most rookie traders smack their lips, rub their palms together, and declare, "I'm going to make $500 a day." Or, "I'm going to make $2,000 a week." Even better, "I'm going to make 50 percent on my money this year."

Hold the ballgame! Maybe you will, maybe you won't. For the sake of your trading career, please avoid promising yourself/your significant other/your kids/the dog that you will bring home a certain amount of investing bacon per day, week, or year.

While you're learning to become a successful market player, your goal is *to conserve your capital*. Believe me, that in and of itself is a challenging goal to achieve!

Once you gain some experience, *then* you can promise yourself and the dog that you'll make more than 50 percent of your trades "green" (winners) in a certain time period. Trust me, it's far better to clear $10 on a trade, than it is to lose $200. Lots of little profits add up to big profits.

After you've been trading for a year or longer, and you're *consistently* taking profits out of the market, you may want to set monetary goals. Personally, I avoid establishing daily dollar goals, such as $1,000 profit per day. A do-or-die number forces me to make questionable trades. Questionable trades equal lost money. So, as they say in Georgia, "That dog won't hunt." I prefer weekly goals; it takes the pressure off, and I usually attain these goals, or better.

Perhaps one of the finest profit-making goals you can establish early on in your trading career is a principal I discussed in my previous book, *A Beginner's Guide to Day Trading Online*. It is: "Trade to trade well, not to make money." If you trade to trade well, by planning your trade and then following your plan precisely, the money will follow. When you keep a running total in your head of the dollar amount made/lost at any given moment, it blurs your perception of market reality. It may even urge you to ignore a potentially dangerous situation. So, make it a goal to *trade to trade well*. Make it a forever-term goal. You'll be glad you did.

The Long Haul

Now, let's define long-term goals. Time frame? Two to ten years.

First, commit to the following goal that defines a professional trader: *To consistently take profits out of the market*. When you reach this goal, you can step proudly into the "arena of success." What's your dream? A log cabin in the Smokey Mountains? A luxury cruise to Alaska? Establishing a charity? Great! Make sure to plant that seed right now. It will act as a terrific motivator, if (when) the going gets tough.

Here's a way to help you attain that long-term goal more quickly. In *The Richest Man in Babylon*, by George S. Clason, the protagonist, Arkad, reigns as the wealthiest man in ancient Babylon. Arkad's first prosperity lesson to his followers is, "Start thy purse to fattening." Further explanation: "A part of all you earn is yours to keep." Arkad insists that when his followers earn money, they immediately put away 10 percent of those earnings into safekeeping.[2]

From now on, when you grab profits from the market, pay yourself first. Take 10 percent and sock it away in a low-risk account. It will grow over time, and checking the balance will uplift your spirits on days the market uses you for a punching bag.

Here are some more goal-setting guidelines:

+ Deep down inside, you must believe you are worthy of financial success.
+ Set realistic goals. Stretching to achieve a high goal is good. Setting yourself up for failure by setting unrealistic goals is detrimental to your self-esteem.
+ Break your goals down into small increments labeled with signposts. Once the signpost is reached, reward yourself. A perfectly executed trade, for example, deserves a treat—a new golf club, a day at the spa, or, if you really hit gold, a weekend away!

Remember, you must be able to imagine (see) yourself reaching your goal. If you can't imagine ever attaining your goals as a successful short-term trader, chances are you won't achieve them. If, however, you form a picture in your mind of yourself as an adept and astute market participant, your actions will confirm your picture, and the picture will confirm your actions.

---

[2] Clason, George S. *The Richest Man in Babylon*, (NY: Signet, 1988).

CHECK YOUR UNDERSTANDING

Okay, now let's review:

1. Trading is a business, like any other. Begin your business plan by writing down the commitment you intend to make in time and money.
2. Make sure that your trading capital is money you can afford to lose.
3. Initial components to budget for your trading area/office: quiet, well-lit space; television, up-to-date PC, large-screen monitor(s); high-speed Internet connection with optional backup connection; surge protectors; and newspaper/magazine subscriptions.
4. To open your trading account, check out online brokers for these requirements: access to real-time quotes, a Web site that is accessible and easy to navigate, a well-organized order-entry screen, a quick confirmation system, account balances and portfolio updates, and reliable, alternative ways of reaching them.
5. If you choose to use a direct-access broker, make sure that they provide weekly charts as an option, candlesticks, and a full complement of indicators and oscillators. Ask for their commission schedule in writing, as some direct-access brokers have complicated commission systems.
6. Slippage occurs when you put in a buy/sell market order, and get filled at a different price than the quote at that moment (higher if you're buying, and lower if you're selling).
7. The standard margin is called a "50-percent margin account," which means your broker matches your deposit with a loan of equal value.
8. Short-term goals to consider: (1) *To conserve your capital,* (2) *To make a certain percentage of your trades "green,"* (3) *Trade to trade well.*
9. Long-term goals to consider: (1) *To consistently take profits out of the markets,* (2) *To attain the "big picture goal" you've always wanted!*
10. Follow the advice of Arkad, "The Richest Man in Babylon": Pay yourself first by taking 10 percent of your market winnings and putting them into a separate, low-risk account.

✦ ✦ ✦

CENTER POINT

If one advances confidently in the direction of his own dreams, and endeavors to live the life which he has imagined, he will meet with a success unexpected in common hours.

—HENRY DAVID THOREAU

Commit: Transform Your Dreams into Goals

Nothing jump-starts us on our roadway to success faster than making a solid commitment to our goals. When we commit ourselves to a desired result, we program ourselves to "lock on," much the same way a missile is programmed to lock onto a target. Then, magically it seems, we proceed on "automatic pilot." Our brain gives us the appropriate actions to pursue the target, no matter how it tries to elude us!

Without a firm commitment to a goal, our autopilot remains in the "off" position; no basis exists for programming or locking onto a target. Perhaps only a hazy idea meanders in and out of our consciousness. Vague ideas and dreams beget vague results.

The act of commitment, however, empowers us to reach into our potential treasure "bag" and bring unused talents into our present-day experience.

We may also discover we can cancel previous limiting beliefs we had about our supposed *lack* of talent or ability. Have you ever declared a hundred times that you're not adept at a certain task, only to find that when pressured into it, you perform at a high level of competency?

The act of commitment programs us to attract new opportunities. When we make a firm commitment, things start happening. Suddenly, when we *know and declare* (yes, writing it down is important!) that we will achieve a certain outcome and adopt it as our truth, all sorts of opportunities start appearing in our lives.

Each time we make a new, positive commitment, we choose to begin a new life experience. Suddenly, what we imagined to be a dream becomes tangible, and transforms into an exciting new reality!

✦ ✦ ✦

CHAPTER 3

Master a Money-Making Mindset

There is only one side to the stock market; . . . not the bull side or the bear side, but the right side. It took me longer to get that general principle fixed firmly in my mind than it did most of the more technical phases of the game of stock speculation.

—JESSE LIVERMORE

The stock market is a timeless macrocosm of energy that expands and contracts as it propels itself through time and space.

As Mark Douglas comments in *The Disciplined Trader,* "The markets are always in motion; they never stop, only pause."[3] Whether they are officially open or closed, they remain stadiums for continuous barter as perceptions of value change.

Imagine this: You purchase shares of equity in a listed company that supplies computer virus scans. On the evening news, the announcer reports that viruses that invade personal computers are on the rise. By the time the New York Stock Exchange rings the opening bell the next morning, your stock price has soared. Did the company fundamentals change in the last twelve hours? Did earnings, the product, or the debt ratio change *overnight?* No. The *perception* of future supply and demand, and thus the value, has changed.

Just as the perception of value fluctuates in human minds twenty-four hours a day, actual marketplaces trade around the clock. Every moment of the day, someone, somewhere, is trading money for interest in companies, financial instruments, agricultural commodities, and more.

As the sun rises and falls on each hemisphere, the events and resulting sentiment in each market affect other markets globally, in a domino effect. In his

---

[3] Douglas, Mark. *The Disciplined Trader,* p. 41 (NY: New York Institute of Finance, 1990).

book, *Intermarket Technical Analysis,* John Murphy says, "One of the most striking lessons . . . is that all markets are interrelated—financial and nonfinancial, domestic and international."[4] While we sleep, events, news, even weather, and the resulting human reactions to those circumstances, determine how our markets open the next morning.

THE MARKET AS AN UNSTRUCTURED ENTITY

Because the market is timeless, it remains unstructured to a large degree. Therein lies the challenge!

We humans like structure. We like to take a certain action with the assurance that it will produce a certain result. We understand limits, borders, and finite circumstances built on foundations of order.

As most of us find out the hard way, the market doesn't work on that principle. And, because added volatility creates wider, more erratic moves based on emotion rather than logic, the market "changes its mind" constantly. Constant change brings on a cornucopia of possibilities—some rational, some that boggle our sense of logic.

How can we—humans who thrive on structure, order, and boundaries—survive in a mercurial market? By creating our own limits. Each time we enter the market, we must carry our own structure—meaning our own definitions, principles, and criteria—along with us.

First, assimilate all the knowledge you can that pertains to this playing field. Next, study your own psychological reactions to the situations trading offers to you. Finally, armed with knowledge of how the market performs—and even more important, how *you* perform when presented with opportunities and challenges— you can draw up a set of guidelines that define your criteria for entering a trade. These criteria define *your* structure, *your* limits, and *your* boundaries. Next, superimpose these onto the market.

Now you are in command of your actions. You are not reactive, you are proactive. You cherry-pick your trades, entering only those with the highest probability of reward and the lowest amount of risk. You plan your trade, and trade your plan. You assume complete responsibility and accountability for your actions. Best of all, your strict approach to the market speeds you to small losses and big profits. And that's what it's all about, isn't it?

---

[4] Murphy, John J. *Intermarket Technical Analysis*, p. 1 (NY: John Wiley & Sons, Inc., 1991).

THE STOCK MARKET IS ALWAYS RIGHT

Surely you've heard the old adage, "the stock market is always right." How true it is!

It has no inherent sense of right or wrong. Did your core holding come out with good earnings? The market sneers and slaps it down. Did Fed Chairman Alan Greenspan smile benignly during a televised speech? The market puffs up in ecstasy.

Are growth stocks overvalued and their P/E (price-to-earnings ratio) blown out of proportion? The market doesn't care. That's the way it is. Like it or leave it.

I once met a CEO from a very large organization who had just retired. He decided to fill his spare time by actively trading in the stock market. This gentleman epitomized success. Handsome and fit, he had a square jaw, silver hair, and drove the biggest Mercedes money could buy. And talk about a "Type A" personality! Everywhere he walked, even on an errand so trivial as lunch or the post office, he led with his chin as though he were going into battle. He spoke rapidly and allowed no time for idle comments. He was a general of people, through and through.

He powered into the stock market, just as he'd powered through everything else in life, sure of his success. Wincing, I watched the market slap him. He licked his wounds and went back for more. The market rolled her eyes, shook her head, and popped him in the chin. He fell, but eventually struggled to his feet and insisted on taking another swing. Pow!

The day came when I couldn't watch any longer. Over lunch, I said, "You're losing money, aren't you?"

He nodded. "I don't understand it. My stocks never act like I think they should. I study analysis and charts. Lord knows, I read books and attend lectures on finance. What more can I do?"

"It's your mindset," I said gently. "You're used to being in charge. You come from a world where you're always obeyed. You've muscled through projects and deals, and if things don't go your way, you use your intellect and power to change them to your favor." I looked directly into his eyes. "You can't do that in the stock market. It won't obey you or anyone else." He flinched at the realization, but he knew it was true.

During the weeks that followed, he tried to alter his mindset, but his attitude was too deeply entrenched. Once he entered a position, he zeroed in on what *should* happen, on what he *wanted* to happen, instead of what *was*. (Get the difference?) He finally decided to take up another endeavor to fill his retirement years.

People who enjoy a position of power in their own communities, organizations, or families often arrive at the market with the expectations of being obeyed. When they buy a stock, they expect it to rise. If it doesn't, frustration sets in.

Know this: The market is bigger than all of us. Few have the power to move it in any direction for any length of time. What we wish, or want to happen, makes no difference. Woe to the player who remains stuck in his or her own opinion of "the way things oughtta be."

We deal with it by adapting ourselves to market movements, and by staying nimble and open-minded. We know that just because we believe the market *should* go up or down, doesn't make it so!

Now, how do we address the previous section that talked about applying our criteria so we're in command to a market that's always right? Like this: When we come to the market to trade, we observe it without emotion, with no thought of *what should be*. Once we identify the apparent trend, we choose stocks with eligible setups and apply our risk/reward criteria to them. If they fit our predetermined plan, we enter the play. If they don't, we stand on the sidelines until a better opportunity comes along.

MEET YOUR EMOTIONS—UP CLOSE AND PERSONAL

By now you've guessed what the biggest obstacle is on your pathway to taking consistent profits out of the financial arenas. You guessed it, your emotions.

As Pogo said, "We have met the enemy, and the enemy is us."

When you're new to trading, you'll probably encounter an emotional roller coaster. For example, you buy a stock that you believe will rise endlessly. Instead, it reverses sharply, swallowing not only your gains, but also a chunk of your capital. Your happiness succumbs to hope. Your hope dissolves into resentment.

The next day you enter another position. It immediately tumbles precariously close to your stop-loss point. Holding your breath and mumbling, "Not again," you watch with dread and apprehension. Suddenly, the stock bounces and soars to new highs, delivering a fat, unexpected bounty. Fear and dread convert to joy and satisfaction. You exhale, then declare staunchly that you knew it all along!

Trouble is, riding that emotional roller coaster can get us into trouble. It also induces stress and exhaustion. At extreme levels, it causes psychological damage.

Professional traders who have been successful in this business for a long time avoid these emotional swings. They've learned how to control their reactions to unexpected market gyrations. And so can you.

That's why I'm addressing the subject of market psychology early on. Just as analysts "pound the table" on stocks they believe will outperform the market, I'm going to "pound the table" on this point. You can read every book and attend every class, hook up a wall full of monitors, and fund your account with a zillion dollars, but I promise you this: *If you don't learn to master your emotions, your account will quickly slide into meltdown.*

THE WINNING MINDSET—TRAIN YOUR BRAIN

We humans instinctively build mental defenses that shield us from the pain of unfulfilled expectations. Our unfulfilled expectations may cause us to create false pictures that distort our vision, and our ability to see our true environment. So, emotional turmoil colors our perception of reality. And, as any psychologist will confirm, emotions are far stronger than logic.

How do we rise above these detrimental feelings? First, we identify which ones "belong" to us. (You can't eliminate something from your life, unless you first acknowledge that you "own" it.) Then, we replace those unwanted emotions with positive responses. At that moment, success is ours.

As mentioned before, most emotions related to the stock market stem from fear and greed. The two are more closely connected than one would imagine. And guess what the bridge is? Excitement!

If we drag fear out into the sunlight, we'll find out exactly what it is. I once heard a minister say, "Fear is nothing, trying to be something."

"Sure," you reply, rolling your eyes. "Tell me that when I watch my brand-new position crash. My palms get sweaty, my heart pounds in my ears, and my stomach churns. You call that *nothing*?"

No. I call that fear. And fear is a *feeling*. Not only is it an unpleasant feeling, it causes blood vessels to constrict, which reduces the oxygen supply to our brains, thus limiting our ability to make rational decisions. And this at a time when we need to make rational decisions the most!

On the other hand, you can't declare, "I'm not scared," and expect fear to disappear. Nature allows no vacuums. You have to feel *something*.

In the previous situation, you bought shares of stock that your research indicated would rise in value. The market, however, had different ideas. It took your stock and hammered it lower. Fear and panic took over when you checked the price. Maybe you went into denial, maybe you rationalized, surely you justified. Still, while your mind raced with thoughts in a frantic attempt to change your pain to pleasure, agony washed over you. You took one of two actions: You held onto the position, refusing to take the loss; or you sold, then chastised yourself for being dumb enough to buy it in the first place.

Guess what? The previous situations, and variations on it, can take place. Instead of *it* controlling you, however, *you'll be in command*. With practice and experience, you'll displace fear and all of its variations (from mild anxiety to head-pounding panic) with a calm confidence spawned by a concise plan that's been filtered through discipline and knowledge.

The fear of being wrong or *the need to be right* has surely lost more money for more people than all of the other attitudes combined!

Imagine this scene: You make every correct move; you research and plan your trade, then buy at the perfect entry point. The following day, the market goes against you. Your stock plummets and hits your mental stop-loss point. Gulp!

Thoughts race through your mind. Should you sell now? Will the stock immediately rebound if you do? Will your loss be for nothing? If you hold on a little longer, will it turn into a win? Will you have to admit to others you were wrong? *Feeling*: Anxiety, disappointment, guilt. *Action*: You ignore your stop-loss point and turn your back on the falling stock.

Unfortunately, Americans and most of "civilized" society are brought up with the dictum that we must always be "right." Strong, smart people are "right." Those who are "wrong," we label ignorant and empty-headed. Consequently, most of us will do *anything* to avoid being wrong. In the stock market, that attitude can be deadly.

Here's the cure for the fear of being wrong/the need to be right. First, banish "right" and "wrong" from your market mentality. From now on, there are no such entities. There are only *choices*. You make a *choice* based on the best information available to you, with your plan at your side.

Remember, no one on this earth knows which way the stock market, or your chosen stock, will move during the next ten minutes, ten days, or ten months. So, you make the most astute choice possible and manage the trade according to plan. If your position moves up, you take profits at your preconceived exit point. If the position surrenders to selling pressure and touches your stop-loss, think, "Hmm . . . this didn't go the way I thought it would. I'll take my loss here and look for another opportunity." That thought triggers the satisfaction of protecting your capital, which in turn causes you to pull the "sell" trigger. No fear, no anxiety, no trepidation, headaches, or stomach twisting. Ahhh. Feels good, doesn't it?

Variations on fear's buddy, greed, are more fun to consider. Unfortunately though, they can cause just as much pain. For example, have you ever chased a stock? I have! If you've been active in the market, you probably have too.

Say the market just opened. A stock on your watch list jumps out of the gate and starts screaming skyward. You think, "Wow! This stock is really flying. Everybody else is paying up for it, so I will too. What's a couple of points in a stock this strong? Betcha it's going to the moon!"

Trouble is, in this scenario, you may end up buying high and selling low. Since the market is controlling you, this is the result more often than not.

Displace that thought pattern with the following: "This stock passed my entry point. Ah, well, I'll catch it the next time. Another opportunity will present itself shortly."

Bear in mind that at this moment, there are more than 9,000 stocks you can choose from. Why be a sheep that might end up shorn?

By the way, if you languish every time you leave money on the table—get over it. Just as you're going to take small losses, you're also going to watch stocks rocket to the moon the day after you sell your position. Don't drive yourself bonkers by adding up the profits you *could* have made. Learn to shrug off missed money. It's part of the business.

Another greed-motivated behavior is to *"bet the ranch,"* especially on a hot tip. Say a cocky taxi driver told you furtively that Cranky Computers was going to be acquired tomorrow morning early by Huge Conglomerate, Inc. Out of the side of his mouth, he says, "The stock price is gonna scream!"

You run home and conduct some quick research. Surprisingly enough, Cranky has good fundamentals and decent charts. Instead of buying a tiny lot size for fun, you max out your account, margin and all. Yessiree, Cranky Computers is going to send your kids to college! Wow, you owe that cabby, big time!

Cranky pops up at the open, then tanks. Slack-jawed and confused, smarting from the loss and overwhelmed with guilt, you sell. Then, you slump in your chair and spend the rest of the morning berating yourself for being dumb as a box of rocks.

Hold it. Get it behind you. Next, replace your "bet the ranch" mentality with the firm assertion that you are an astute trader. From this moment forward, you are far too wise to ever commit a major portion of your portfolio to *any* stock. Period.

When someone gives you a hot tip, and you *can't* resist, research it. If the stock fits all of your guidelines, buy a limited amount and set a tight stop-loss. Apply the same well-thought-out plan you assign to your other positions. Say the rumor's true, and the stock flies up. Take your profits fast. (Market mandate: Buy the rumor, sell the news.) Maybe (probably) the rumor is false. Sell quick and tell yourself that your resolve to ignore hot tips is now firmly in place!

I will admit to checking charts on tips ever since I experienced a good one. On a flight a few years ago, I overheard two men in the row behind me talking. One man reminded the other to check out a certain stock when he arrived home; the stock had great fundamentals and was poised to rise soon.

As soon as *I* got home, I called my stockbroker with the tip. (Those were the days before online brokers.) With great amusement and much clucking, my broker placated me and looked up the stock. Huh, he reported, well the darn thing looked pretty good. And, yes, he agreed I should buy a *few* shares. Which I did. And made money. So there. It's not impossible to make money from hot tips, just improbable. And dangerous if done with great expectations and no discipline.

Hope, faith, and *optimism* are certainly wonderful attitudes to infuse into our everyday lives. But please, leave them out of your financial decisions. They can get you creamed!

Have you ever heard yourself whispering, "Please, *please* make this stock go up"? Hope motivates us to send that prayer to the stock market god. She may not be listening. Faith makes us declare staunchly to our friends and ourselves (when our stock is tanking), "It's a good company." (Ever heard those words before?) Optimism speaks through us, with, "It'll come back. After all, the market has an upside bias." How do I know these words so well? Believe me, early in my trading career, I repeated them like a mantra.

For such delightful characteristics, hope, faith, and optimism sure cause mayhem when they act as decision-making tools in the financial markets. Because they are detrimental to my wealth, I place mine in a make-believe basket placed outside my office door. I reclaim them when I leave for the day. Is that a head game I play with myself? Sure. Does it save me money? Absolutely. And I'll do it until my market days are over.

THE END RESULT: WHAT IT LOOKS LIKE

You can only achieve the self-mastery that leads to success, if you know what that success looks like. Here's the picture: Wisely, you decided to learn all you could before entering the game. You crossed the market's threshold cautiously. So now, when you buy or sell a stock, you do so secure in the knowledge that you've planned for all eventual outcomes.

The feelings you experience are those of *serenity, confidence,* and *detachment.* You have no attachment to the outcome of the trade. Robot-like, you observe the markets, and your stock's reaction to that environment.

In addition, you know yourself. Honest introspection sheds light on the emotions you chose to displace, and those that will serve you well. Maybe you're impulsive, stubborn, and have a high tolerance for risk. Recognizing these traits, you've resolved to displace them with a mindset geared to strict money management.

On the other hand, maybe you're a die-hard perfectionist. You'll approach each entry and exit driven by the need for precision. Fantastic. It doesn't get any better than that!

As you gain more knowledge and make more decisions filtered through your increasing self-mastery, you'll find that experience adds to both knowledge and discipline. In other words, it's a self-fulfilling circle. Each component supports the other. After all, knowledge without discipline is dangerous. Discipline without knowledge has little value. And you won't ever gain experience without the other two.

Soon, you'll step into the market with the firm conviction of a professional who knows the market only hurts those who allow it to. And, you'll be taking gains on a consistent basis.

R & R: DON'T GO SHOPPING WITHOUT IT

Responsibility and respect represent two of the most important constituents in our financial—and indeed, our non-financial—lives. They must be an integral part of our actions.

Ever talk to someone at a cocktail party, who says smugly, "I made 25 percent on my portfolio this year"? Talk to that same person in a bear market, and he or she will whine, "The market took away 25 percent of my portfolio." Hear the difference? He or she made the brilliant decisions that increased the portfolio value. The stock market "took" money away.

You, as a confident market participant, take full responsibility for your portfolio's bottom line. You are aware of the fact that you alone push the "buy" and "sell" buttons.

You also respect money, especially the money in your account. You realize that without that capital, you are out of the game completely. You know that the primary objective when you compete in the financial arena is to *protect your capital at all times.*

Take a moment to reflect. Do you treat your money carefully? Do you pay your bills on time? Do you spend thoughtfully? Are crumpled $20 bills thrown on the dresser? Keeping bills carefully organized in your wallet indicate that you respect money and the power it has.

SELF-RESPECT AND DESERVEDNESS

The world's most successful traders and investors believe in themselves and their ability to win. It's a known fact among top traders: The beliefs you have about yourself as a person will impact the outcome of your profits in a big way!

As Mark Douglas says in *The Disciplined Trader,* "Contradictory beliefs cancel your energy because you have a built-in mental conflict between the validity of one belief, expressing itself only at the direct expense of another belief."[5]

Do you state in one moment that you can learn how to take big gains out of the market—and in the next decide you'll never catch on? Do you snatch a rapid return out of a stock in one week, then "accidentally" give it back the next? Subconsciously, you may not believe making money rapidly and without back-breaking labor is honest work!

Reflect on your inner level of deservedness. Deep down inside, do you believe you *deserve* to be wealthy, or at least to accumulate a lot more money than you have at the present?

---

[5] Douglas, p. 169.

Consider this: Money is a means of exchange that provides us with circumstances and experiences we could not otherwise have. There is plenty for all. When we attract abundance and prosperity into our lives, we are able to help others more fully.

So, declare the truth: You deserve the best life has to offer, including abundant health, happiness, *and* money!

CHECK YOUR UNDERSTANDING

Time for review:

1. The market is timeless and unstructured.
2. To succeed in the market, when we trade we must bring our own structure and order with us.
3. The stock market is always "right."
4. You can fund your account with a hefty sum, buy the most expensive equipment available, and acquire reams of knowledge about the market. But if you can't control your emotions, your account will quickly dissolve.
5. Emotional turmoil colors our perception of reality.
6. Learn to replace emotions of fear and greed, and their variations, with the calm confidence borne of having a plan in place, and trading according to that plan.
7. Leave hope, faith, and optimism outside your trading office door.
8. Self-mastery leads to success: You've studied and learned as much as possible before embarking on your trading career; you have an exact plan for each trade; you stay detached from the outcome of the trade.
9. Responsibility and respect play important roles in the way we feel about our money, and how we treat it.
10. The world's most successful traders believe in themselves, and so do we.

✦ ✦ ✦

CENTER POINT

The only way to discover the limits of the possible is to go beyond them, to the impossible.

—ARTHUR C. CLARKE

Make Your Circle Bigger

As humans, our goal is to reach our highest potential. We are programmed for excellence! No endeavor is beyond our potential. Once we believe in ourselves, every activity and goal is within our grasp. Any human experience can be enjoyed once we decide to venture into the "unknown."

Picture yourself as the center of a circle. Within the space between you and the circle's circumference is your world, meaning your friends, family, experiences, value system, career, even level of health.

Beyond that circle are the places you've never visited, experiences you've never had, mindsets you can't imagine, knowledge you haven't learned, points of view you've never encountered. Also drifting outside your circle reside the wonderful talents you don't realize you have, and the "distant" parts of yourself you've never explored!

Outside your circle, there are no guarantees. It's a never-never land we gaze at and refer to as "someday." "Someday I'll write a book." "Someday, I'll learn to speak French." "Someday, I'll go to Europe." "Someday I'll tell her how much I love her."

Think of all the people we honor as geniuses, people who excelled and gave spectacularly to the world. They ventured outside their circles and stepped into the unknown: Leonardo da Vinci, Albert Einstein, Gandhi, Galileo, and Winston Churchill, to name a few, left the safety of the "known" to journey into the unknown.

In order to grasp all the joy life has to offer, we have to open ourselves to new experiences. We must go to the edge of our circles and break through the boundaries. That automatically makes our circle bigger. New vistas open up, and we're on the road to reaching our full, exciting potential!

✦ ✦ ✦

CHAPTER 4

Market Machinations 101: The Fuel That Sparks the Energy

I know from experience that nobody can give me a tip or a series of tips that will make more money for me than my own judgment.

—JESSE LIVERMORE

This was once overheard from a top technical analyst: "Trading successfully may be one of the most difficult things to accomplish. We never know for sure whether a specific action will produce a specific result."

Wow, is that accurate! No two trades are ever alike. But then, no single day in the stock market duplicates another. Every day hurtles through a profusion of different events, judged by millions of mindsets, producing a unique mixture of consequences.

And always, the final result manifests itself in *price*.

THE BUCK STOPS HERE

Imagine a giant tornado-like tunnel. At the top of this ferocious, whirling mass of energy are global events and our reactions to them. The vortex spins with supply and demand levels, interest rates, and cyclical industry shifts. Further down, analysts' reports, company earnings, and the public's opinion on sectors and leading equities revolves in a constant pirouette. All elements of the maelstrom converge to a single point: *price.*

Price is the consensus of opinion in a single moment.

Say you want to sell your current holding in Worldwide Wireless. I want to buy shares of Worldwide Wireless. We agree that the current selling price of $60 a share is fair. So we exchange equities for money.

Moments later, the consensus shifts. For whatever reason, perception of the value of Worldwide changes. Market players decide the stock is worth more per share, say $60.25. Once again, shares and money change hands. Have the fundamentals of the company changed in that instant? No. The change in collective consciousness—the perception of reality—dictated by those who currently participated in this stock made the change.

Also remember this: When you sell your shares of a stock to me, you believe the value of the stock will soon shrink. I buy because I believe the value will increase. In the short term, only one of us will be right!

FUNDAMENTAL ANALYSIS VS. TECHNICAL ANALYSIS:
THE TUG O'WAR

When I first started investing, I talked to a lot of stockbrokers. The majority of them relied solely on fundamental analysis as their decision support tool, quoting from company financial reports and earnings research for their investment advice. They fluffed off technical charts as hocus-pocus. Their standard chant: "I've never met a rich technical analyst."

Tugging on the other end of the rope were the card-carrying members of the technical analysts' club. "Who has time," they insisted, "to comb through pages of sleep-inducing reports? A chart tells you all you need to know."

Fundamental analysis and technical analysis are the two major methods of examining a publicly traded company to determine the health of its stock. (I've been told that some folks buy stocks on the strength of a company's astrological charts and a system of "sacred numbers," but for now we'll stick to standard analysis.)

Fundamental analysis is like taking an "x-ray" of a company. It examines the internal financial fitness of an organization and tells us how strong it is. Fundamental analysts check out the supply and demand levels of the products and/or services the company produces. Then, they study company reports, profit and loss summaries, price-to-earnings (PE) ratios (calculated by dividing the stock's price by its earnings-per-share figure), market share, sales and growth, and brokerage analyst's ratings. Those who buy and sell on the strength of a company's fundamentals generally buy a stock "for the long haul," and ignore gymnastics performed by the market on any given day.

Technical analysis is the study of time, price, and sentiment of a chosen equity (or market or index) as shown on charts. The price action draws patterns on those charts. And, because human behavior can be repetitive, the price patterns can be repetitive. When keen-eyed technical analysts recognize one of those formations starting to form, it gives them a set of probabilities on which to base the stock's next move.

If fundamentals show us a company's internal strength, then a chart reveals that stock's personality. As an added benefit, charts allow us to quickly compare price action of a specific stock to its buddies in the same industry, and to broader indexes such as the S&P 500. Obviously, charts have the advantage of speed, showing the "picture is worth a thousand words" theme in action.

When you utilize fundamental and technical analyses together, you've got an accurate picture of a company's financial fitness and personality profile. That's why, more and more, we see technical analysts sneaking looks at a company's fundamental information, and fundamental analysts furtively peeking at charts.

It appears the tug of war is slowing. Stalwart members of both camps have softened their stances and released their grips. A truce is in the offing!

We, as wise and profitable short-term traders, recognize the value of both worlds. When we enter the market, we want all odds possible in our corner. To that end, the following section shows how to find the most comprehensive fundamental information about a company, in the least amount of time.

FUNDAMENTAL ANALYSIS: QUICK YET THOROUGH SOURCES

In this age of information, we no longer have to spend hours wading through pages of a company's mind-numbing financial reports to find out if it's worth our time and money. Instead, we're going to look at a quick way to check a stock's fundamental health. (Later in the chapter you'll find Web sites where you can find more fundamental data about companies on your stock target list.)

The kind folks at *Investor's Business Daily* (IBD) have devised a ranking system for stocks that I find invaluable. Under the guidance and ownership of the renowned William O'Neil, they provide proprietary ratings that give you a quick and reliable snapshot of corporate numbers. (Please understand, I am not connected with IBD.)

When I use IBD's ratings method, as opposed to doing my own research, it's analogous to either eating all the servings of a balanced meal, or taking a vitamin and getting most of the same nutrients in one fast, quick swallow. The following is the vitamin approach.

You can glance at your stock's listing, check out the six number-letter combination, and thus obtain your daily dose of fundamentals. Then, during your free time, you can wander through the Web sites listed a bit later in the chapter and delve into in-depth reports and research.

IBD PROPRIETARY CORPORATE RATINGS

The *Investor's Business Daily* SmartSelect ratings cover the following:

+ *SmartSelect Composite Rating.* Combines all ratings that follow into a combined ranking. The stock's percent off its fifty-two-week high is included. Results are compared to all other companies; then the stock is assigned a rating from 1–99. We prefer the stock to rank 70 or higher.

+ *Earnings Per Share (EPS) Rating.* Tells you a stock's average short-term (recent quarters) and long-term (last three years) earnings growth rate. The number you see is how your company compares to all other companies; the scale goes from 1–99, with 99 being the highest rating achievable. For our purposes, we want this number to come in at 70 or higher.

+ *Relative Price Strength (RS) Rating.* Measures a stock's relative price change in the last twelve months in comparison to all other equities. Again, the scale runs from 1–99, and we look for a rating of 70 or higher.

+ *Industry Relative Price Strength Rating.* Contrasts a stock's industry price action in the last six months to the other 196 industries in IBD's industry list. The scale is in letters from A to E, with A representing the best-performing industries. Look for stocks with A or B rankings.

+ *Sales + Profit Margins + ROE (Return on Equity) Rating.* Crunches a firm's sales growth rate during the last three quarters, before and after profit margins and return on equity into a letter. Again, the ratings are A–E. We want stocks rated A or B.

+ *Accumulation/Distribution Rating.* Applies a formula of price and volume changes in the last thirteen weeks to determine if it is being accumulated (bought) or distributed (sold). Again, ratings are A–E, with A equals heavy buying, C equals neutral, and E equals heavy selling. This "Acc/Dis" rating is very important. Choose stocks with an A or B.

These ratings are located next to the stock's listing in the IBD tables. For example, you would find your target stock and see: *99, 99, 99, A, A, A, 72 (represents fifty-two-week high) Cranky Computers* (then the rest of the quote information, etc.). Of course, the three 99s and the three As indicate the highest ratings possible; such a stock probably doesn't exist! Still, you can understand how fast this number/letter combination gives you an instant picture of a company's internal health. Sweet, huh?

In addition, check IBD's "The IBD List," published in each weekend edition (on Fridays). The roster inventories the best issues the S&P 500 has to offer in earnings per share ratings of 80 or higher. Also included are each stock's ticker symbol, industry (IBD tracks 197 industries), earnings growth rate, and First Call (*www.thomsonfinancial.com*) earnings estimate. It's a great list to pull stocks from in order to formulate your own personal "watch list."

MORE INSTANT INFO: CNBC, CNN, AND BLOOMBERG

Walk into any trading room, and you will no doubt see televisions perched near the ceiling tuned to CNBC, CNN, and Bloomberg financial networks. They report global events, and interview nabobs such as CEOs, political pundits, and institutional analysts. It's important for you to stay abreast of all events that affect your portfolio, so it's a good idea to listen to one of these networks whenever you can.

Sometimes CNBC will feature an off-the-wall, self-declared "expert" sporting a baseball cap topped with a propeller and waving a fistful of balloons pushing municipal bonds, just to see if we're awake. Overall, though, the penguin tape is my favorite. When a bunch of analysts gang up on a company and all downgrade it on the same day, CNBC shows a group of penguins waddling to the edge of their ice float, then plunging all at once into the chilly water. Oh, how a little humor adds balance to the puckered-brow world of dollars and (sometimes little) sense!

And while we're on this subject, basing your stock picks on analysts' upgrades and downgrades will send you to Pecan Manor (the nut house). Remember, analysts think in terms of long-term holds, not a few days or weeks.

Many people trade and invest according to financial network news. Just keep in mind that trading news can go against you. Again, the old market caveat, "Buy the rumor, sell the news" remains true.

How many times have you watched companies announce good earnings news only to see the stock price get driven into the ground the next day? The good news/price plummet syndrome sometimes happens because the earnings news leaked out early and the price rose *before* the announcement. Or, maybe the host industry is stuck in a nasty downtrend, and no amount of good news will induce buyers to step to the plate. Generally speaking, good news lasts for one day, and bad news for three days.

However, if Fed Chairman Alan Greenspan appears on your screen and utters phrases like "irrational exuberance," and "looming inflation," pay attention. Before he reaches the end of either of those sentences, start pushing the sell button as fast as you can!

Use financial network news as a great overall global and market picture, and to stay aware of market sentiment. As a rule, though, refrain from basing single trades on lightning-bolt announcements.

Before we leave newspapers and networks, I want to mention the *Wall Street Journal*, first published in July 1889 by Charles Dow, and its sister paper,

Barron's, which hits the streets on weekends. Alan Abelson's crusty opening commentary, "Up and Down Wall Street," alone is worth the price of the subscription. Both are excellent financial resources published by Dow Jones & Co.

WONDERFUL WEB SITES TO WANDER THROUGH

The World Wide Web offers more financial research than you could ever hope to wade through in a lifetime! One report ventured that more than 13,000 financial Web sites now grace cyberspace. I suspect the true number runs much higher. Here's a micro-list of well-known, well-rounded sites to jump-start your research. Some are free, some offer a free trial subscription, and then charge a nominal monthly price. Enjoy!

+ **Big Charts** *(www.bigcharts.com)*. Bills itself as "the world's coolest charting and research site. Free interactive charts, quotes, industry analysis, intra-day stock screeners, market news, and commentary. The charts at this Web site offer most all indicator studies, plus you can overlay indexes on stock charts. Great charts for beginners who don't have charting software yet.

+ **BigEasy Investor** *(www.bigeasyinvestor.com)*. Popular among traders, this easy-to-use free site offers stock screening, charts, analysis, and research. It also features extensive educational tools for both novice and seasoned traders. The Trader's Playbook shows "hows" and "whys" of good plays, and the Trader's Dictionary offers a great resource on market terms.

+ **BigTrends.com** *(www.bigtrends.com)*. A good Web site for traders that offers daily market analysis, e-mail newsletters, feature articles, and trading education by Price Headley. Additional subscription services and products available.

+ **Bloomberg** *(www.bloomberg.com)*. Offers news, detailed stock lists, quotes, and more. Also, you can sign up for Bloomberg's Market Monitor, which will track up to ten stocks or indexes and give you updates on their performance.

+ **CBS Market Watch** *(www.cbs.marketwatch.com)*. Offers a portfolio tracker, stock screener, charting utilities for technical analysis with direct links to data from Hoover's and Zack's.

+ **ClnetNews.com** *(www.investor.cnet.com)*. Links to the latest news stories and snapshots of current market activity, quotes, SEC filings, company profiles, and competitors. Targets tech companies/news.

+ **DailyStocks.com** *(www.dailystocks.com)*. This site bills itself as the Web's first and biggest stock research site. It offers research including quotes and screens. If you still can't find the data you need, Daily Stocks boasts a three-page list of links to other Web sites.

✦ **Fairmark Press** *(www.fairmark.com)*. Tax guide for traders/investors. Offers tax forms and publications, books, and handy "Reference Room," a message board for tax questions.

✦ **Hoover's Online** *(www.hoovers.com)*. Lots of information, including profiles of public and private companies, IPO (initial public offering) pages, and industry research.

✦ **Investor's Business Daily** *(www.investors.com)*. Features selected articles from the daily newspaper. Provides easy-to-use stock charts and screens. You can also access *IBD*'s stock ratings through the "Stock Doctor" section.

✦ **Microsoft MoneyCentral** *(www.moneycentral.msn.com)*. Real-time quotes and portfolio and charting tools. Provides timely news, analysis, SEC filings, and a stock and fund screener. An inside view from six professional advisers, insider trading, and analyst recommendations.

✦ **The Motley Fool** *(www.fool.com)*. A comprehensive site where your portfolio can link to customizable charts, quotes, news, estimates, and other data. Offers one of the liveliest message boards around.

✦ **Quicken.com** *(www.quicken.com)*. A full-service personal-finance site that includes banking, mortgage, and insurance information. It offers a portfolio tracker, quotes, a stock screener, news, and a mutual fund finder. In addition, you will find a retirement planner and a Roth IRA calculator.

✦ **Quote.com** *(www.finance.lycos.com)*. Provides real-time market information and displays an unlimited number of charts, quote sheets, hot lists, historical time and sales data, and summary period data—all updated live in real time.

✦ **Silicon Investor** *(www.siliconinvestor.com)*. Has news, real-time quotes, research, StockTalk, and a host of award-winning message boards. One of the best tech stock sites on the Web.

✦ **sixer.com** *(www.sixer.com)*. A Web site for traders that provides technical analysis, market news, community discussions, and trading education. Their "active game plan" offers watchlists for traders.

✦ **SmartMoney.com** *(www.smartmoney.com)*. A business and financial Web site offering commentary, portfolio tracking, a stock watch list, charting center, daily market reports, and hourly updates. It includes quotes, news, a fund finder, company snapshots, analyst recommendations, and more.

✦ **StockCharts** *(www.stockcharts.com)*. Everything about charts you've ever wanted to know, and then some. Good market commentary, along with sections on "Tools & Charts" and "Chart School," which lists every type of chart imaginable. "The Experts" features advice from noted technical analysts like Arthur Hill and John Murphy.

✦ **TheStreet.com** *(www.thestreet.com).* Gives expert analysis of the investment scene before, during, and after the trading day. It provides quotes, fund facts/scoreboards, portfolio tracker, stock/fund charts, Thomson reports, and SEC filings.

✦ **Thomson Investor Network** *(www.thomsoninvest.net).* Offers news and expert tips. You can see what analysts at some of the mega-brokerage houses think of your stock picks. Check out the "First Call" earnings estimate section.

✦ **TradingMarkets** *(www.tradingmarkets.com).* Geared to traders and active investors, this excellent and highly professional site includes top-notch educational sections. Also, check out the message boards, Stock Scanner, commentaries, and intra-day updates. Well worth the nominal monthly fee.

✦ **Yahoo! Finance** *(www.quote.yahoo.com).* Tools include a stock screener, portfolio, message boards and stock chat area, a personal stock pager, and company profiles. One page will display quotes and historical charts, current news, and links to research and related user messages.

After you scan these sites, you'll find your favorites that you'll return to time after time, and you'll also find new ones that pique your interest. Also, check my Web site, *www.toniturner.com.* The Financial Links page lists an updated selection of sites you may want to check out.

MAGAZINES

Two excellent magazines come to mind that target traders, *Active Trader* *(www.activetradermag.com)* and *Stocks & Commodities (www.traders.com).* *Active Trader* comes chock-full of articles that educate traders about everything from market psychology to pattern analysis. Its "Trading Basics" section speaks primarily to novice traders, and is well worth the read. *Stocks and Commodities* does a great job of explaining various indicators and how to use them, among other topics. It also gives sector (industry) reviews and interviews industry gurus.

Of course, a whole host of magazines geared to investors and American business line the newsstand shelves. Most are treasure troves of educational material, but are not to be depended on for up-to-the-second fundamental information. The time lag between the writing and go-to-press dates make fundamentals too dated for short-term traders.

In the upcoming chapters, you're going to learn charting basics and how to choose a stock. It's going to get hectic, so get your rest and take your vitamins!

CHECK YOUR UNDERSTANDING

See how are you doing so far:

1. Price is the consensus of opinion on a stock in a single moment.
2. Fundamental analysis and technical analysis are the two major methods of examining a publicly traded company to determine the health of its stock.
3. Fundamental analysts study supply and demand levels of the products and/or services the company produces. They also study company reports, profit and loss summaries, price-to-earnings (PE) ratios (calculated by dividing the stock's price by its earnings-per-share figure), market share, sales and growth, and brokerage analyst ratings.
4. Technical analysis is the study of time, price, and sentiment of a chosen equity (or market or index) as shown on charts.
5. *Investor's Business Daily (IBD)* provides proprietary ratings that give you a quick and reliable snapshot of corporate fundamentals.
6. CNBC, CNN, and Bloomberg television networks are used as great overall global and market resources and to stay aware of market sentiment. As a rule, though, refrain from basing single trades on lightning-bolt network announcements.

✦ ✦ ✦

CENTER POINT

Follow your heart, your dreams, your desires. Do what your soul calls you to do, whatever it is, and allow it to be finished; then you will go onto another adventure.

—RAMTHA

Invite Spontaneity into Your Life

The stock market is a rigid mistress. Those who meet with success in her playground must proceed each day armed with exacting guidelines and principles, a structured mindset, and unyielding discipline. Optimism, hope, and spontaneity must be avoided at all times.

When we leave this arena, however, in order to achieve balance and refresh our spirits, it's beneficial to shift our perspectives and mindsets to the opposite end of the spectrum, and invite spontaneity into our world.

Spontaneity means trying anything on the spur of the moment, just because it's an experience you might enjoy. The actual experience may turn out differently than you imagine it might, but you'll surely have a good time finding out and sometimes, impulsive actions have exciting results that ultimately change your life for the better.

If you act spontaneously, and especially if those around you don't expect it, you may be labeled as irresponsible. Good. What fun! Wouldn't you rather be the one having the adventure, rather than the one who stayed behind and gossiped about it?

We all know "higher ups" who get stuck on their thrones, who forsake the art and joy of spontaneity. They march through their lives with ramrod backs, noses held high, and blinders in place. When presented with a new suggestion, their standard retort is, "We've never done it that way before, and we're not changing things now."

Conversely, what do you want to wager that the zipper, the paper clip, and the hula-hoop flew out of nowhere to zap their open-minded inventors with a spontaneous bolt of genius?

We spoke in an earlier discussion of the masks we wear that disguise our inner light. Spontaneity chips off those masks and reveals our true spirit of joy just beneath.

For fun, consider indulging yourself in a spontaneous act, or two (three?), this week. Grab the phone and call someone you haven't talked to in years. Jump up from your desk in the middle of the day and take a fast walk around the block. Call out to the hotdog vendor that you'd miss him if he weren't there. Ask one of your children to go to a Disney movie. Do a somersault in the park.

And remember, sometimes an act of joyful spontaneity results in unexpected blessings that last a lifetime!

✦ ✦ ✦

CHAPTER 5

Market Machinations 102: Basic Charting Techniques That Make You Money

> *My plan of trading was sound enough and won oftener than it lost. If I had stuck to it I'd have been right perhaps as often as seven out of ten times.*
>
> —JESSE LIVERMORE

Chapter 4 showed you where to find quick yet comprehensive fundamental information. Now, it's time to begin learning the basic skills of technical analysis. I fully realize that the words "technical analysis" scare the bejeepers out of most people, but I promise you, it's not as intimidating as it sounds.

Just keep this in mind: The moment you start absorbing the charting essentials in this chapter and those that follow, you will be way ahead of most market players—and on your way to pocketing bigger profits.

First, let's take a quick look at how cycles play a role in the way the financial markets pulsate through time.

CYCLES: THE WORLD'S OPERATING SYSTEM

Our world, indeed our universe, operates on a system of cycles. We know that the Earth, along with her sister planets, orbits around the sun. A complete orbit equals a cycle, which we refer to as a "year." Predictable weather patterns create four seasons, each with its own cycle, within that year. Tides flow in and out on exact cycles. Humans and all living creatures experience cycles of life, including birth, childhood, puberty, adulthood, and passing on.

Industrialized economies progress through cycles of expansion, peaking, trough, and expansion again. It follows then that the major industries propelling those economies pass through four phases during their existence: introduction, growth, maturity, and decline. Those industries consist of separate companies, and of course, the securities issued by those companies tend to anticipate business cycles and move in the same direction.

When you look at a stock chart (Figure 5-1), you can observe its price history and the cycles—or series of peaks and troughs—that it's completed so far.

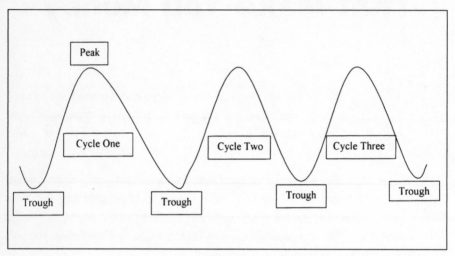

Figure 5-1.
Economic cycles.

If you observe a monthly or weekly chart, where each bar or candlestick (we discuss candlesticks in Chapter 6) represents one month or one week, respectively, you may be able to look at a stock's price history for an extended duration of time, such as five to ten years. Although the cycles may not be formed as uniformly as those drawn in Figure 5-1, they will still etch a bell-curve, or cycle formation, consisting of peaks and valleys, or troughs.

These cycles take place from the macrocosm to the microcosm. Each large cycle consists of many smaller cycles, and each small cycle is formed by a sequence of even tinier cycles.

Here's an analogy: This book is made of many chapters. Within each chapter are separate sections that, when strung together, create that chapter. The sections are made of a series of paragraphs; the paragraphs are built of sentences, which are formed by words. Each word, sentence, paragraph, and section is a complete unit in and of itself. And, when looked at as a whole, they form the complete book. Get the picture?

So, you will find complete cycles occurring on monthly, weekly, daily, and intra-day stock charts, where one bar or candlestick may represent a time frame of one month, one week, one day, or intra-day designations, such as sixty minutes, thirty minutes, five minutes, one minute, or any increment in-between.

LET'S DRAW THE CURTAIN ON STAGE ANALYSIS

A "close-up" of a cycle, whatever the time frame, reveals that it's constructed of four different movements, or stages. We call the study of these stages "Stage Analysis."

When you learn how to identify which of the four price stages (Figure 5-2) your target stock currently inhabits, you've made the first step to keeping your losses small and your profits large!

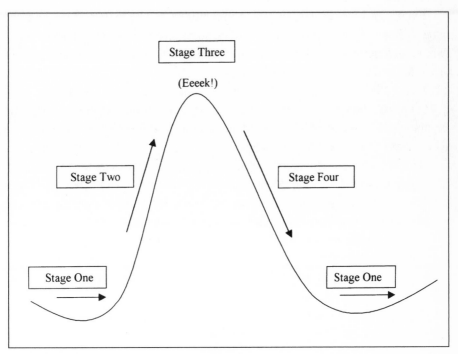

Figure 5-2.
Four stages of a cycle.

Stage One represents the valley, or trough, of the cycle. This is when the stock prices are at their lows of the cycle. During these times—which on weekly and daily charts could last from weeks to months—the stock price moves sideways in a range between an approximate high and low price, and increments in between. You'll hear gurus and analysts talk about a stock in Stage One as "basing." That means the stock is forming a new price base from which it will (hopefully!) start to rise again.

What is the collective mindset of market players participating in a Stage One? Volatile vacillation! Buyers hold the price up each time it falls to the bottom of the base, and sellers push it down each time it rises to the top of the base. Equal pressure from buyers and sellers cause the stock to oscillate sideways, sort of like a snake swiveling through a drainage pipe.

When the stock bases for a period of time, market conditions, industry rotation, or good news will urge buyers to step in and start paying higher prices. Then, the price "breaks out" of its base and shoots into an uptrend, or Stage Two. The collective mindset—greed—creates more and more demand, which drives the stock higher. Rising, then pulling back and rising again, it rockets to higher and higher prices on the wings of euphoria.

Finally, at its peak, buyers refuse to continue paying higher prices, and the uptrend slows to a halt. Euphoria and demand dissipate. So the uptrend, or Stage Two, is broken, and the stock drifts sideways into a Stage Three. Technical analysts refer to this pattern as "rolling over."

During Stage Three, which is the peak of the cycle, buyers support, or "hold up," the price when it falls. Sellers press the price down when it rises. As you can see, the stock price seems suspended in "mid-air." The collective emotion in a stock experiencing Stage Three: indecision.

At some point, when a stock is in a Stage Three, fear steps to the forefront. (If it doesn't, and the stock breaks out to new highs, it resumes a Stage Two.) When fear sets in, buyers refuse to support the stock any longer. Selling pressure increases and the stock tumbles into a downtrend, into a Stage Four.

Now the stock "heads south." In a Stage Four (which looks like a Stage Two, reversed) the stock dives to lower prices, rebounds a bit, and then dives again (think: "rubber rock"). Supply floods the market as fear goads terrified sellers into unloading their long positions.

The only happy campers who hold a Stage Four stock are short sellers. As you may remember, short-sellers sell the stock at a high price. Then, they buy it back at a lower price and pocket the difference as profit. (We'll go into selling short later.)

Stage Four is also the place where frustrated investors, watching their stocks tank and principal shrink, may "average down" by buying more of the losing issue. Because averaging down lowers the average price paid for the stock, their fervent hope is that when the stock rebounds, losses will recoup faster.

Maybe. Maybe not. Some beat-up stocks stay down for the count, or at least for weeks and months. Hanging onto these weaklings ties up money that could

Hot Tip

As a general rule, stocks fall three times faster than they rise. Why? Fearful, panicky sellers react even faster than buyers motivated by greed and euphoria!

be spent on a strong stock that makes money. We sometimes call capital invested in such issues "dead money."

Since we're on this subject, if you have the "averaging down" mentality, please banish it. There's a correct way to average down that's based on sound money-management principals; then there's the desperate averaging down method that usually leads to bigger losses. In the pages that follow, you'll learn how to average down properly.

Stage Four is also when some investors, believing they're getting a "blue-light special," load the truck with a tanking issue. Watch them go slack-jawed when their cheap stock gets even cheaper!

As an astute trader, you won't let that happen to you. You'll stand on the side-lines, cash in hand, while others hold losers or run screaming to the door. Then, when the selling is over, you'll step in and buy high-quality bargains that are ready to recover. Sound like fun? It is!

At some point, a stock in a Stage Four will slow its descent. Hot and furious selling evaporates, and buyers start stepping up to the plate. Now the stock turns back into a sideways, basing pattern—a Stage One—and the cycle is complete.

DIFFERENT STAGES CALL FOR DIFFERENT REACTIONS

With a little practice in looking at charts, you'll start recognizing which stage of a cycle a stock is experiencing. This in turn will initiate your selection process for buying stocks.

We use Stage One to scan for stocks that are basing, preferably for four to six weeks. Again, these stocks are in the first stage of a new cycle, and usually coincide with a market or industry correction. This is when a stock is "on sale." Usually, we don't buy stocks in Stage One. We monitor them. When they break out of their base in synchronicity with other factors, *that's* when we jump in!

Stage Two is where you, as a short-term trader, will spend most of your time and make most of your profits. When you're position trading, you spot a stock breaking out of a solid Stage One base into a Stage Two uptrend. You buy it and ride it for several weeks, taking profits when it completes its entire Stage Two.

If you opt to swing trade, you play Stage Two by buying the break outs and selling before the stock pulls back, taking multiple-point profits out of two-to-five day holds. With practice, you may decide to do a combination of both position trading and swing trading. I like this method for capturing optimum profits!

When a stock rolls over into a Stage Three, we stand aside. During this stage, price patterns tend toward the volatile and unpredictable, and a stock may lurch sideways in a haphazard pattern. It's particularly unwise to hold a Stage Three stock overnight.

Again, stocks that fall into a Stage Four are doomed to suffer lower and lower prices. There are two ways to treat a stock in a Stage Four downtrend. First, if you are relatively new to the stock market and have no prejudices against selling short—that's good news! When you arrive at Chapter 12, which talks about shorting, you'll want to study it thoroughly to maximize your profits. Or, perhaps you've been in the market for a while and already realize the profit potential in selling high and buying low. You may even hedge your account by selling short.

The second way to approach a stock in a Stage Four downtrend is to avoid it completely! If shorting a stock—or even the thought of it—makes you break into a sweat, then sidestep stocks in a crash and burn mode. During times when major market indexes plummet to new lows (read Bear Market), as they did in the fall of 2000 and spring of 2001, you can keep your assets in cash and take a vacation. Or, spend the your time off to read up on advanced trading techniques.

Remember, one of the most important lessons any trader or any investor can learn is *when to stay out of the market altogether!*

ADDITIONAL CYCLE COMPONENTS

Now that we've identified the stages inherent in cycles, let's zoom in even closer to analyze the action.

In the illustration that follows (Figure 5-3), you can see motivating factors in each stage. (Keep in mind that many small stages form the larger stages.) It's interesting to note that while a stock experiencing a Stage Two uptrend on a daily chart may be soaring on the wings of optimism, greed, and euphoria, a glance at an intra-day chart may reveal intervals—not apparent on a daily chart—where apprehension and outright panic prevail.

Aside from emotions, Figure 5-3 also shows notations referring to supply and demand. As discussed in Chapter 2, greed and fear act as precursors to these two economic factors.

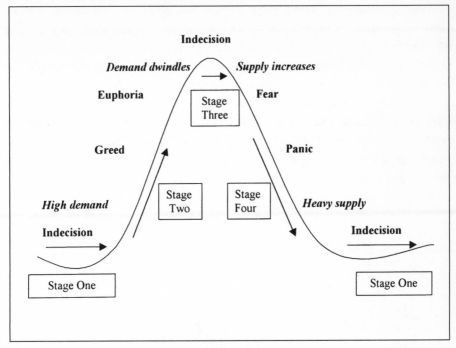

Figure 5-3.
Supply/demand cycle.

In Stage One, indecision causes supply and demand for a stock to alternate in the short-term, pushing it sideways. When optimism (mild greed) triggers a stock to break out of a Stage One into a Stage Two, greed for the stock at that price causes increasing demand. The greed amplifies as more and more buyers absorb all available stock (supply) at each higher price level.

When the price gets "frothy," or "toppy," at the height of a Stage Two, demand will shrink as increased supply, provided by sellers taking profits, arrives in the marketplace.

As the stock rolls over into a Stage Three, indecision reigns again. Just as in Stage One, supply and demand remain in relative balance, although volatile swings are the norm.

Sooner or later, buyers will turn their backs on a Stage Three stock and decide to take profits. Supply floods the market. When no one steps in to buy, these buyers-turned-sellers must lower their prices to attract buyers. This initiates a Stage Four. Now, apprehension turns to fear, causing even more sellers to join the ranks, which pushes more and more supply onto the market at each lower price level. Just as greed initiates demand, so does fear initiate supply. It becomes a self-perpetuating action and reaction.

Finally, when the falling price reaches a support area established weeks, months, or even years ago (as seen on a weekly or daily chart), supply begins to be absorbed by tentative buyers. As they continue to soak up the supply, the stock ceases making lower lows. Selling volume dries up, and buyers start to step in. Supply and demand even out, and the stock reverts to a Stage One to begin a new cycle.

Figures 5-4 through 5-7 show two weekly charts (each bar equals one week) and two daily charts (each bar equals one day) of stocks that have made complete cycles. Check out how fear and greed incite supply and demand to drive stock prices up and down.

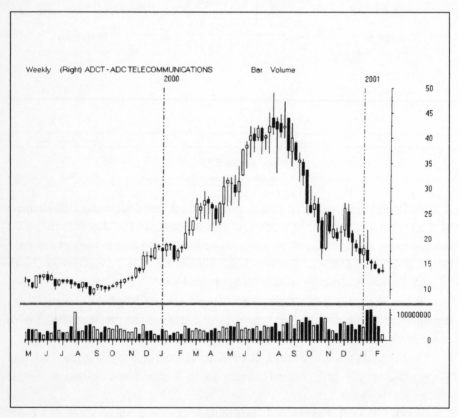

Figure 5-4.

On this chart, which marks the weekly activity of ADC Telecommunications (ADCT), you can clearly see the bell curve of the stock's complete price cycle.

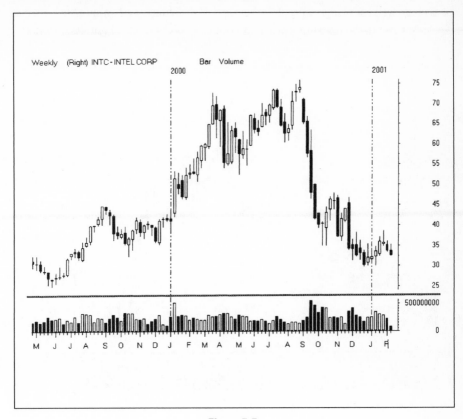

Figure 5-5.

This chart of Intel Corp. (INTC) also shows a weekly cycle. INTC's price pattern shows a stock with a more volatile "personality" than ADCT.

SUPPORT AND RESISTANCE, OR ACTION AND REACTION

Now we're going to add the final, yet mega-important components to the cycles: support and resistance. These two factors are the actual outcome, or the result of, the interaction between fear and greed and supply and demand. Understanding how they all work together is like watching a magnificent, orchestrated dance. It also gives you a giant advantage for making money.

As you read, keep this statement in the forefront of your mind: for every action, there is a reaction.

Support and resistance will form the foundation for every trading decision. You can trade without oscillators and indicators and moving averages. You can even eliminate charts altogether from your financial decisions (although I wouldn't recommend it). But even floor traders in commodities pits who rarely see a chart will mentally compute where price resistance and support lie, even as they shout and use hand signals (called "open outcry") to get their orders filled.

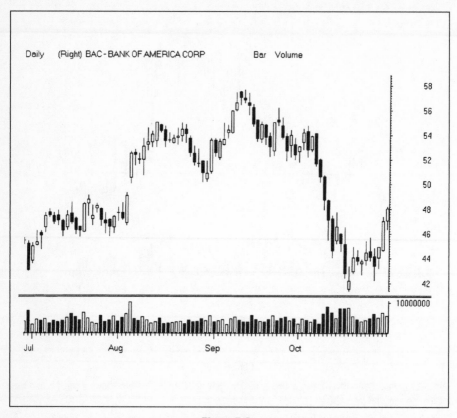

Figure 5-6.

This daily chart of Bank of America (BAC) shows the complete cycle of a price pattern that took approximately five months.

The concept behind support and resistance is a simple one, and once you digest it, you will have absorbed the basic premise underlying market moves.

I used the following analogy in my previous book, *A Beginner's Guide to Day Trading Online.* I'm using it again because it gives such a clear image of support and resistance in action.

Picture this: You're standing in the living room of a house, on the first floor. In your hands, you hold a ball. This ball equals the price of a stock. You toss the ball over your head. It soars upward, and hits the ceiling. The ceiling keeps it from rising higher, so the ceiling equals *resistance.* Now, the ball falls back down and bounces on the floor. The floor stops it from falling further, so the floor equals *support.*

Next, you spot a hole in the ceiling. You throw the ball as hard as you can, and it flies through the hole in the ceiling. It rises to the second-story ceiling and hits it. That ceiling equals *resistance*. Then, the ball falls to bounce on the second-story floor, which now forms *support*. Understand that the first-story ceiling supports the second-story floor. Result? *Resistance becomes support.*

Figure 5-7.

This daily chart of Johnson & Johnson (JNJ) shows a complete price cycle. Notice how the Stage Three rollover lasted for one day!

Continue by running upstairs and grabbing the ball. Throw it back through the hole, down into the first-story living room. When it drops through the hole in the floor, it breaks through *support*. It falls to bounce on the living room floor, or previous *support*.

Then, it rises to hit the ceiling, or previous *resistance*.

Run back down the stairs. Take the ball and toss it through a hole in the floor. The ball descends to the basement floor, which forms *support*. Then, it rises to bounce off the basement ceiling, *resistance*. Just above the basement is the living room floor, which used to provide *support*. So now, previous support forms resistance. Figure 5-8 illustrates support and resistance.

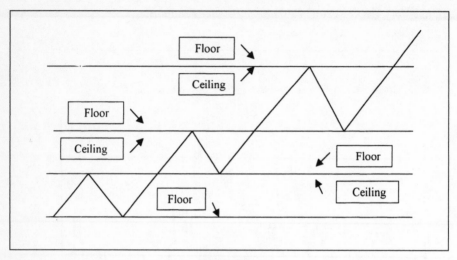

Figure 5-8.
Support and resistance.

When the ball, which we'll now think of as a stock price, bounces off of support or resistance, we refer to it as a pivot point (Figure 5-9).

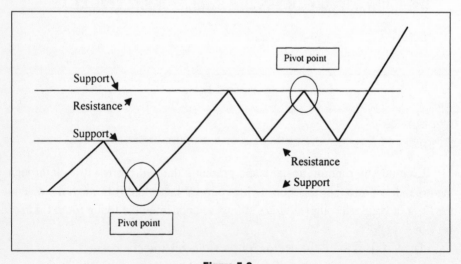

Figure 5-9.
Pivot point.

As you study support and resistance, remember, they are price *areas.* You will have to find a specific price to refer to, for example $54, but give it a little leeway. Picture yourself jumping on a trampoline. The trampoline supports you when you land on it, but the depth of your bounce varies a little each time. Also, just as heavier people stretch the trampoline base lower when they land, more volatile stocks need a little extra latitude in their resistance and support areas.

Hot Tip

When a stock returns to a support or resistance level three times or more, we call that "major support" or "major resistance."

Since you now know what support and resistance look like, let's quickly find out how they actually form. Go back to imagining the ball bouncing from floor to ceiling in the basement. Now, apply that to a stock in a Stage One, or basing price pattern. The basement floor is support, and we call it that because buyers are supporting the price. Were it to start lower, buyers (greed + demand) step in and accumulate, thus keeping the price from sinking lower.

When the price rises to the basement ceiling, it hits resistance. Resistance equals buyers who jam their hands in their pockets and refuse to pay a higher price for the stock. Also, resistance equals supply. At this point, some previous buyers, as mentioned before, revert into sellers. Afraid (fear) the stock will rise no higher, they offer their stock for sale, thus flooding the market with supply. If the stock falls here, the next time it rises to return to this price area, it may sell off again. Why? Because we have memories!

Say the stock shoots through the resistance (supply is absorbed). Maybe the sector it inhabits is in a favorable spotlight, the bulls are in control of the market, or the company itself enjoys a spurt of good news. The price will continue to rocket—maybe for hours or days—until a new factor suppresses it. When it "sells off," that pivot point creates fresh resistance. The stock then falls to the earlier resistance area, which is now the "floor," or support. It will hold there if buyers absorb the supply, and in so doing, "support" it.

Support and resistance levels apply on every chart you'll ever see, whatever the time frame. In fact, you may have guessed by now that *all* the applications you'll learn about charts hold true on all time frames. That means the concepts you find in these pages pertain not only to swing-and-position trading, but also to strategies including active trading and traditional buy-and-hold investing.

Figures 5-10, 5-11, and 5-12 show support and resistance areas on a weekly chart, a daily chart, and a fifteen-minute intra-day chart. As you study these charts and observe support and resistance levels, you may be amazed at how reliable they are!

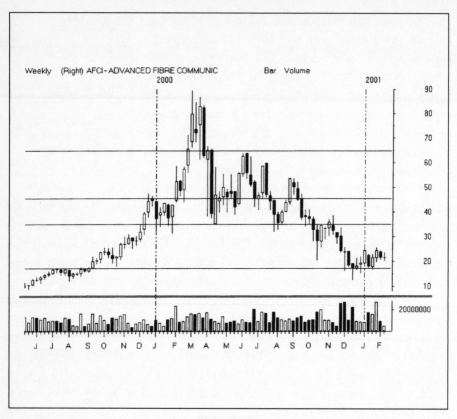

Figure 5-10.

This weekly chart of Advanced Fibre Communications (AFCI) shows a complete cycle with distinct support and resistance areas. Note how the stock returns all the way down (Jan. 2001) to rest on the support established in 1999.

Now, secure in the knowledge that you assimilated all the material in this chapter, we'll continue a custom I established in my previous book, *A Beginner's Guide to Day Trading Online.* . . .

From now on, this is an interactive book! The quiz below is designed to tell you how much you recall of the current chapter. Remember, in the high-stakes game of trading, the more knowledge you bring with you to the market, the more money you'll make. So, here's your chance to find out what "stuck," and what you may want to review.

Figure 5-11.

On this wild and woolly daily chart of Ciena Corp. (CIEN), notice how previous resistance hampers the stock's future move to the upside. Remember, resistance translates into supply, or sellers dumping their stock on the market. Resistance can also consist of short sellers, who recognize the upcoming resistance area and sell the stock short into it, intending to buy it back at a lower price and pocket the profits.

Figure 5-12.

All time frames encounter support and resistance. Here, a fifteen-minute chart of Cisco Systems (CSCO) completes an entire cycle and forms definite support and resistance levels. Note how the high made right after the open on February 13 (2/13) served as resistance when the stock tried to make another high that afternoon.

QUIZ

1. Name the different stages in a typical stock price cycle, and describe in which direction each stage moves.
2. Specify the collective mindset that applies to each stage.
3. True or False? The trading method known as "averaging down" is the best way to recoup your losses when you're holding onto a tanking stock.
4. Briefly name options available to short-term traders in each stage of a stock's cycle.
5. Which emotion fuels supply—greed or fear? Which one fuels demand?
6. Referring to the "ball bouncing between the floor and ceiling" analogy, what does the floor represent—support or resistance? Which of the two does the ceiling represent?
7. Continuing with the same analogy, when the ball soars through a hole in the ceiling and bounces on the floor above, what does that depict on a stock chart? What if the ball drops through the floor, then bounces up to hit the ceiling?
8. What denotes *major* resistance or support?
9. What is a "pivot point"?
10. True or False? Support and resistance levels apply on every chart, regardless of the time frame.

ANSWERS

1. Four stages create a stock's price cycle. Stage One is a sideways, or basing movement. Stage Two represents the uptrend. Stage Three is the peak, or topping action, in which the stock moves sideways. Stage Four is the downtrend. When the downtrend ends and the stock turns up again, it initiates a Stage One and the cycle repeats itself.

2. The collective mindset in a Stage One: indecision. Stage Two: greed. Stage Three: indecision. Stage Four: fear.

3. Very big False!

4. Stage One: We monitor stocks in this basing action, ready to spot a buying opportunity when they break into a Stage Two uptrend. Stage Two: As swing and position traders, we spend most of our time playing stocks in a Stage Two; we work the uptrend, with the intention of grabbing multiple-point profits. Stage Three: We avoid stocks experiencing this stage. Stage Four: We either take advantage of short selling strategies, or stand aside until the stock assumes a more positive price pattern.

5. Fear fuels supply. Greed fuels demand.

6. Floor equals support. Ceiling equals resistance.

7. Resistance becomes support. Support becomes resistance.

8. *Major* resistance or support is noted when a stock bounces off a support or resistance area three times, or more.

9. A "pivot point" is when a stock price reverses direction.

10. True.

✦ ✦ ✦

CENTER POINT

All substance is energy in motion. It lives and flows. Money is symbolically a golden, flowing stream of concretized vital energy.
                                    —"THE MAGICAL WORK OF THE SOUL"

Develop a Prosperity Mindset

We all create our own financial picture. How we think and feel about our financial affairs determines our experience!

When we first encounter it, this is a difficult concept to grasp. It's far easier to blame someone else or outside circumstances for the lack in our lives. The truth is, "as within, so without." The image we hold of ourselves—about *any* aspect of our being—is reflected out to our external world.

Let's check out this premise. Do you entertain thoughts like these? *There's always too much month left at the end of the money. I have to grab mine before someone else does. Opportunity probably won't knock on my door.* If you take time to rethink these statements, they all focus on scarcity. They define a world of lack and shortages.

Since we receive what we focus on, when we dwell and speak about scarcity and lack, that's exactly what we produce. Conversely, we attract abundance and prosperity into our lives when we discard thoughts of lack and limitation and replace them with statements like: *I have everything I need right now to experience abundant prosperity.*

True affluence requires us to live from the inside-out. When we accept in our hearts that we are complete right now, and when we develop an inner knowing that limitless abundance can be ours just like the air we breathe, then we discover that everything we need and desire is within our reach. We can draw it to us like a magnet, using our consciousness, our beliefs, and our actions.

We cannot control global events, or the stock market, or the behavior of those around us. We *can*, however, command our own thoughts. The minute we affirm and *know* that we have within us the potential to prosper and succeed in all areas of our lives, creative ideas, resourcefulness, and opportunities will abound. Only then can we claim our legacy of prosperity and abundance!

✦ ✦ ✦

CHAPTER 6

Jump-Start on Charting Basics

If a stock doesn't act right don't touch it; because, being unable to tell precisely what is wrong, you cannot tell which way it is going. No diagnosis, no prognosis. No prognosis, no profit.

—JESSE LIVERMORE

You know how each one of your friends has a different personality? So do stocks! Just as some of your friends are quiet and dependable, some stocks—mostly those listed on the NYSE—move in polite, conservative price patterns. I think of Wal-Mart (WMT) and General Motors (GM) in that way. (General Electric used to stand as a great example of a dignified stock, but lately that venerable blue-chip is experiencing what appears to be an onerous, midlife crisis, and it insists on erupting, then imploding without warning.) Mild-mannered stocks typically move in single-digit price increases or decreases during the course of a day, and so move through their cycles in measured, orderly paces.

In contrast, do you have friends who are moody, and you never know from one day to the next which frame of mind they're going to be in? I call stocks that mimic this behavior, "manic-sleepers." Residing on either the NYSE or Nasdaq, they can nap for days, weeks, or even months, then snort themselves awake and explode into action.

Still other stocks continually bounce up and down all over their charts, resembling kangaroos on steroids. Most of these stocks thrive on the Nasdaq, are technology or tech-related companies, and are referred to by pundits as "high-flyers." These stocks that behave in wild and crazy patterns are just like friends who act in a similar manner—you can't count on them. Sure, they're fun to spend time with for a few hours at a time, but if you hang out with them for much longer than that, they drive you bonkers!

From now on, when you study charts, it's fun to think of yourself as a psychologist. The stock is your "patient," and you are the "doctor" whose job it is to analyze the stock's good points and trouble-causing characteristics. When you learn to look at a chart with a trained, discerning eye (and you'll be able to do that soon), it won't take long before you'll be adept at judging the risk/reward, and thus money-making possibilities of any stock you choose.

One glance at a chart will show you whether a stock has an orderly or erratic personality. And from now on, the operative word is *orderly*. Memorize it, set it to music. Make it your chant, your mantra. From this day forward, for our purposes of trading multi-day and multi-week holds, we will focus on stocks that exhibit *orderly* personalities.

Disorderly stocks are undependable; they exhibit little or no follow-through. Playing an erratic stock skyrockets the risk involved and greatly diminishes odds of a reward. That's called "gambling." No thanks!

Orderly, more predictable stocks may be a tad more boring to monitor and trade, but a low risk/high reward setup aligns itself with our goal to take *consistent* profits out of the market. And, never once have I found it boring to make money!

CHARTING ESSENTIALS: LINE CHARTS AND BAR CHARTS

Technical analysts use three types of charts: line charts, bar charts, and candlestick charts (discussed in detail later).

Line Charts

Line charts typically connect a stock or indexes' closing price into a single line, during a designated period of time. For example, look at Figure 6-1. The daily line chart of Sun Microsystems, Inc. illustrates the daily closing prices of that issue from August 2000 to December 2000, drawn into a single line.

Line charts are handy for comparing stocks to other stocks or indexes, such as the benchmark S&P 500. Overlay a pertinent index over your stock's chart, such as the biotech index over a chart of Amgen, Inc. (AMGN), and you can instantly measure the stock's strength as compared to the overall industry, as indicated in a single, straightforward line.

Many indicators and oscillators (overbought/oversold indicators) are displayed as line charts. We'll learn about them in Chapter 8.

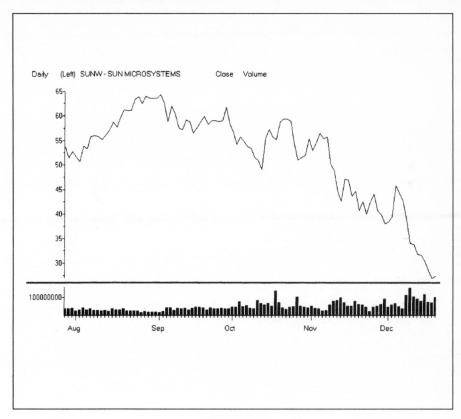

Figure 6-1.

This line chart of Sun Microsystems (SUNW) illustrates the closing daily prices connected by a single line, from August 2000 to December 2000.

Bar Charts

Bar charts use single, vertical bars to illustrate a stock's price range and opening/closing prices for a designated time period. Figure 6-2 displays the same daily chart of SUNW; only this time it is shown as a bar chart. Because it is a daily chart, each bar represents a single day's price activity in SUNW's history.

In Figure 6-3, we'll "zoom in" on the single bar to interpret it. The top of the bar indicates the stock's "high," or the highest price for the day. In this case, we're using the price high of 50. The bottom of the bar represents the stock's lowest price for that period; in this illustration, 40. The small, perpendicular bar on the left designates the stock's opening price (42). The one on the right shows the stock's closing price (48).

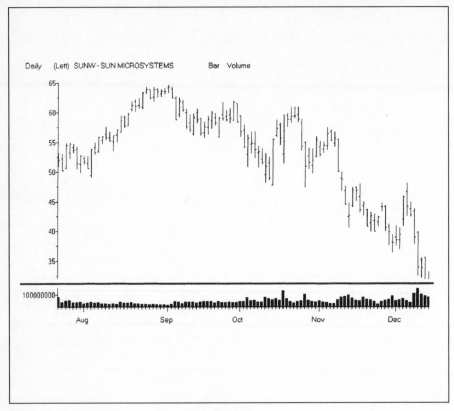

Figure 6-2.

This figure shows the same daily activity as the line chart of Sun Microsystems (SUNW), only this time in bar chart form. Each bar represents the price action during the course of one trading day.

RealTick graphics used with permission of Townsend Analytics, Ltd. ©1986–2002. All rights reserved.

Although some traditional technical analysts still prefer bar charts, the majority have switched to candlestick charts. For the remainder of this book, we're going to use candlestick charts. They definitely shine more light on the subject!

CANDLESTICK CHARTING BASICS

We owe a debt of thanks to a legendary seventeenth-century Japanese rice broker, Munehisa Homma, who was one of the first Japanese traders to use price history to predict price future. Referred to as "the god of the markets," Homma amassed a huge fortune, and as legend has it, he made 100 consecutive winning trades. His trading theories and principles evolved into the candlestick charting techniques we use today.

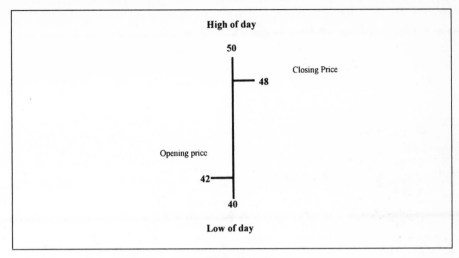

Figure 6-3.
Single bar.

Current candlestick guru Steve Nison, who wrote the foreword to this book, earns most of the applause for bringing this ancient and highly effective technique to the United States, and indeed much of the rest of the world. I highly recommend Nison's books, *Japanese Candlestick Charting Techniques* (New York Institute of Finance, 1991) and *Beyond Candlesticks: More Japanese Charting Techniques Revealed* (John Wiley & Sons, 1994) for thorough, reader-friendly texts that explain candlestick charting in depth.

Basic Candlestick Patterns

For now, we're going to explore some major candlestick patterns that when used properly, can produce tidy profits. For example, Figure 6-4 is the previously shown chart of SUNW, this time in candlestick form.

Just as a bar chart uses the top and bottom of its bar to indicate high and low prices of the time frame indicated, so does a candlestick. With candlesticks, however, we draw in a "real body" to connect the opening and closing prices. This gives us a quick and complete picture of the stock's action and denotes prevailing sentiment.

The real body shows the opening and closing prices with a clear, or a dark, rectangle. The bar that extends above and below the real body is called the upper and lower "shadow."

When the rectangle or real body is clear, it means that the stock closed *above* its opening price. When the real body is dark, it means that the stock closed *below* its opening price. This gives you an instant picture of a positive or negative close. Those of us who stare at charts for hours at a time find candlesticks are not only easy on the eyes, but they also convey strong signals sometimes missed on bar charts. Figure 6-5 shows basic candlestick formations.

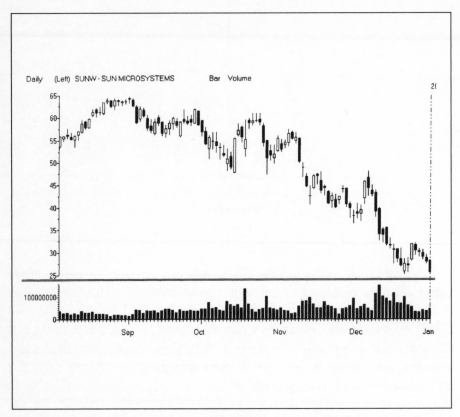

Figure 6-4.

This shows the same daily chart of Sun Microsystems (SUNW) using candlesticks instead of bars.

Candlesticks, like bars, each represent a specified time frame. For example, on a weekly chart, each candlestick represents one week; on a daily chart, each candlestick represents one day; and on a fifteen-minute intra-day chart, each candlestick represents a fifteen-minute unit of time.

Now, notice the long, clear real body in Figure 6-5(A). The long, *clear* real body, showing the closing price multiple points *above* the opening price (in this case, five points), indicates extremely positive or bullish sentiment. In (B), the long, *dark* real body, with the closing price multiple points *below* the open, reveals negative or bearish sentiment.

Next, check out (C). This formation, where the stock opens and closes at the same price, is called a "doji." With a doji, no real body is present. Because buyers could not apply enough bullish pressure to close the stock *higher* than the open, and sellers could not force enough bearish pressure to close the stock *lower* than the open, it reveals a collective mindset of *indecision*.

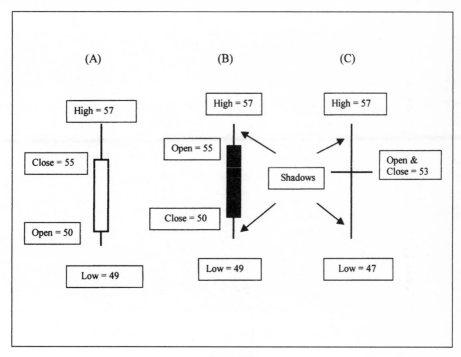

Figure 6-5.

Basic candlestick formations. In (A), Bossy Bank opens at 50, closes at 55, with a high of 57 and a low of 49. In (B), Bossy opens at 55, closes at 50, and again has a high of 57 and low of 49. In (C), Bossy opens *and* closes at 53, with the same high and low.

Please memorize the doji right this minute! It is a very important candlestick, as it many times presages a shift in, or even a reversal of, a current trend. As short-term traders, we need to stay on top of trend changes and reversals at all times. Why? Because they act as valuable entry, exit, and money-management signals.

Candlestick patterns can be read alone, but are extremely powerful when used in conjunction with other charting indicators. Therefore, a selection of important patterns are detailed in the next few pages, and in the chapters that follow, you'll learn how to combine them with other indicators to recognize buy and sell signals.

Hot Tip

Candlestick patterns indicate that a *change* in the direction of trend may be imminent. That means that a stock in an uptrend/downtrend could begin moving sideways, or it could make a U-turn.

The candlesticks illustrated in Figure 6-6 are called the *hammer* and the *hanging man*. Their real bodies are small, and can be either clear or dark. Their lower shadows should be twice the length of the real body. They should have "shaven heads," meaning no (or short) upper shadow will be evident.

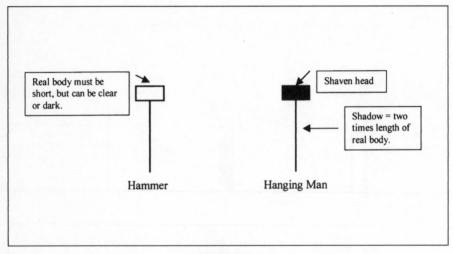

Figure 6-6.

Hammer and hanging man.

When you see a hammer form in the context of a downtrend, it may signify that the downtrend will slow and change direction by moving sideways or reversing to move upward. Think: hammer it back up.

If a hanging man appears in an uptrend, the connotation is evident right away. It's time to start playing the funeral march! If you're holding a long position in this stock, take profits right away. Figure 6-7 illustrates these two patterns.

Two-Candlestick Patterns

The next pattern that presages trend change is an "engulfing pattern." It's a two-candlestick pattern consisting of opposite-color real bodies. The second real body must completely "engulf" the first real body. Translation: The opening price of the second real body must be lower than the closing price of the first, and the closing price of the real body must be higher than the opening price of the first. That's called a "bullish engulfing pattern." The flip side of this is a "bearish engulfing pattern." Figure 6-8 shows these two patterns in action.

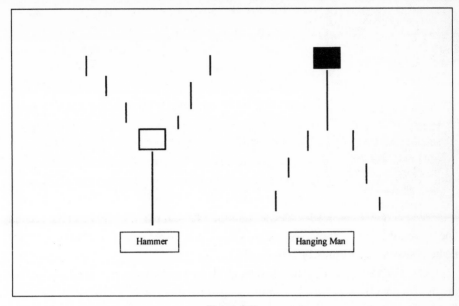

Figure 6-7.

Hammer and hanging man as reversal signals.

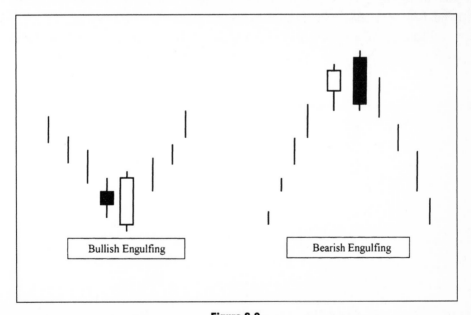

Figure 6-8.

Bullish and bearish engulfing patterns as reversal signals.

Hot Tip

Remember that these patterns do not *absolutely always* mean a trend change or reversal will take place. Just like every other tool we use, they give a "heads up" to *possible* future price action.

Bullish and bearish engulfing patterns are similar to Western "key reversal" patterns, in which a stock opens at a new high (or low), then closes lower (or higher) than the previous day's low (or high).

Another important reversal pattern is the *dark cloud cover*. Also a two-candlestick pattern, it portends change when it appears at the top of an uptrend, or toward the top of a congestion (sideways) move. The first candlestick is a long, clear real body. The second real body opens above the close of the first, then closes near the low of the range and deep within the price range of the first candlestick. The deeper into the first real body (range) that the second one closes, the more bearish the signal. Dark cloud cover indicates exactly what the name conveys—a storm is brewing!

The reverse of the dark cloud cover is the *bullish piercing pattern*. Resembling the bullish engulfing pattern in that the second candlestick (real body) opens below the previous candlestick's close, the piercing pattern shows that the second real body should rise *at least halfway* into the previous dark real body. The greater the second real body pierces the first, the greater the chance that it is a strong reversal pattern. So, when this two-candlestick pattern takes place at the bottom of a downtrend, look for a change in direction to begin.

Figure 6-9 illustrates dark cloud cover and bullish piercing patterns. Since these are both powerful patterns, be sure to commit the simple formations to memory.

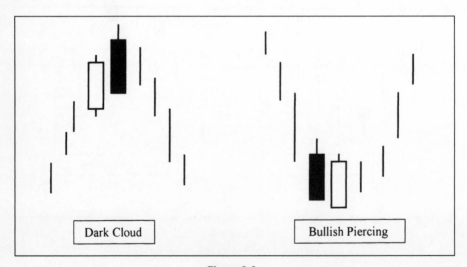

Figure 6-9.
Dark cloud cover and bullish piercing patterns.

The *harami* and the *harami cross* are two-candlestick patterns that also indicate a trend change. *Harami* means "pregnant" in Japanese—the pattern consists of a long real body that engulfs the subsequent small candlestick. The long real body is the "mother" candlestick and the smaller real body is the "baby."

In this pattern, the long real body must occur *first*, with the short real body appearing second. (The reverse of this pattern is the bullish engulfing pattern.) The colors need not be opposite, but you will find they usually appear that way. Figure 6-10 illustrates the harami and the harami cross.

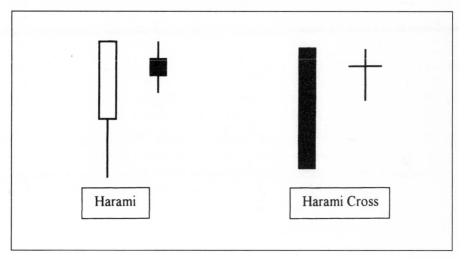

Figure 6-10.
Harami and harami cross patterns.

If you're thinking this formation is called an "inside day" in Western terminology, you're right. A Western inside day, however, demands that the second session keep its highs and lows within those of the preceding one. The harami does not. As long as the first real body is relatively longer than the second, and the second is short, the shadows (session high and low) of the second real body can extend above or below the first.

The harami pattern warns not so much of a dramatic reversal in a trend, as it does that the current trend may slow or drift sideways for a while.

A harami cross forms when the second candlestick is a doji. That means definite opinion—strong bullish for a tall, clear real body, or strong bearish for a tall, dark real body—has dissolved. A doji, as mentioned before,

Hot Tip

The plural of "doji" is "doji."

Hot Tip

These three-candlestick patterns promise to pack more of a punch when the first candlestick forms on relatively low volume, and the third candlestick forms on high volume.

translates into indecision and uncertainty. Thus, a harami cross can be a potent reversal signal. When you spot this pattern during an uptrend or downtrend, pay attention!

Three-Candlestick Patterns

The following patterns consist of three candlesticks that include "stars." Star patterns represent strong and valuable reversal warnings. As Steve Nison says, the formation of strong reversal patterns not only keeps us informed of potential setups for entries, they also offer themselves as efficient profit-taking signals. Why? Because if you're long (own) a stock, and you see a reversal pattern forming that indicates the stock may make a U-turn soon, you can grab your gains quickly. Besides, it's fun party conversation to be able to boast that you bought a stock and "got out at the top!"

To qualify for "star" billing, the candlestick should appear at the top (or bottom) of an uptrend (or downtrend), have a short real body, and gap away (open higher in uptrend (or lower in downtrend) from the previous candlestick.

The co-stars: In the context of an *uptrend*, the first real body should be long and clear. The third real body should be long and dark, penetrating the real body of the first candle. In a *downtrend*, the first real body is long and dark, then the star appears next. Finally, the third real body moves up, well into the first dark real body.

The Japanese call the first star an *evening star*, and the second a *morning star*. When the star emerges as a doji, it's an even more powerful warning that a reversal may be impending.

Figure 6-11 depicts the evening and morning stars and *evening and morning doji star patterns*.

While we're looking at doji, let's check out variations on this extremely powerful candlestick. Maybe we should call it a "dynamite" stick instead of a candlestick!

When you spot a doji—and remember, it's most potent forecasting position is at the top of an uptrend or bottom of a downtrend—the following points should be taken into consideration:

+ Traditionally, the doji opens and closes at the same price. But if you spot a "near doji," where the prices are within a few decimal points of each other, it's still a significant signal.
+ A doji that appears in a sideways move, accompanied by other doji and short real bodies, are not quite as powerful beacons of change.

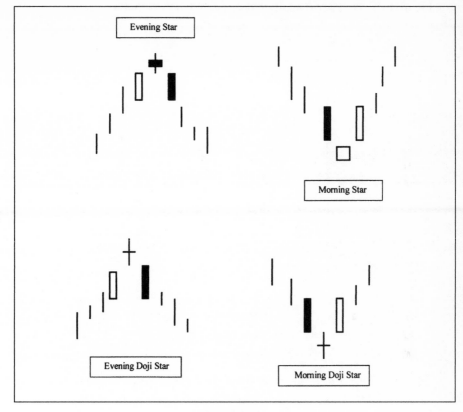

Figure 6-11.
Stars and doji stars as powerful reversal signals.

✦ Doji can be viewed as more powerful at stock/market tops, rather than bottoms. This holds especially true when preceded by a long clear candle, such as in the doji evening star pattern. Think: Long, clear real body equals strong bullish opinion. Then, a doji develops. Doji equals indecision by market players to pay a higher price. Result? Possible pullback or profit-taking may soon follow.

✦ Doji that confirm trend tops or bottoms many times turn into support or resistance areas.

✦ When a stock in an uptrend pulls back to support and then forms a doji, that indicates the stock may be ready to turn and resume its uptrend. The same is true of a stock in a downtrend; a rebound to resistance, followed by the formation of a doji, may indicate the stock will drop back to the downside. Notice the operative word here is *may*. Always wait for the next candle to confirm price direction.

Figure 6-12 shows two additional distinctive doji formations.

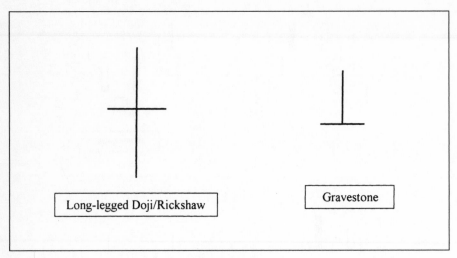

Figure 6-12.
Long-legged doji/rickshaw and gravestone doji patterns.

The *long-legged doji* has long upper and lower shadows, and its appearance at stock/market tops should definitely grab your attention. When a long-legged doji opens and closes in the middle of its session, it's referred to as a *rickshaw man*.

If you think through what actually happened to form one of these doji, you'll realize why their emergence is so meaningful. The stock opens at a certain price, say 50. Buying pressure pushes it strongly higher, then selling pressure shoves it much lower. Still, it closes at or very near the session's opening price of 50. Conclusion? Total indecision! Neither the bulls nor the bears have the strength to raise or lower the price above or below the open. Can you see how that may cause bulls to shrug and take profits during the following session? *Remember, the market dislikes indecision.*

When you see a *gravestone doji* form in an uptrend, and you're long that stock, take profits immediately. Then, you can smile smugly and hold the exit door open for the screaming stampede that usually follows!

In *Japanese Candlestick Charting Techniques,* Steve Nison says, "As we have discussed, many of the Japanese technical terms are based on military analogies,

---

6 Nison, Steve. *Japanese Candlestick Charting Techniques* (NY: New York Institute of Finance, 1991), p. 159.

and in this context, the gravestone doji also represents the graves of those bulls or bears who have died defending their territory."[6]

As you see by Figure 6-12, a gravestone doji opens and closes at the low price of the day. If the price rises to a *new* high, drawing a long upper shadow, that spells even more gloom and doom for bulls. Translation: No matter how much the bulls absorbed supply, the bears squashed the price down to the low, and closed it there. Remember, the point at which a stock or market closes on the day is a very significant signal in itself.

Spinning Tops and High Wave Candlesticks

The final candlesticks we want to look at are *spinning tops* and *high wave* candlesticks (Figure 6-13). Candlesticks with small real bodies, of either color, are referred to as "spinning tops." The length and range of their shadows may vary. Think of spinning tops as slightly "kinder, gentler" versions of doji. Their siblings are "high wave" candlesticks, which are spinning tops exhibiting very long upper and/or lower shadows. A group of high wave candlesticks may forecast a trend reversal.

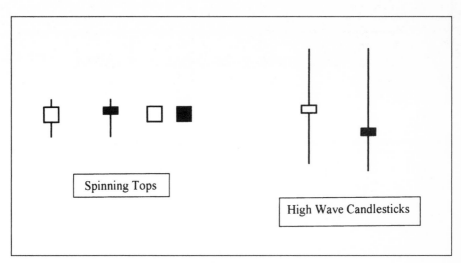

Figure 6-13.
Spinning tops and high wave candlesticks.

In the previous pages, you've learned major candlestick formations and patterns that will alert you to changes or reversals in trends. Many more exist, and as previously mentioned, you can study books by Nison and others for additional examples and explanations. I find candlesticks an invaluable source of information and if you continue to study them, it will be time well spent.

In the following chart examples, you will see examples of the candlestick patterns we just discussed. Observe how trends usually slow or reverse when certain formations occur.

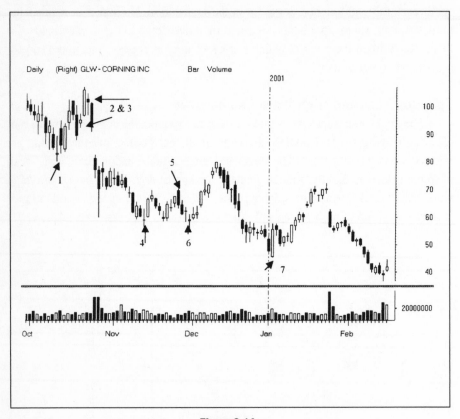

Figure 6-14.

This daily chart of Corning, Inc. (GLW) displays several candlestick reversal patterns: 1. morning star; 2,3. harami; 4. doji morning star; followed by bullish piercing pattern, followed by evening star; 5. dark cloud cover; 6. morning star; 7. bullish engulfing pattern in context of sideways consolidation pattern, not as forceful as at a possible pivot point in uptrend or downtrend.

After looking at those charts, I'll bet my duck slippers you pointed to a doji that appeared after an extended downtrend and yelled, "Hey, there's a doji in a screaming downtrend, and the downtrend didn't reverse. It just kept going!" Or, "Hold the ballgame. I see a dark cloud cover smack in the middle of an awesome uptrend, but the stock kept going up."

My snappy retort, which you're going to read a zillion times over in this book: "Nothing *always* happens in the stock market." Memorize it. Write it on your bathroom mirror, your refrigerator, the back of your hand. No candlestick pattern, indicator, oscillator, analyst's report, or arrangement of the moon and stars can tell you where your stock or the market is going to go in the following moments, days, weeks, or months. What they *can* do is give us possibilities and probabilities of price movement based on history. The fact that you will interpret the possibilities to infer one outcome, and the guy or girl next to you will decipher them to mean the opposite is what makes the market go 'round!

Hot Tip

Doji, spinning tops, and high wave candlesticks can act as such potent reversal indicators when they emerge in the context of an uptrend because they demonstrate indecision.

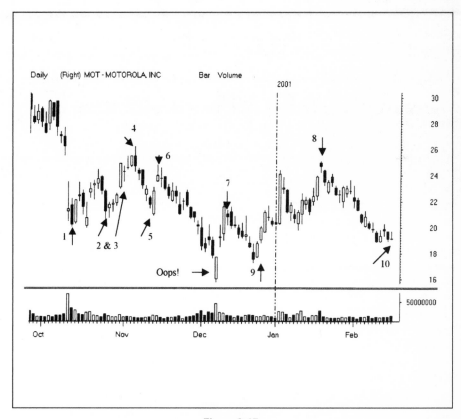

Figure 6-15.

On this daily chart of Motorola (MOT), several more candlestick patterns indicate change. As you can see, these patterns are not "absolutes," but they hint at what may take place: 1. bullish piercing pattern, stock moves up but cannot continue for more than one bar; 2,3. harami and harami cross; 4. bearish engulfing pattern; 5. bullish engulfing pattern; 6. shooting star followed by doji, strongly indicates a change in direction; 7. harami followed by bearish engulfing pattern, funeral music time!; 8. shooting star; 9. bullish piercing pattern; 10. if gravestone doji at the top of a trend, a signal of possible reversal.

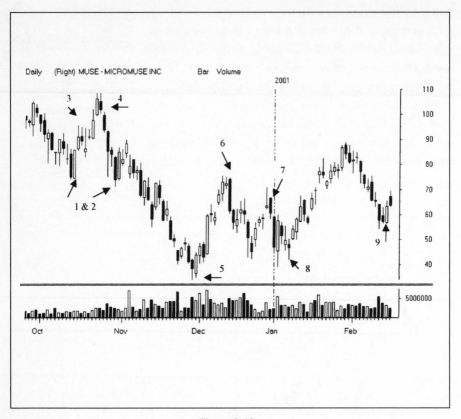

Figure 6-16.

This daily chart of Micromuse, Inc. (MUSE) shows more candlestick patterns. What patterns and formations can you find that I haven't mentioned? 1. bullish engulfing pattern; 2. bullish piercing pattern; 3. spinning tops followed by high wave candle moving sideways show indecision; 4. harami; 5. hammer followed by bullish engulfing patter signifies possible trend reversal; 6. spinning top in extended bearish engulfing candle predicts gloom and doom!; 7. shooting star followed by another bearish engulfing pattern; 8. near-hammer (technically, it doesn't have a shaven head) indicates change; 9. bullish engulfing pattern.

QUIZ

1. True or False? When presented with a stock chart that displays a disorderly, erratic price pattern, you disregard it completely and go onto the next.

2. A line chart shows a stock's _____ prices, drawn in a single line.

3. In bar charts, the top of a vertical bar indicates the stock's _____ for that session. The bottom is the _____. The short, perpendicular bar extending on the left shows the _____ price, and the corresponding one on the right displays the _____ price.

4. What does the rectangle on a clear candlestick, referred to as a "real body," indicate? How about a dark candlestick?
5. Define "doji."
6. What prevailing opinion or emotion does a long, clear candlestick suggest? A long, dark candlestick? Which one implies supply? Which implies demand?
7. The plural of "doji" is _____.
8. What does the candlestick referred to as a "hammer" look like, and where, in a price pattern, might it forecast a trend change or reversal?
9. Describe a "bearish engulfing" candlestick pattern. What is its counterpart in Western technical analysis?
10. Give one common characteristic of all "stars."
11. If you're long a stock and you see the current trading day is closing in a gravestone doji, what action might you take?
12. What collective opinion do "spinning tops" and "high wave candles" indicate?

ANSWERS

1. True, true, true!
2. Closing.
3. High, low. Opening, closing.
4. On a clear candlestick, the lowest point of the real body is the opening price of that session; the high represents the closing price. On a dark candlestick, the top of the real body is the opening price and the lowest end designates the close.
5. A doji is a candlestick formation consisting of upper and lower shadows intercepted by a single "crossbar." That means that stock (index or market) opened and closed at the same price.
6. A long, clear candlestick translates into a strong bullish opinion. The collective emotion equals greed. Implication equals demand. A long, dark candlestick displays a firm bearish opinion. Collective emotion equals fear. Implication equals supply.
7. Doji.
8. The candlestick referred to as a "hammer" consists of a small real body with a lower shadow that extends at least two-thirds the length of the real body. Resembling the common carpentry tool, when it appears in the context of a downtrend, it implies a possible slowing and reversal to the upside, as in "hammer it up."
9. The bearish engulfing pattern is a two-candlestick pattern of opposite colors that appears during an uptrend and warns of a possible reversal. The second candlestick's real body will completely engulf the prior candlestick. The Western counterpart is the "key reversal day."

10. All "stars"—whether morning, evening, or doji stars—must open away from (meaning higher or lower, whether in an uptrend or downtrend, respectively) the previous candlestick's real body.
11. Grab your profits and brace yourself for the crash!
12. Indecision and uncertainty.

✦ ✦ ✦

CENTER POINT

What lies behind us and what lies before us are tiny matters, compared to what lies within us.

—RALPH WALDO EMERSON

Reach for Your Highest Potential

Our planet, born of stellar debris, came together billions of years ago and has continued to evolve ever since. As part of that evolution from one-celled plants and animals to conscious beings of expression, we are a unique part of life unfolding, always in the process of moving to greater expression.

Because the urge to express our highest potential is innate and ever-present (no matter how hard we try to ignore it!), it offers us the opportunity to participate in the creative process in our own lives, to develop our special talents. We have been given the awareness and ability to birth our being's greatest potential.

Indeed, each of us is born with special gifts that if brought to the surface, developed, and polished, are meant to take us to new levels of personal growth and fulfillment as well as to contribute to the good of the world.

Many times, we believe—even fear—that our dreams are selfish, egotistical, or impractical. Consider the child, who longs to grow up to be an actor, and his parents, who pooh-pooh that dream as selfish and impractical.

The truth is that by entertaining us in a stage play or film, actors and actresses encourage us, the audience, to "suspend our disbelief" and accompany them into a wonderful world of feelings and experiences we otherwise could not access. They transport us to a time and place that transcends our everyday environment. The experience may invite us to laugh, offer a life lesson, or simply alleviate our stress. What a wonderful gift these performers give to us! Selfish? Quite the contrary! Impractical? Certainly not. Good actors and actresses are paid for their work.

What does your heart want? What makes your soul sing? What is that inner talent that longs to assert itself? Are you ready to claim it and give it expression?

If the answer is yes, you're ready to continue with your individual process of evolution by reaching—and embracing—your highest potential!

✦ ✦ ✦

CHAPTER 7

Charting Close-Ups:
The Pieces of the Puzzle

A trader gets to play the game as the professional billiard player does—that is, he looks far ahead instead of considering the particular shot before him. It gets to be an instinct to play for position.

—JESSE LIVERMORE

Want to hear really good news without the usual "bad news" tacked on? *Stock prices only move three directions—up, down, and sideways.*

Why is that such great news? Because it underscores the simplicity of actual price moves. (Why don't prices move backwards? Because time moves forward.)

The up, down, and sideways news gets even better. If you keep your losses small and your wins big (what a concept!), you can afford trades to go against you more than fifty percent of the time—and still make money. Hey, it doesn't get any better than that.

We talked in previous chapters about uptrends (Stage 2), downtrends (Stage 4), and sideways price movements (Stages 1 and 3). Now let's dissect them to find money-making buying and selling signals.

ANATOMY OF YOUR FRIEND: THE UPTREND

The definition of an uptrend is: *a price pattern making a series of higher lows and higher highs.*

As I said in the last chapter, trading stocks in strong uptrends is where you and I will spend most of our time. Swing traders target the two-to-five day breakouts in a stock that is beginning a hardy uptrend. Position traders scan for stocks breaking out of a Stage One base, then buy and hold for the duration of the uptrend, possibly four to six weeks.

Stocks break out of bases and into uptrends for several reasons: Institutional buyers (such as managers of mutual funds and managed accounts) suddenly show interest, the related industry or sector gains favor, or the stock comes out with positive news and good earnings. The added buying pressure (greed plus demand) shoots the stock out of its base and above previously formed resistance.

Figure 7-1 shows how a stock breaking out of a base and into an uptrend will appear.

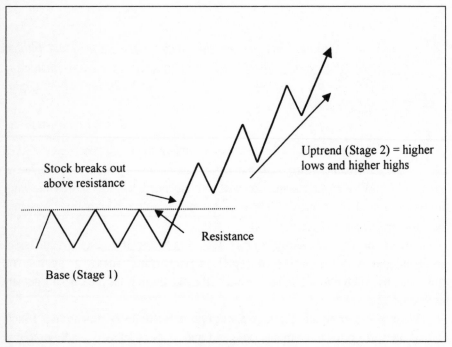

Figure 7-1.

Here, a stock breaks out of a base into an uptrend.

If you talk to a tennis pro about a tennis racquet, he or she will show you the "sweet spot" on the racquet face. You'll find that spot in the center of the strings. Hit the ball perfectly on the sweet spot, and you'll deliver your shot with delicious power and accuracy.

As a swing trader, your goal is to capture multi-point "sweet spots" in each upswing in a strong uptrend. The sweet spot translates into the "middle" of the upswing.

"Hey," you retort. "What do you mean, 'middle'? I want more than the *middle* points. I'm gonna buy at the bottom and sell at the top!"

Let's be realistic. The wealthiest traders aim for the middle, and so will you. When you buy, you want to make sure the breakout is a healthy one, so you wait for confirmation. When you take profits, *you sell when you can, not when you have to*. Will you sometimes leave a point or more on the table? Sure. Do you care? Nope! You planned your trade and traded your plan, and that's the road to success!

Figure 7-2 gives you a quick glance at the swing trading and position trading strategies possible in an uptrend.

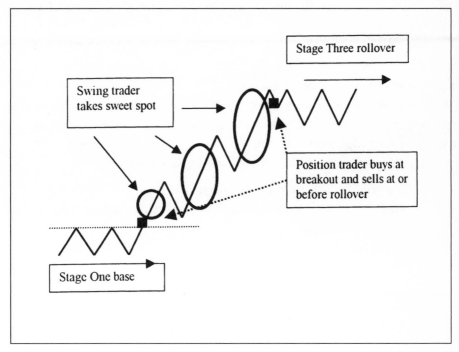

Figure 7-2.
Swing and position trading possibilities in an uptrend.

I've already anticipated your next question: "How can you make the most money, by swing trading or position trading?" Answer: In a muscular bull market that propels market leaders skyward, a talented swing trader can jump onto stocks rocketing in euphoric uptrends and pluck fat profits. In a market rising in a relaxed uptrend, where breakouts take more savvy and skill to capture (and the discipline to jump out when they fail), a position trader who quietly plods through the higher highs and higher lows, pulling a trailing stop-loss behind, may actually come out ahead.

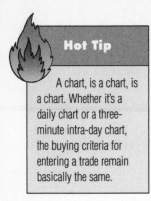

Hot Tip

A chart, is a chart, is a chart. Whether it's a daily chart or a three-minute intra-day chart, the buying criteria for entering a trade remain basically the same.

The best of both worlds: Take a position in a stock when it breaks out, then, depending on market conditions, swing trade a portion of the position, and keep the remainder in position-trade mode.

Here's an alternate way of accomplishing the same goal. Go to *www.holdrs.com*. Click on "HOLDRS Outstanding," and check out the list of HOLDRS. Each represents a single stock that trades on the Amex. Choose a sector you like (for example, the SMH is the semi-conductor holders), and use it for a position trade. Then, you can swing trade one of the leading stocks in that sector to maximize profits.

BUY SIGNALS: WHAT TO LOOK FOR

This section shows optimal buy signals for swing trading and position trading. The basic pattern forms the foundation of all trading entries you make. You can use this pattern on day trading setups as well.

Figure 7-3 illustrates three key buy signals. Read them like this:

1. Number 1 is the breakout over base resistance.
2. Number 2 is the breakout after the stock pulls back to support and resumes its uptrend.
3. Number 3 is best used as an add-to-position point. It takes place when the price rises over the previous high's pivot (resistance) price.

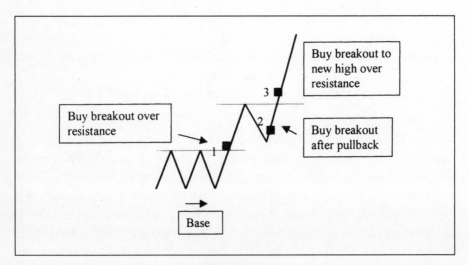

Figure 7-3.

Three key buying entries.

In the following chapters, you'll add bells and whistles to these signals as decision support tools. For now, though, please memorize the basic pattern.

Typically, both swing and position traders will buy the first breakout over resistance (see 1 in Figure 7-3). Swing traders take quick profits by selling half or all of their position while greed and demand remain strong, and before the first pullback begins. Position traders will watch the stock pull back to support, and when it "bounces," or trades over the high of the lowest pullback day, they may add additional shares to their original position (see 2). This gradual increasing of a position is called "scaling in."

Swing traders, who bought at the first breakout and sold before the first pullback, will now watch the stock for the next entry—the bounce subsequent to the pullback (see 2).

Okay, stay with me here. Say both swing traders and position traders are long the stock as it continues its uptrend and heads for its previous high. Both traders watch how it approaches this point of resistance. If it falters slightly, swing traders may want to take profits in one-half or all of their position. Or, if the market and relevant sector is screaming to the upside, they might want to tighten their stop-loss and tune into how the stock handles supply (resistance) that comes its way. Position traders hold tight, and look for the next opportunity to tighten their stop-loss point. You'll learn how to set stop-loss points in Chapter 10.

Note: From now on, when your target stock gives you a buy signal, you'll enter the stock from .15 to .25 above the previous day's high. (This will be explained in further detail as we go.)

Figures 7-4, 7-5, and 7-6 show stocks that have broken out of their bases and into uptrends. Check out the 1-2-3 entry points.

> **Hot Tip**
>
> Professionals and institutional managers utilize the "scaling" method all the time. They scale in when buying, and scale out when selling. It's a dandy way of minimizing risk while maximizing profits.

> **Hot Tip**
>
> You've heard the old saying, "The trend is your friend"? It's the absolute truth. Going against a prevailing trend is like trying to win on the defense. It's a lot of work, and you may get beat up!

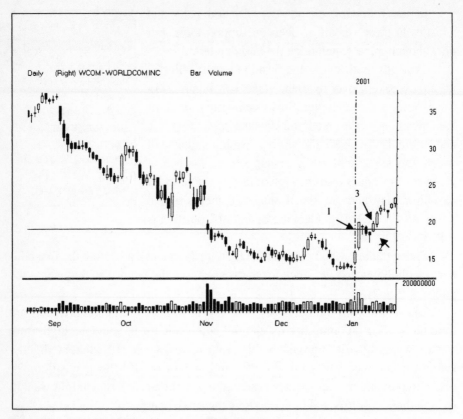

Figure 7-4.

On this chart of Worldcom Inc. (WCOM), you can see how it broke out of a fairly tight base on strong volume. The breakout occurred on Jan. 3, 2001, where you see signal number 1. The number 2 buy signal is the first clear candle after the hammer at the bottom of the pullback. The next candle rises over the previous high, and when it does, it makes a number 3 signal.

Keep in mind that ideal bases take weeks to form. Bases lasting only a few days many times produce failed breakouts.

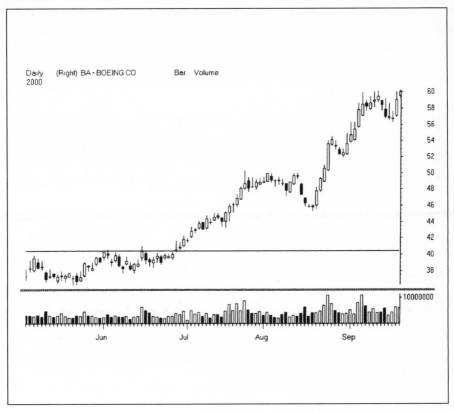

Figure 7-5.

On this chart of Boeing Co. (BA), you can see how it broke above a tight base on June 28, with a buy point just over 41. That was number 1. July 17, 2000, the hammer, was the low pullback day, with a high of 44.44. The number two buy point was the next day, July 18, at about 44.50. The stock passed the number 3 add-on or buy point on the same day, as it passed that resistance point of 45.13. Both swing and position traders might hold the orderly stock until it topped out before the first major pullback. The spinning tops and sideways congestion pattern starting July 25 indicates indecision was taking over. Swing traders could sell easily at 49, gaining an 8-point profit. Position traders might monitor through the pullback, then take profits when the stock tops out at 60. You can see other swing trading opportunities after that mid-August pullback.

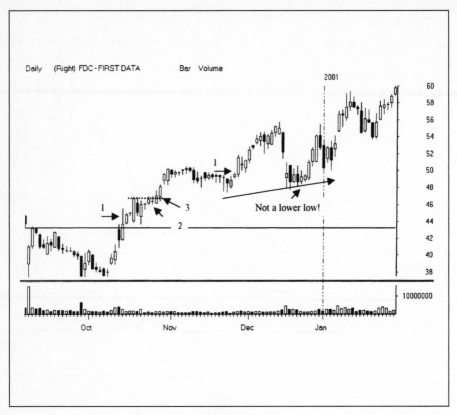

Figure 7-6.

On this daily chart of First Data (FDC), it broke above base resistance of 43.44 on Oct. 13. So, number 1 buy signal would be on that day, at 43.50. Two days later, the stock began consolidating sideways. Remember, stocks rest or correct, through time and price.

HOW TO DRAW AN UPTREND LINE

Okay, get out your crayons! It's connect-the-dots time.

Now that you're playing a stock that's broken out of its base and into an uptrend, it gives you a good sense of the stock's ongoing health if you draw a trendline as soon as it has established two (higher) lows. First, when you draw a trendline on an uptrend, you connect the lows of the pivot points, then extend the line a bit farther than the price action to get an idea of the path it *might* take ("might" being the operative word). Technically, you can draw a trendline connecting any two lows (or any two highs), but this method is a bit more precise. Start your line at the first low after the breakout high, and then connect subsequent lows. Figure 7-7 shows an uptrend line.

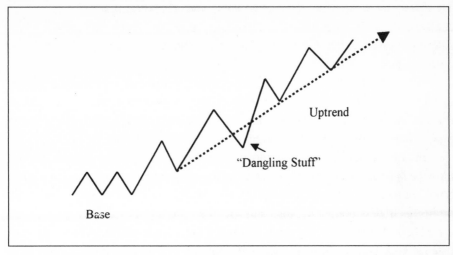

Figure 7-7.
Draw an uptrend line.

Now, I already know your next comment. "Hold it!" you yell. "You ignored a pivot low and drew the trendline right smack through it. What's up with that?"

Hey, they're my crayons! Just kidding. When you see three or more pivot lows that connect in an orderly trendline, that's where to draw it. Now and then you'll see a low that doesn't coincide with the general channel line of the others. As long as *it has not made a lower low than the previous low*, you can draw right through it.

Here are some trendline tips:

✦ For our purposes, the best uptrends are formed at about a 45-degree angle. Any angle steeper than that can result in a heart-stopping, gut-grinding trade. A price pattern that crawls up at a more shallow angle may bore you silly.

✦ When you connect three or more lows in a trendline, it's considered a "major" trendline. Position traders may want to use it as a stop-loss point; that is, if your stock drops below it, you take profits.

✦ *The trendline is broken* the first time the stock pivots to a price lower than the prior one.

✦ Can stocks in an uptrend roll over, make a lower low, then shoot back up and start making higher highs? Sure. And, if you were long that stock and sold it when it broke the trend line, you may want to buy it back. If you do, treat it as a brand-new trade, holding it to your usual criteria.

TRADING IN A RANGE, CONGESTION, AND CONSOLIDATION

As we said earlier, stocks move in three directions—up, down, and sideways. The sideways moves can be divided into three basic categories: trading in a range, congestion, and consolidation.

When we say a stock is "trading in a range," that means it is bouncing up and down between a low price area, or support, and a higher price area, or resistance. *It is not trending.* Most stocks trading in a range are experiencing a Stage One or Stage Three. Another term for trading in a range is "bracketing."

In "the old days," before explosive volatility infiltrated the market, particularly the Nasdaq, traders used to take great joy at finding a stock trading in a range. Some traders called them "rolling" stocks. Playing these securities produced tidy profits, as traders bought the dips and sold the rallies.

These days, trading ranges tend toward the unpredictable, even in dignified listed stocks. Follow-through, meaning a smooth transition in a continuous move to the upside or downside, may be rudely interrupted by market or sector antics. I no longer recommend—in fact I warn against—playing stocks trading in a range.

Gary Anderson, veteran market analyst and author of the weekly market advisory service, *Equity Portfolio Manager (www.equitypm.com)*, says, "Congestion areas tend to be 'hot-war zones,' where strong and weak hands engage in active battle. At bottoms, scared traders sell into the waiting hands of strong buyers. At tops, the reverse is true. Strong sellers offer shares in size to late-adopters of the bullish trend."

Figure 7-8 depicts how a stock trades in a range.

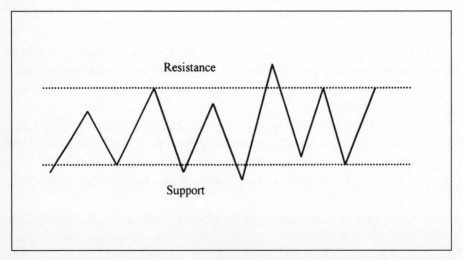

Figure 7-8.

A stock trading in a range, held captive by support and resistance.

When a stock trades in a range, buyers support it at the bottom of its price range. When it reaches the top area of its range, however, buyers refuse to pay higher prices, so it falls again. This is one of the most uniform examples of rotating supply and demand.

The following chart, Figure 7-9, shows a stock trading in a range.

Figure 7-9.

As you can see on this daily chart of Cisco Systems (CSCO), it traded in a fairly even (Stage Three) range between June and mid-September. Note how follow-through at the top and bottom of the range was erratic—and would provide a hair-raising experience!

The second way a stock trades in a sideways price pattern is "congestion." Think back to the last time you had a cold or the flu. Remember how your nose was all "stuffed up," and you couldn't breathe? In the same way, a stock in a congestion pattern gets stuck moving laterally, in an erratic, disorganized fashion, with very little follow-through, as though it can't breathe. You'll see this many times in a stock experiencing a Stage Three.

Congestion patterns form resistance and support. If a stock falls under a ragged congestion pattern, that congestion will act as resistance. Why? Because all those who bought at the high price area are annoyed and are just waiting for the stock to bounce near enough to what they paid for it so they can dump it without too big a loss. That creates supply. Conversely, if the stock rises above the congestion area, the congestion forms support. Figure 7-10 shows how trading in a congestion pattern might look.

Please avoid holding stocks moving in a congestion pattern. Day traders may play them intra-day, but for our purposes of holding overnight, a congestion pattern usually produces losses. As I said in my previous book, "You don't kiss a friend with a cold, and you don't trade a stock in a congestion pattern."

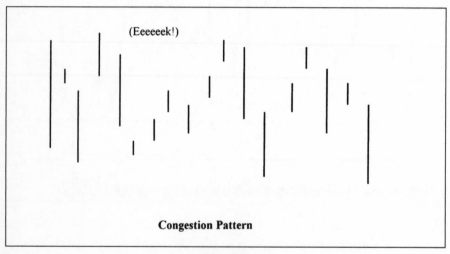

(Eeeeeek!)

Congestion Pattern

Figure 7-10.

A stock trading in a congestion pattern, generally something to steer clear of.

Remember how we discussed the importance of looking for "orderly" stocks to trade? Imagine holding a stock that's experiencing the same mood and manner as in Figure 7-10 or in the charts that follow. Heartburn City!

Check out the stocks experiencing congestion patterns in Figures 7-11 and 7-12, so when you spot the pattern in the making, you know to stand aside.

Unlike the congestion pattern, the next sideways pattern will become our best friend. It's called a "consolidation" pattern, and it presents profitable opportunities when observed and played properly.

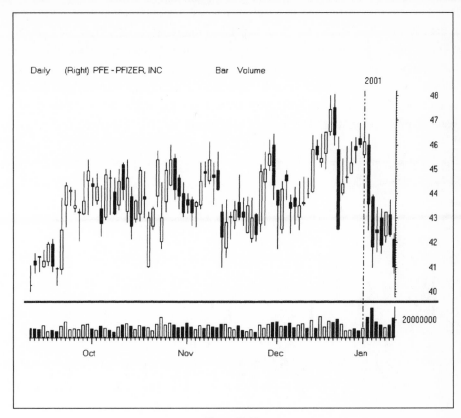

Figure 7-11.

Check out this daily chart of the pharmaceutical company, Pfizer, Inc. (PFE). Talk about a congestion pattern! When you see a stock start a disorderly pattern like this, avoid trading it until (if) it begins a clear uptrend (or downtrend).

A stock in a consolidation pattern moves sideways in a very tight price range. You'll see this pattern most often in a basing pattern, or when a stock is in an uptrend and decides to go into a "resting" mode.

Picture a pressure cooker—a big pot placed on a hot stovetop with its lid clamped on so it becomes airtight. The superheated steam in the pot cooks the food. Now, if you turn up the heat under the pot, the steam expands. If you open the vent in the lid, the steam escapes with a loud "whoosh." Were you to lift the lid with the heat still burning on high, the steam and food would erupt into the air.

Hot Tip

Stocks in uptrends correct in one of two ways—through price or time. They either pull back (down) to previous support, or consolidate laterally.

Just so, a stock moving in a tight sideways consolidation pattern heats up in a pressure cooker. Bulls lift, bears squash. Finally, at some point, the pressure cooker builds up so much steam, it bursts open and the contents explode into the air! In other words, a jolt of rising volume—caused by good/bad news or market activity—explodes the stock price to the upside or downside. When you're playing a stock breaking out of a congestion pattern (assuming you're on "the right side"), you can profit mightily from the price explosion.

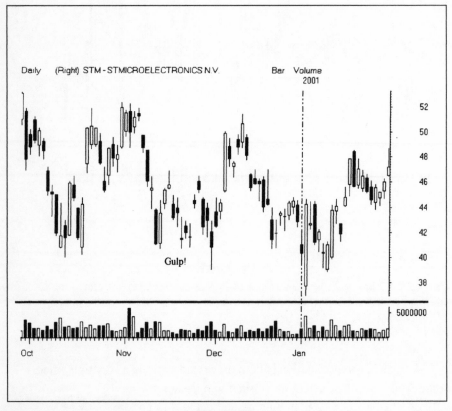

Figure 7-12.

This daily chart of St. Microelectronics N.V. (STM) shows one ornery congestion pattern! Can you imagine holding a stock like this overnight?

Figure 7-13 displays a typical congestion pattern. When a stock breaks above or below the congestion area (think "ledge" or "shelf"), accompanied by high volume (you'll learn volume signals in the next chapter), it many times produces a buy or sell signal.

The longer a stock stays in a consolidation period, the more explosive the move to the upside, or downside, when it finally occurs. That's why you'll often read in *IBD*'s "Investor's Corner" that price breakouts from bases that last at least four to six weeks are optimum.

Figures 7-13, 7-14, and 7-15 show consolidation patterns. Once you learn how to recognize them, bring up charts from your own source and scan for more consolidation patterns. Each time you find one, note the strength of the subsequent move to the upside, or the downside.

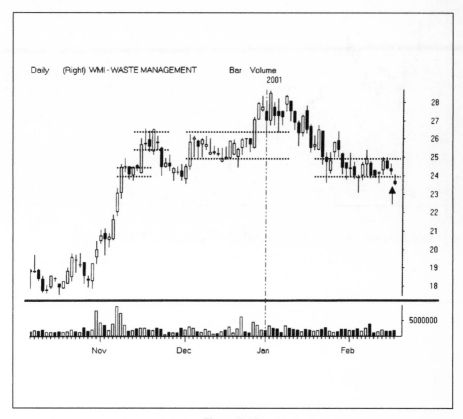

Figure 7-13.

This daily chart of Waste Management (WMI) drew some tight consolidation areas. Many times the real bodies will line up neatly and you can draw through some shadows. Note how these sideways consolidation areas acted as pressure cookers. After a few days of consolidating, the stock broke to the upside or downside in a persistent manner. It appears the stock is completing a Stage Three. By the appearance of the last candlestick (arrow), I suspect the consolidation period in February will result in a break to the downside and the start of a Stage Four downtrend.

Remember, once a stock breaks down from a tight consolidation pattern like those formed by WMI in December and February, the consolidation forms major resistance—think "glass ceiling"—and the stock may struggle when it tries to rise above it.

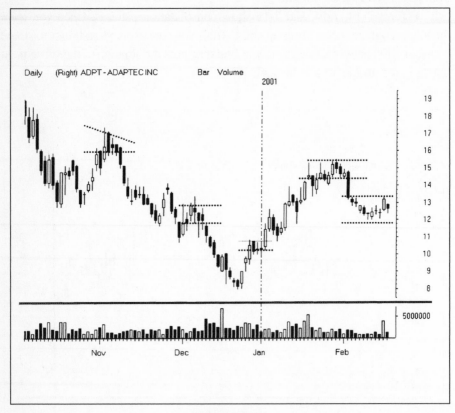

Figure 7-14.

Note the short but effective consolidation areas on this daily chart of Adaptec Inc. (ADPT). The first period shown is also called a "pennant." Often, consolidation patterns are inhabited by spinning tops and doji, which makes sense since sideways consolidation moves have a collective emotion of indecision. Just remember that when the indecision pattern is broken, the move to the upside or downside can be doggone violent!

Hot Tip

Most professionals I know would rather "go short" than take on a long position. Why? Because they make more money, faster, by selling short!

ANATOMY OF A DOWNTREND

The definition of a downtrend is *a price pattern making a series of lower lows and lower highs.* Although, you will probably spend most of your time trading stocks in strong uptrends, if you learn how to sell short properly, you can grab multiple points out of a stock in a Stage Four downtrend. In Chapter 12, you'll learn how to sell short safely and profitably.

Since we usually jump out of short trades faster than we do those to the long side, swing traders targeting breakdowns in the initial or early stages of a downtrend will expect to take the sweet spot out of two- to three-day holds. Position traders will scan for stocks breaking down from a Stage Three, and then sell short and hold for the duration of the downtrend, possibly two to four weeks.

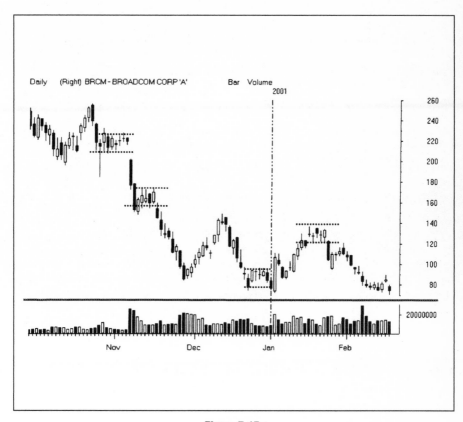

Figure 7-15.

On this chart of Broadcom Corp. (BRCM), note how the consolidation areas led to dramatic price movement. Once formed, consolidation areas form strong bulwarks of support and resistance.

Stocks break down from Stage Three rollovers for several reasons, including: overall negative market conditions; institutional buyers becoming disenchanted with a stock's industry or sector; company reports that show weak earnings, sales, or high inventory; or other negative news. One time you can *always* count on a stock tanking is when the company reports "accounting irregularities."

So when a stock tops out, rolls over, and heads south into a downtrend, it's because fear goads sellers (supply) to lower prices at every level in order to entice reluctant buyers. The fewer the buyers, the faster the fear floods the market with supply, and the more rapidly the stock falls.

Figure 7-16 shows how a stock breaks and falls into a downtrend.

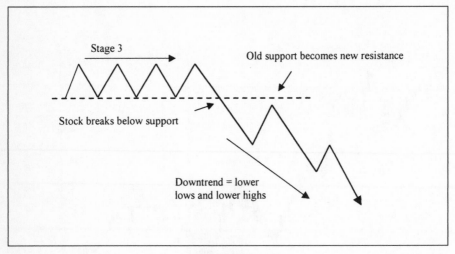

Figure 7-16.
Stock falling into downtrend.

OVERVIEW OF SELL SIGNALS: WHAT TO LOOK FOR

Since we'll delve into selling short in Chapter 12, the following shows a brief overview of shorting signals in a downtrend. As you can see, the setups resemble buying signals in an uptrend. There are, however, subtle differences that we'll discuss later on. Figure 7-17 illustrates three key shorting signals. Read them like this:

✦ Number 1 is the breakdown from support.
✦ Number 2 is the breakdown after the stock rebounds to resistance (supply), then drops back into its downtrend.
✦ Number 3 is the add-to-position point for position traders. Here, the price collapses below the previous pivot low, or support.

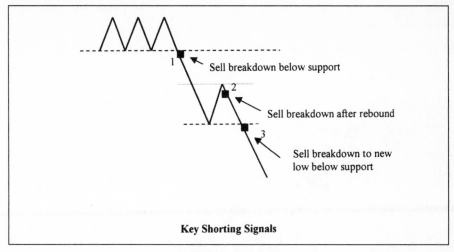

Figure 7-17.
Key shorting signals.

Typically, both swing and position traders will sell short the first breakdown below the support area established in the rollover phase (see 1 in Figure 7-17). Swing traders will buy the shares back to "cover their short" within a day or two, depending on the price action.

Position traders will watch the stock rebound to resistance. When it "smacks its head" on that resistance and resumes its downtrend below the low of the highest rebound day, they may add additional shares to their original position (see 2).

Swing traders, who sold short at the first breakdown and closed the trade, or "covered" before the first rebound, can also sell short again at (2). Both traders can add to their position at (3), as the stock falls below the support of the last low and continues its tumble. If the stock/industry/market shows signs of rebounding at that support level, swing traders might want to take profits.

The following three charts show stocks breaking down from their Stage Three tops and dropping into downtrends. Check out the 1-2-3 entry points.

As you'll see on Figure 7-18, signals 2 and 3 may come at one time. A stock falling into a downtrend can push up to previous resistance, then gap down multiple points. It can breakdown from the rebound and pass prior support—all in one candlestick.

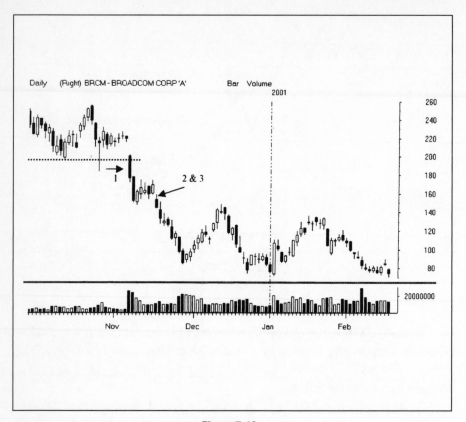

Figure 7-18.

Again, you can clearly see the daily chart of Broadcom Corp. (BRCM) as it breaks the low of its Stage Three of 196. 25 on November 7 and falls to a low on that day of 172.33. The number 1 buy would be as soon after 196 as you could get your order filled—this stock moves fast! The stock consolidated from November 9–15 but gapped down again on November 16, quickly passing the last pivot low of 148 and giving both 2 and 3 selling short signals.

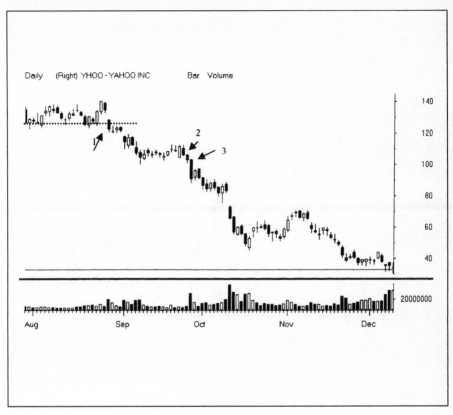

Figure 7-19.

On August 28, this daily chart of Yahoo, Inc. (YHOO) shows how this Internet power of old gapped down to open at 128.50, breaking the support low of the base at 123, then continuing its dive that day to 120.63. Notice how the old base then acts as resistance. You would sell short YHOO on August 28 (number 1) as soon as possible after it broke 123. There are other entries for numbers 2 and 3, but the obvious number 2 signal was on September 26 when YHOO broke the consolidation pullback low of 105. On the next day, a number 3 sell signal took place as YHOO broke the previous low of 99.75, opening at 102.75 and falling to 88, nearly 25 points in one day!

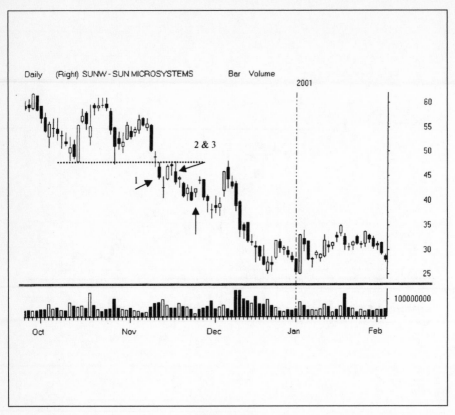

Figure 7-20.

This daily chart of Sun Microsystems (SUNW) shows a definite Stage Four downtrend. You could have successfully shorted SUNW (number 1) when it broke support of its base low of 48, on the gap down day of November 9. On that day the stock fell to 44.50. Numbers 2 and 3 came simultaneously on November 16, when this previously popular tech stock fell past the previous low of 45.13 to 43.25. When a stock falls for two days and hands over a multi-point profit, it's time to take gains, particularly with a volatile tech stock. When on November 24, SUNW closed on the high of the day (arrow), it's time for all traders to cover shorts!

RealTick graphics used with permission of Townsend Analytics, Ltd. ©1986–2002. All rights reserved.

HOW TO DRAW A DOWNTREND LINE

Still got your crayons handy? Good. It's connect-the-dots time, again. Just as with an uptrend, you can get a good sense of the possible direction of a stock if you start drawing a trendline as soon as it establishes lower highs in a downtrend. Connect the tops of the lower highs, beginning at the first one. Figure 7-21 shows a downtrend line.

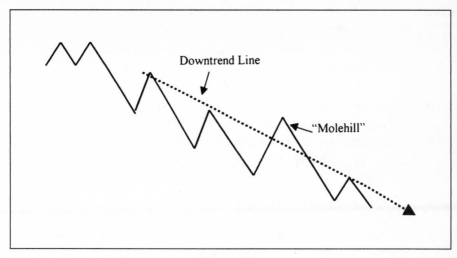

Figure 7-21.
Draw a downtrend line.

Remember how I drew a trendline in the uptrend right through one of the lows? It's sort of like when a piece of your hair sticks out in a weird direction right before a big date—and you get the scissors and cut it off. Well, you'll notice I did the same thing in Figure 7-21. I drew right through the high that sticks out beyond the rest. The highly technical term I use for this is "molehill." It's simply a molehill wanting to be a mountain. Notice that it's *not* a higher high. It didn't break the downtrend.

When the stock does break the downtrend line by making a higher high and higher low, then that trend is considered finished, or "broken."

I'll stress the following point more than once, so you make sure to absorb it. A high-quality, dignified stock can rise in an orderly, stair-step uptrend that gladdens the hearts of swing and position traders everywhere. But once that stock reaches the trend's high and rolls over into a downtrend, watch out! Downtrends lean toward volatility, with the stock's price bouncing like a rubber rock. That's why, as you'll learn later, when you sell short, you may hold the position for a briefer time period than if you were long.

QUIZ

1. Stocks move in what three directions?
2. Give one reason why stocks break out of bases and into uptrends.
3. Define "uptrend."
4. Briefly describe buy signals 1-2-3.
5. What is a swing trader's strategy when presented with a stock breaking into a strong uptrend? A position trader's strategy?
6. Name three ways in which a stock moves sideways.
7. True or False? It's fun and profitable to play a stock trading in a congestion pattern.
8. Stocks correct one of two ways: (1) _____ or, (2) _____.
9. The longer a stock marches sideways in a tight congestion pattern, the *more explosive* or *less explosive* the breakout/breakdown?
10. Give the definition of a downtrend.

ANSWERS

1. Up, down, and sideways.
2. A stock may break out of its base and into an uptrend because an institutional buyer(s) starts to accumulate it. Also, the stock's industry/sector may come into favor, or the company issues good news, or announces higher-than-expected earnings.
3. An uptrend is when a stock's price pattern makes a series of higher highs and higher lows.
4. (1) Buy breakout above resistance, (2) buy first breakout immediately after first pullback (consolidation) to support, (3) buy breakout to new high over previous high.
5. When presented with a stock breaking into an uptrend, a swing trader will buy the initial breakout and sell on or before the first pullback takes place. The swing trader will then strive to take the sweet spot, or middle, out of the upswings in the trend. The position trader buys the initial breakout, and while he or she may add to the position along the way, the trader will hold until the prevailing uptrend slows or is broken.
6. Trading in a range, congestion, consolidation.
7. Don't you *dare* say true!
8. Stocks correct: (1) by pulling back to support, or (2) by consolidating.
9. More explosive.
10. A downtrend is a price pattern that makes a series of lower highs and lower lows.

✦ ✦ ✦

CENTER POINT

The moment one definitely commits himself, then Providence moves too. All sorts of things occur to help one that would never otherwise have occurred. A whole stream of events issues from the decision, raising in one's favor all manner of unforeseen incidents and meetings and material assistance, which no man could have dreamed would come his way.

—W. H. MURRAY (CLIMBED MT. EVEREST)

The Power of Synchronicity

If a single miracle takes place of which I have no doubt, it is the existence of synchronicity. Some choose to call the perfect timing of seemingly unrelated events and people coming into our lives as "coincidence." Not me. Too many situations in my life have been touched by synchronicity.

One cold winter evening, only an hour lingered before fifty guests would arrive at my home for a holiday party. It occurred to me that I'd forgotten to bring the ice chest up from the storeroom downstairs. Once in the storeroom, I found the styrofoam container to be damaged and broken. I had no time to go to a store and buy another.

Frustrated, I returned upstairs. Suddenly, an inner voice *insisted* I take a load of newspapers back down to the recycling bin. "Later," I argued. "Newspapers to the recycling bin are not a priority. I have a problem! What am I going to use to hold the ice?" *Take the newspapers down now*, the voice insisted. Annoyed, I grabbed an armful of newspapers and trudged back downstairs. When I opened the recycling bin, my jaw dropped. On top of the stack of newspapers sat the cleanest, newest styrofoam ice chest a hostess could ever want! Evidently, someone had given it as a gift, filled with frozen desserts. Now it had been "delivered" to me with perfect timing.

Have you ever spontaneously thought of someone one minute, and had him or her call the next minute? Have you ever longed for an answer to a question, then tripped over it in a book, movie, or conversation with a friend?

Underlying this connection between seemingly random events somehow is a grand and harmonious plan. It weaves through our lives, offering us exactly what we need, when we need it. Can you imagine how we would empower ourselves if we learned to trust it and to access it?

When we believe in synchronicity, we know an exquisite rhythm reverberates through ourselves, each other, and all of creation. As we give thanks for it, this intelligence supports us and leads us to our highest potential with flawless timing and grace.

✦ ✦ ✦

CHAPTER 8

Putting the Puzzle Together

The professional concerns himself with doing the right thing rather than with making money, knowing that the profit takes care of itself if the other things are attended to.

—JESSE LIVERMORE

Certain things in life are givens. At Thanksgiving, serving turkey, stuffing, and cranberry sauce is a given. Then, according to our own family traditions, we add the sweet potatoes, mashed potatoes, vegetables, and pumpkin pie.

Swing and position traders need certain givens. Then, according to your personal preferences, you'll add on bells and whistles (indicators and oscillators) that agree with your trading speed and style.

But before we go on, allow me to briefly climb on my soapbox. Recently, traders' mailboxes have been stuffed with circulars that make bizarre promises like: "Make $15,000 a month in the stock market by working just thirty minutes a day." Yeah, right. And I'm Tinkerbell. Then they go on to hit you with a set of buying signals, using indicators and oscillators, without explaining the reasoning behind them. They tell you "when this, and this, and this happens—*buy!*" Never mind that you are risking your hard-earned money in a trade where you have no clue what's really going on. Never mind that they don't teach you how to monitor market conditions. Talk about driving without brakes!

Guess you can tell by this huffy discourse that we're not going to do that in this book. Will we give specific buy/sell signals? Absolutely! Are you going to know *why* you're following them? You bet! That way, if a freight train is headed in your direction with its whistle turned off (stock market surprise), you'll have the savvy to jump off the tracks *before* it arrives. Those traders blindly following directions may not enjoy the same fate. Ouch!

Okay, back to trading givens. They are: candlesticks, volume, and moving averages. As soon as you understand how they work in a buy/sell setup, you can add additional indicator/oscillators as decision support tools.

We've already discussed candlesticks, so let's move on to volume and moving averages.

VOLUME: A MEGA-IMPORTANT INDICATOR

Volume is one of the most important indicators traders use to predict future price direction. The ability to read volume signals will be one of the handiest tools in your toolbox.

Have you ever gone to a party where few people showed up? Not very exciting, was it? In the same way, when you're buying a stock, you don't want to be the only person at the party! You want lots of people to attend so that the stock skyrockets right out of the gate (breakout).

Think of high volume as energy being directed at a stock. This energy may be positive or negative.

Can you hear your dentist telling you, "Only floss the teeth you want to keep?" Makes sense. Keeping your teeth extra-clean means they'll stay healthier, longer. When you water and fertilize a plant, it flourishes happily. If you don't, it withers. During the weeks that you deposit money into your checking account, you have the funds to pay your bills. No deposit, no bill paying. Conclusion: Positive energy directed at an entity—human or otherwise—causes it to flourish. Low or negative energy causes it to stagnate and atrophy.

Stocks, especially, respond to energy. Human energy translates into volume, or the number of shares traded in a specified period of time. By now you've spotted the volume spikes that run along the bottom of the charts we've observed. The spike below the candlestick represents the total number of shares traded during that session.

Here are some general volume rules:

+ Strong volume equals strong conviction, which can be either positive or negative.
+ Low volume equals lack of conviction.
+ Lack of conviction usually means prices will drop.

Note: From now on, I'm going to be talking about signals to the buy side, not to selling short. So, please keep that in mind. (We'll tackle shorting signals in Chapter 12.)

Now, as swing and position traders, you initially look for high volume on the breakout, when the stock trades over its first resistance area (lots of happy people at the party). As the stock continues to the upside on subsequent days, strong volume (if not quite as strong as the breakout day) is desirable.

Hot Tip

Breakouts that take place on weak volume usually fail!

When the stock tops off and begins to pull back, or retrace, make sure the pullback is on relatively *low* volume. Why? Because you don't want the selling pressure (energy) during the pullback to be as strong as it was on the move up. If pullback volume is low, it means that many previous buyers are holding onto their positions. If pullback volume is high, buyers are selling just as hard and fast as they bought. So, the stock will surely drop not only to its previous resistance, but perhaps below it. You don't have to stay at that party! If you are long the stock when it tops out and begins its pullback or retracement, and you see heavy selling pressure coming in via high volume, take profits.

Figure 8-1 shows ideal breakout and pullback volume patterns.

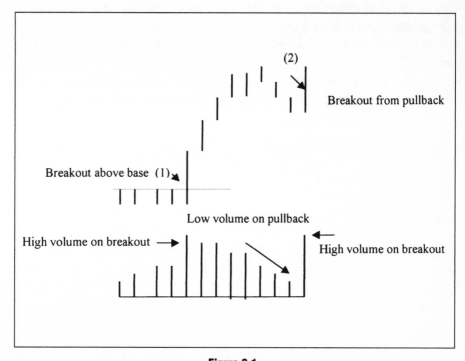

Figure 8-1.
Volume patterns.

Hot Tip

Heard the old saying, "Buy the rumor, sell the news"? If you find yourself long a stock that shoots straight up for no discernable reason, a positive rumor may be afloat. Take profits before the news hits the street!

Attention swing and position traders: The following volume tip is designed to make you big bucks. When you're scanning charts to find stocks' building bases, look at the volume spikes and *locate a stock experiencing increasing volume while the stock continues to trade in the same tight, price range.* That particular pattern indicates a strong possibility that institutional buyers are quietly accumulating the stock and hoping no one will notice. A mutual fund, for instance, might be buying up limited shares per day, so as not to make the price accelerate until the order is filled. Of course, this game can only be played until all the shares offered at the low price levels are absorbed (supply). When that happens, all heck may break loose! If you're tracking the stock like the stealth trader that you are, you'll have your finger on the buy button.

In fact, this is one time (as you become more experienced) when you might take on a tiny lot size (50 shares) early on, while the stock is still in the base. You'll set your stop-loss extremely tight (stop-loss settings are discussed in Chapter 11) to keep risk at a minimum. Then, if the stock rockets out of its base, you can add to your position. On the chance that the volume fizzles out and no breakout occurs, you jump out even.

Another volume signal for swing traders: After two to three (or less) days up, if the current day made a new recent high and appears to be ending in a doji, star, or spinning top (short real body) on *low volume*, it's a good time to take profits. Why? Any one of those three candlesticks translates into "indecision" on the part of market players. Remember how low volume means "low conviction"? Indecision plus low conviction equals falling prices. Figure 8-2 illustrates this point.

The final volume signal for both swing and position traders? When climactic volume designated by a *huge* volume spikes near the end of an *extended* uptrend or downtrend, it often indicates the current trend may soon slow or halt. By "huge," I mean several times the usual daily volume. If you trip over a mega-spike like this (you'll see some in the charts that follow) and you're holding a position, take partial or complete profits.

On the chance that the climactic volume reversal warning doesn't play out, and the stock continues in a strong uptrend, you can always buy it back if presented with a good opportunity. (You're better off, though, scanning for a stock that's in early stages of an uptrend. The older the uptrend, the less steam it has left.)

Conversely, just because a climactic volume spike forms on a stock that's fallen for several weeks in a pig-ugly downtrend, don't take this as an automatic trend reversal and start bottom fishing. These patterns sometimes take a few days to play out. (Occasionally, they even misfire.) However, if you're convinced the stock is about to turn, you can place the stock on your watch list and monitor it for a future base/breakout.

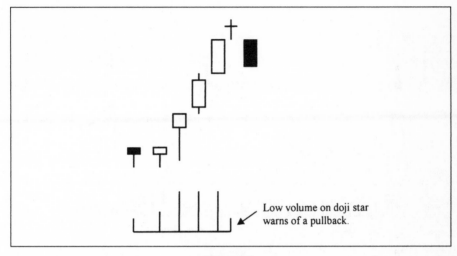

Figure 8-2.
Low volume on doji star.

Check out Figures 8-3, 8-4, and 8-5 on the next few pages for the volume signals we've discussed. Study the price action that takes place immediately after the volume signal occurs.

MOVING AVERAGES: WHAT THEY ARE, HOW TO USE THEM

Another tool you'll want to have tucked into your trader's toolbox is the moving average (MA). Moving averages come in three flavors: simple, weighted, and exponentially smoothed averages.

For our purposes, simple moving averages work beautifully. We're going to use them as one component of our buy signals. A simple moving average is a line chart constructed from the closing prices of a stock (index, market) over a specified time period. For example, a 20-day moving average equals the last 20 days of a stock's closing price added together, then divided by 20. The procedure is repeated each day and finalizes in a line chart.

Hot Tip

Stocks that form *orderly* bases with tight price patterns supported by *orderly* volume spikes yield the most profitable breakouts and dependable uptrends. Bases fashioned of erratic price moves fueled by wildly variable volume spikes many times produce failed breakouts.

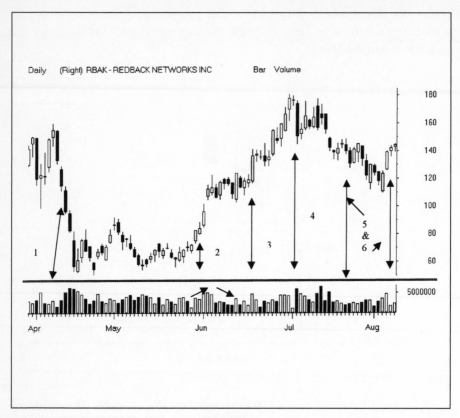

Figure 8-3.

On this daily chart of Redback Networks, Inc. (RBAK), you can see how volume plays a role in the price pattern. 1. RBAK falls straight down (!) on rising volume. 2. Breakout to upside on strong volume = bullish. Subsequent volume on sideways consolidation is low—that's bullish. 3. High volume on next breakout. 4. Climactic volume to downside on wide range day hints at future negative move. 5. Lower volume on consolidation is typical. 6. High volume on breakout is positive.

Moving averages are "lagging" indicators, because they use information that has already taken place. Because of that, they are also called "trend following" indicators. They work best in trending price patterns, where an uptrend or downtrend is firmly in place.

Major moving averages act as fantastic support areas. Think of them as magnets for price patterns. Over and over, you'll see a stock in an uptrend rise high above its twenty-day moving average, only to turn and dip down to it, use it for support, then bounce and rise again.

Hot Tip

Moving averages that move horizontally are not to be used as indicators. They have no predictive value when they "flatline."

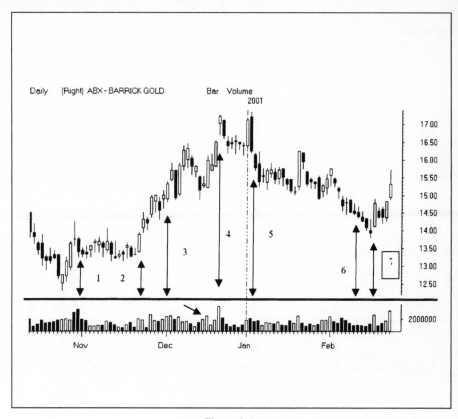

Figure 8-4.

On this daily chart of Barrick Gold (ABX), you can again see how volume plays a role in price movement. 1. When pullback has stronger volume than breakout (and doesn't tank!), stock is in for a long consolidation period. 2. Strong volume on breakout = bullish. 3. Again, breakout on strong volume = bullish for swing trade setup. 4. Mega-strong climactic volume in context of extended uptrend foretells trend change. 5. Notice how on January 2, ABX rockets to previous resistance set in mid-December. On January 3, it forms a bearish engulfing pattern on high volume. (Alan Greenspan made a surprise announcement for an interest rate cut, which is bearish for gold.) 6. Stock falls on low volume and inertia. 7. ABX breaks out on high volume.

Moving averages also act as resistance. Once a stock trades under a major moving average, that average will serve as a ceiling, or resistance, to hamper the stock's rise. This is especially true with a stock that's fallen below the 200-day moving average. A stock that's tanked under this power-average usually puts up a struggle before clawing its way back through. Conversely, a stock that dips to its 200-day MA, many times finds support on it.

The term "major" moving average usually refers to the brawniest ones used by technical analysts. You'll hear them mentioned regularly on CNBC and other financial networks. They are the 20-day, 40-day, 50-day, and 200-day moving averages. Other effective moving averages are the 10-, 30-, 40-, and 100-day MA.

Everybody develops their favorites—I've heard traders swear by the 12-, 18-, 21-, and 67-day MAs.

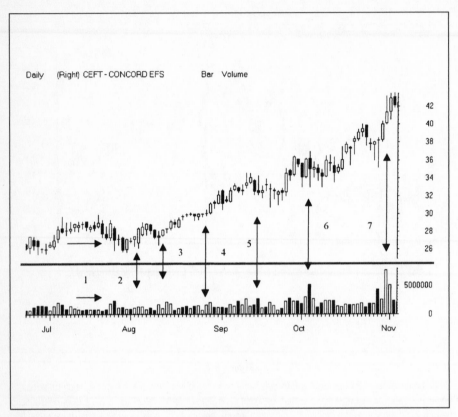

Figure 8-5.

This daily chart of Concord EFS (CEFT), a bank equipment stock, shows an orderly uptrend. Notice how volume gradually increases in this stock. Do you think institutions might be accumulating this stock? 1. CEFT moves sideways on low volume. 2. CEFT moves up on strong volume = bullish. 3, 4. Breakout on strong volume. 5, 6. Long, black candle on high volume, as in a similar pattern on Figure 8-4, ABX, doesn't cause stock to tank but does contribute to elongated consolidation period. 7. Breakout on strong volume.

On our charts, we're going to start with the 20-, 40-, 50-, and 200-day MAs. You may want to experiment with others as you gain experience, but hold yourself to a limit. Ever seen a mass of tangled fishing line? That's what moving averages look like if you overlay more than four or five on a chart. Then they don't give signals. They give heartburn!

The 20-, 40-, and 50-day MAs will provide decision support tools for our buy signals. The 200-day MA maintains as a thermometer.

Note in which order we want moving averages to appear on a chart. When we look for buying signals, optimally we're looking for the 20-, 40-, 50-, and 200-day MA's layered *in that order,* from top to bottom. Figure 8-6 illustrates this point.

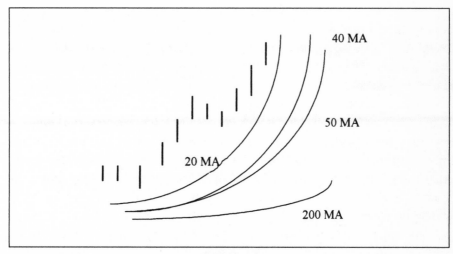

Figure 8-6.
Optimal moving average positioning.

Now, after reading my warnings about stocks trading under their 200-day MAs, consider this scenario: The year 2001 presented a volatile market game, to say the least. As I write, many (most tech) stocks are gasping for breath and trading under their 200-day MAs. They have bravely clawed up from April 2001 lows and have begun building Stage One bases. As such, they offer terrific buying opportunities. Were we to discount them because their price pattern remains under their 200-day MAs, we would miss juicy profits delivered by fantastic breakouts from tight bases. So . . . am I contradicting my previous warning? Not exactly.

Early in my trading career, I studied with a trader/teacher who often said, "Back up. Back up and look at the big picture." That was great advice. Always take overall market conditions into consideration when you trade. Use common sense. Stand back and look at the big picture. In a raging bull market where healthy

Hot Tip

After subtracting weekends and holidays, there are approximately 240 trading days left in a calendar year. A stock trading *under* its 200-day MA wallows underneath it's closing price average for the past 200 days. Is it any wonder we consider stocks inflicted with this syndrome as "bad news bears"?

stocks abound, a stock trading under its 200-day MA is indeed a sick puppy, and should be avoided on the long side.

When stocks start basing after a bear market, many good companies trade under their 200-day MAs. The trough represents an inevitable part of the unending business cycle.

Therefore, would I buy a fundamentally strong company (healing from a bear market) breaking out of a steady base with increasing volume—with its 200-day MA sloping down from high overhead? Sure. I'd check for sound fundamentals. Then I'd scale in, set tight stop-losses, and closely monitor market movement.

What I would *not do* is buy a stock trading under its 200-day MA that's within a few points of touching it. The 200-day MA forms a powerful ceiling, or resistance. Most stocks will falter and even pull back as they near this bully from underneath. If your stock climbs to a point near the 200-day MA, take profits. After it rises above the MA, re-enter only if it meets your buying criteria and resumes a solid uptrend. Remember to use wisdom and common sense in all trading situations.

We will, however, not fudge with the other moving averages I listed. We will only target stocks to buy when they trade above their 50-day MAs. The 20-day and 40-day should be layered above the 50-day MA, as previously mentioned.

As I said at the beginning of this section, we're going to add moving averages as a component of our 1-2-3 buy signals. Like this:

✦ When our target stock pulls back to the 20-, 40-, or 50-day MA for support, then bounces.

✦ When a faster moving average crosses a slower moving average from below and rises over it.

Hot Tip

Institutional buyers use the 50-day MA as a buy and sell signal. That's why you'll see high-cap companies in favor when these managers pull back to the 50-day MA, then bounce like a kangaroo.

Let's consider the first point. Think of a moving average rising like a staircase. Your feet, moving up the staircase, are the stock. Your foot rises above the step, and then moves lower to use it as support before rising again. The moment your foot lifts off the staircase equals the stock rising off its moving average. That's the buy point, and as you will soon learn, it will correlate perfectly with volume and our 1-2-3 signals.

Now let's look at an example of the second point. A 20-day MA is inverted and trading under the 50-day MA on a daily chart. (Naturally, both are below the price pattern.) As the stock rises out of its base, the 20-day MA starts curving up, will cross over the 50-day MA and rise above it. When you see a faster MA (the shorter the time frame of the MA, the "faster" it is) cross over and above a slower MA, it's a very bullish sign. Depending on how the stock fits the other buying criteria we will establish, we may use the crossover as an add-on signal.

Figure 8-7 illustrates both points.

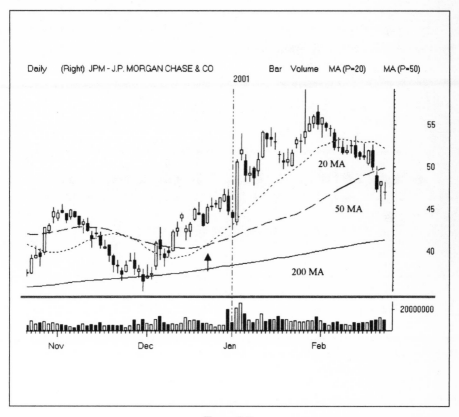

Figure 8-7.

On this daily chart of J.P. Morgan Chase & Co. (JPM), the 20-, 50-, and 200-day moving averages have been added. Notice in mid-December (arrow) how the 20-day MA crosses over and rises above the 50-day MA. It was a bullish signal that accurately foretold a dandy uptrend! Also note how fond JPM is of the 20-day MA, and how the stock uses it as support. In this case, the 20-day MA could be used as a very accurate uptrend line. When JPM breaks the 20-day MA, it drifts lower to the 50-day MA and then gaps down decisively. Remember, institutions many times use the 50-day MA as a major support indicator. When a stock falls below the 50-day MA, institutions may be shunning it. So—guess what—we do, too!

To clarify this explanation, in the following charts you'll see examples of moving averages, how stocks use them for support, and bullish crossover signals.

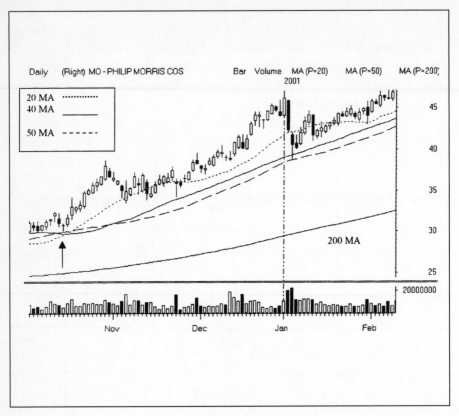

Figure 8-8.

On this daily chart of Philip Morris Companies (MO), the 40-day MA has been added. (If you start by looking at too many at one time, it gets confusing.) You can see how MO uses the 20-day MA and 50-day MA as support. Notice where the 20-day MA (arrow) comes from under the 40-day and 50-day MAs and crosses to the upside. Then, the MAs stay nicely layered in perfect uptrend order. Again, we can use the 20-day MA and possibly the 40-day MA as trendlines. We can also use the pullbacks to support, meaning the price bouncing off of the 20-day, 40-day, and 50-day moving averages as a criterion for buy signals.

Worry not. Shortly, you'll understand how price patterns, volume, and moving averages all move in harmony, just like a well-directed orchestra.

In the next chapter, you'll learn how to add one more instrument to the symphony in the form of oscillators, which are valuable overbought/oversold indicators. Then, get ready, 'cause it will soon be time to go shopping!

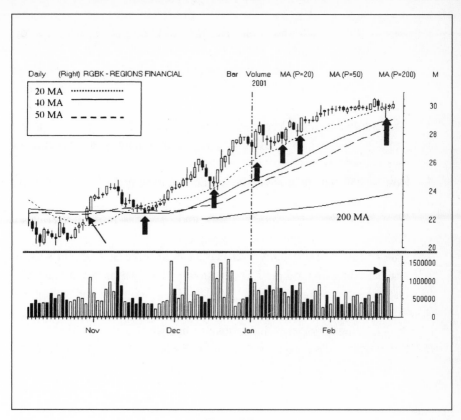

Figure 8-9.

On this daily chart of Regions Financial (RGBK), you can again see how stock will use its moving averages as support. RGBK broke out of its base on strong volume on October 30 (arrow) and climbed over its major moving averages. Swing traders could have bought that move, however, we like to buy for a longer term when at least the 20-day MA is *rising*. In mid-November, the stock dipped down to its converged MAs and at the same time, the 20-day MA crossed above the others, a bullish sign. RGBK took off after that, never looking back. The block arrows show you where RGBK's pullbacks to the 20-day MA gave buy signals. The last buy at the end of February 2001 could be dicey. Why? Note how RGBK is slowing its uptrend, and the candlesticks are narrowing to spinning tops. Spinning tops indicate indecision. Also note the climactic volume (arrow), which also could mean a trend change. In this case, the trader keeps a tight stop-loss (a .50 point or so), right under the lows of the consolidation area.

QUIZ

1. True or false? A higher than average volume spike indicates strong conviction.
2. For a profitable price pattern, you want _____ volume on the breakout and subsequent rise, and _____ volume on the pullback.
3. You're swing trading. Your stock has risen three days in a row. The current day appears to be closing in a doji, and volume is low. What action do you take?
4. How would you calculate a 40-day moving average?
5. Moving averages act as _____ and _____.
6. We will use the ____-day, ____-day, and ____-day moving averages as decision support tools for our buy signals.
7. True or false? If a healthy bull market is in force, it's fine to scan for stocks trading under their 200-day moving averages as buying targets.
8. Institutional managers use the ___-day MA as a buying and selling tool.
9. When you see a fast-moving average crossing over and moving above a slow moving average, is that bullish or bearish?
10. If you add moving averages to our buy signal criteria, what will you look for now when targeting a stock to buy?

ANSWERS

1. True.
2. High, low.
3. Sell and take profits!
4. Add the closing prices of a stock for the last 40 days, then divide by 40.
5. Support and resistance.
6. 20-day, 40-day, 50-day.
7. False, false, false.
8. Institutional managers monitor the 50-day moving average.
9. Bullish.
10. Look for a stock breaking out of a base, pullback, or consolidation that's bouncing off of the 20-, 40-, or 50-day moving average on high volume.

✦ ✦ ✦

CENTER POINT

Your potential is unlimited. Aspire to a high place. Imagine and perceive that which you wish to be. Back your image with enthusiasm and courage. Feel the reality of your 'new' self; live in the expectancy of greater things, and your subconscious will actualize them.

—BRIAN ADAMS

Thoughts Are "Things"

Every single tangible and intangible reality in this world came into being because of a single thought. The chair you sit in, the book in your hands, the computer on your desk, indeed your best friend, originated with a thought.

A thought plus a feeling equals an action. Pure, simple, accurate. Our thoughts are energy, and we are the product of our thoughts.

I once spoke with a friend who had accomplished a masterful feat in an amazingly brief period of time. "How did you achieve such a momentous goal so quickly?" I asked.

He shrugged. "It never occurred to me that I *couldn't* do it." He zeroed in on his goal, held it in his consciousness as a reality, and did it!

What are you holding in your consciousness right now? Thoughts of anxiety, frustration, or even failure? Or thoughts of serenity, confidence, and peace? In our hectic lives, we rarely stop long enough to realize the truth: *our thoughts are our choice!*

Furthermore, when we hold thoughts of ourselves as inept, lazy, or stupid, our conscious mind says, "Okay. You got it. Clumsy, stoic, and dumb it is." Robot-like, our actions follow suit, and those in our world see the person who is all of the above. Why not rewrite that mindset? Why not mentally dwell in a consciousness that accepts and believes you are poised, dynamic, and sharp? Your consciousness will work to produce that image and make it a reality.

Since our thoughts are energy, our actions are that energy in motion. When we dwell on the truth of ourselves as abundant, loving, and successful beings, we become that and more!

Ramtha said, "If any one thing can be conceived or pondered, it exists; for whatever is dreamed or imagined is already within the realm of existence. That is how all of creation came into existence."

✦ ✦ ✦

CHAPTER 9

The Bells and Whistles: How They Chime and Tweet

To learn that a man can make foolish plays for no reason whatever was a valuable lesson to me.

—JESSE LIVERMORE

Now that you've learned charting basics, including important candlestick patterns, the 1-2-3 setups, and how volume and moving averages play a major role, it's time to add the bells and whistles. The following pages discuss the most reliable and popular indicators and oscillators and easy-to-understand methods of incorporating them into your chart analysis as money-making tools.

At the end of the chapter, we'll focus on gaps (think "air pocket") and how to handle them to your advantage.

OSCILLATORS: WHAT THEY ARE

An "oscillator" is not a cubicle you step into and ride up to the second floor of Macy's! *An oscillator is a technical indicator that tells at a glance whether a market, index, or equity currently trades in an "overbought" or "oversold" condition.* Mostly plotted as line charts, you'll position oscillators near the bottom of your charts, above the volume.

When a stock is *overbought*, this means that it's trading at the upper extreme of its current price range and may be vulnerable to a correction. A stock that's *oversold* is scraping the bottom of its current price range and is due for a bounce up.

A truckload of oscillators is available for study and use, each with its own twist on the subject. Those discussed in the following sections—the RSI, Stochastics, and MACD (moving average convergence divergence)—represent popular oscillators most easily found on charting software.

THE RSI: WHAT IT IS, HOW TO USE IT

The RSI, or Relative Strength Index, is a misleading moniker for this reliable oscillator. When we speak of an equity's relative strength, many times we refer to its health as it relates to a broad market index such as the S&P 500, or the industry index where the stock resides, like the semiconductor index ($SOX.X) or the pharmaceutical index ($DRG.X).

The RSI *does not* compare two separate entities. Introduced by Welles Wilder in the June 1978 issue of *Commodities* (now *Futures*) magazine, and in his book published in the same year, *New Concepts in Technical Trading Systems,* the RSI operates as an oscillator that measures a particular stock's current relative strength *as compared to its own price history*.

When Wilder first introduced the RSI, he recommended using a 14-day time period. Now, 9-day and 25-day RSIs are also favorites.

> **Hot Tip**
>
> The shorter the time period you use to calculate moving averages or oscillators, the more volatile these indicators become. For example, an RSI set to a 9-day period gives much faster signals than an RSI set to a 25-day parameter.

The RSI is one of my preferred oscillators, and we're going to use it in our buying criteria. For multi-day to multi-week holds, the 14-day parameter works well (and is standard in most charting software). So, please stick to that time parameter for now. As you gain more experience, you may want to tweak the setting to a faster, or slower, time period.

As a price-following oscillator, the RSI is plotted on a vertical scale numbered from 1 to 100. It's considered to be oversold when it falls below 25, and overbought when it rises over 75.

Dandy features of the RSI are:

✦ The RSI forms chart patterns, such as a double top or head-and-shoulders (see Chapter 10), which may not show up in the stock's price pattern.
✦ The RSI may indicate support and resistance levels more clearly than the stock's price pattern.
✦ The RSI makes a fantastic buy/sell decision support tool when it diverges from the stock's price action. For example, the stock may make a new high, but the RSI does not. That's bearish. Or, the price may tumble to a new low, while the RSI moves sideways or up. That's bullish. Prices usually follow the direction taken by the RSI.

To incorporate the RSI into your buy/sell criteria, you'll add it to the signals we already have in place, meaning the 1-2-3 entries, strong volume on the breakout, and price bouncing off a major moving average (such as the 20-day, 40-day, or 50-day MAs).

Now add the RSI. When you enter a position, you want it to appear in one of these ways:

+ Oversold, and hooking up from below 30.
+ Hooking up from below 50 and in an uptrend (making higher lows and higher highs).
+ Making a bullish divergence by rising when the stock price is consolidating, or pulling back, in the course of an uptrend.

Figures 9-1 and 9-2 show the RSI in action. Check out the different ways it can support your buy/sell signals.

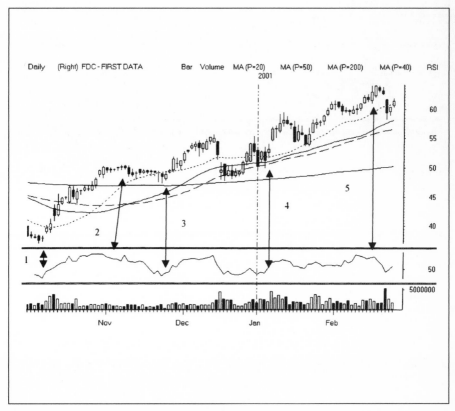

Figure 9-1.

On this daily chart of First Date (FDC), note the RSI added right above the volume. 1. RSI begins move up before price does = bullish divergence. 2. RSI heads down before price sinks = bearish divergence. 3. RSI makes bullish divergence. 4. RSI forms another bullish divergence. 5. RSI makes a lower high, diverging from price pattern. FDC soon follows—big time!

Figure 9-2.

On this daily chart of Juniper Networks (JNPR), note how the RSI acts as a precursor for a price move. 1. The RSI moves before a price pattern, which is bullish. 2. Again, the RSI rise precedes price pattern. Also note the coinciding bullish engulfing pattern and the price moving over the 50-day MA. These are all good signs! 3. RSI makes double top—a bearish sign. 4. RSI makes downtrend (lower highs and lows) while JNPR struggles to move up—a very bearish pattern. The crystal ball was right—JNPR eventually tanked for quite a while. Note that the mid-October move dove under the 50-day MA, which may have lost it institutional support. 5. JNPR heads south after the RSI continues to fall.

As I mentioned earlier, in our final buy criteria, we'll use the RSI as the "official" oscillator. Still, you'll want to read over the descriptions of the remaining oscillators to get a sense of alternative options and the benefits they have to offer.

STOCHASTIC OSCILLATOR: WHAT IT IS, HOW TO USE IT

Traders sometimes refer to the Stochastic (pronounced sto kas tik) Oscillator, as "Stochastics," because it employs two lines to give a single signal.

An overbought/oversold indicator developed by Dr. George Lane, the Stochastic Oscillator *compares where a stock's price closed at to its price range over a specific period of time.* The driving principle: as a price rises in an uptrend, the closing price moves to the upper end of the recent price range. In a downtrend, closing prices usually sink to the bottom of the range. We won't study the actual calculation here. And believe me, if you ever see it, you'll be glad we didn't!

Again, the Stochastic Oscillator is displayed in two lines. The major line is called the "%K." The second line is referred to as the "%D," and is a 3-day moving average of the %K. Many times you'll see the %K as a solid line, and the %D as a dotted line.

Stochastics come in two flavors—fast Stochastics and slow Stochastics. The one described in the previous paragraph is fast Stochastics. In slow Stochastics, the slow %K equals the fast %D, with the slow %D equaling a 3-day average of the fast %D.

> **Hot Tip**
>
> Oscillators have one drawback. When a stock stays in a strong uptrend (or downtrend) for an extended period of time, the oscillator will rise (fall) to the overbought (oversold) position, and then stay "glued" at the top or bottom of the scale while the trend continues. This condition renders the oscillator neutral until the trend changes.

Got that? If not, cheer up. Your charting software understands the equations needed to calculate the display. For the record, I prefer the fast Stochastics, although slow Stochastics has a smoother look.

In tandem, the %K and %D lines rise and fall between zero and 100. Readings above 80 are considered overbought, and readings below 20 are oversold.

The Stochastics buy/sell signal is as follows:

+ *Buy*—when the lines are below 20, and the faster %K line crosses above the slower %D line. (Watch out for short-term crossovers. Use indicators to confirm the reversal.)
+ *Sell*—when the lines are above 80, and the %K crosses the %D to the downside.
+ Look for divergences, just as you do with the RSI. An example: Bossy Bank makes a new high. At the same time, the Stochastics moves sideways or hooks to the downside. That's called a "bearish divergence." Assume the price will soon follow the Stochastics south. Or, while Bossy Bank experiences a normal consolidation period in an uptrend, the Stochastic suddenly hooks up. Referred to as a "bullish divergence," it tells you to prepare for a continuation of Bossy Bank's uptrend within the next few time periods.

> **Hot Tip**
>
> Novice traders: Limit your oscillators to one per chart. Choose a single oscillator and get to know it, up close and personal. As you gain experience, replace it with another, and try that one out.

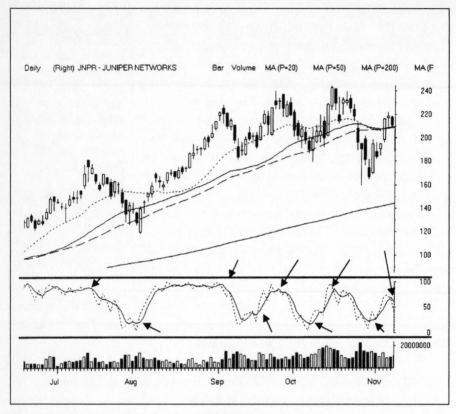

Figure 9-3.

This daily chart of Juniper Networks (JNPR) shows the fast Stochastics. Like the RSI, it can give early buy signals by diverging with the price pattern. When the %K crosses over the %D after they hook up from the bottom (oversold), a buy signal occurs. When the %K crosses over the %D after topping and hooking down, a sell signal takes place. Note the arrows that indicate those signals.

THE MACD: WHAT IT IS, HOW IT WORKS

Traders fondly refer to the MACD as "the mac-dee." The acronym stands for "moving average convergence-divergence" (say that fast three times!). Multifaceted, the MACD not only acts as an indicator, it also plays the role of an oscillator.

Developed by Gerald Appel, publisher of *Systems and Forecasts,* the MACD is a trend-following momentum indicator/oscillator that illustrates the relationship between the 26-day and 12-day exponential moving averages of an equity's price pattern. A 9-day exponential moving average, referred to as the "signal line," overlays the MACD and indicates buy/sell setups.

Since the MACD is a "lagging" indicator, meaning it delivers signals from information that's already taken place (the S&P and Nasdaq 100 futures are "leading" indicators), it is best used in strongly trending markets. Because the traditional MACD usually arrives a bit late to the party (read: trend reversal), short-term traders may leave money on the table by adhering strictly to its signals. To obtain faster signals, I recommend using the MACD histogram, available on most charting programs.

The MACD Histogram (MACD-H) represents the difference between the MACD and its 9-day exponential MA. Don't worry if your brain tangles over that one. Your charting program understands it! Just insert it on your chart, above the volume indicator. The MACD-H will snake above and below its zero line, moving into positive (above zero) or negative (below zero) territory.

MACD-H signals are:

+ *Crossovers.* Buy signal (bullish) equals when the MACD-H rises above its zero line. Sell signal (bearish) equals when the MACD-H tumbles below the zero line.
+ *Overbought/oversold indicators.* As an overbought/oversold oscillator, when the MACD-H rises to the top of its scale and resembles a majestic mountain, the stock may be overbought and ready to pullback. When the MACD-H edges below the zero line and digs a deep scoop to the downside, the stock is oversold. When the histogram bars shorten and edge back up, the stock should be preparing to bounce.

Fun to do: Use a MACD-H on a weekly chart to generate a long-term buy/sell signal. Then, go to a daily chart of the same stock, and only trade in the direction of that longer-term signal.

Figure 9-4 illustrates the MACD-H. Check out the buy/sell signals it gives as it zooms above, then dives below, its zero line.

ON-BALANCE VOLUME: WHAT IT IS, HOW TO READ IT

One of my favorite indicators is the On-Balance Volume (OBV). We're going to use it as a decision support tool for our buying criteria.

Originally developed by Joe Granville, the OBV is a nifty momentum indicator that integrates volume *and* price change. Take a quick glance at this line chart that overlays onto your volume indicator, and you can gauge whether money's flowing into—or out of—a stock.

The OBV works like this: Say Bargain Biotech closes higher than the previous day's close; the OBV considers all volume on this day to be positive. When Bargain closes lower than the previous close, the volume records it as negative.

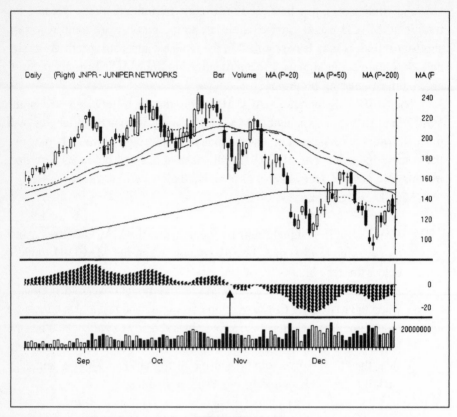

Figure 9-4.

This daily chart of Juniper Networks (JNPR) shows a MACD-H. Note the highs JNPR made in September and October at the same time the MACD-H makes lower highs. The sell signal is at the arrow, when JNPR crosses below the zero line; however, that signal comes too late for most short-term traders.

Hot Tip

Remember, you want to go long with stocks receiving positive (buying) energy. The OBV represents a snapshot of the energy—positive or negative—that market players are infusing into your stock.

The basic theory behind the OBV is that change precedes price moves. If you're scanning charts and see the OBV has bottomed out, then hooks back up, you can assume money is flowing back into the stock

Read the OBV like price patterns. That means it moves just like price: up, down, and sideways. For our purposes, we want the OBV hooking up, or in a solid uptrend, just like the corresponding price pattern. As it can be a short-term indicator, the OBV only needs to be *moving up* to give us the signal we need.

Here's some stuff to learn about the OBV:

✦ When the OBV reverses from a downtrend by hooking up near the bottom of the volume spikes, the downtrend has been broken. You may see this happen in a basing stock. As this event normally *precedes* a price breakout, quickly check out your remaining buying criteria (we'll get to that in Chapter 10) for a possible entry point.

✦ Conversely, if *price movement precedes OBV action*, we call this a "non-confirmation." This occurs at the conclusion of extended uptrends or downtrends. Think "divergence," and if you're holding the stock, take profits.

Now check out the following charts (Figures 9-5 and 9-6) to see how the OBV gives awesome signals. I'll bet you my duck slippers that you'll end up appreciating the OBV as much as I do!

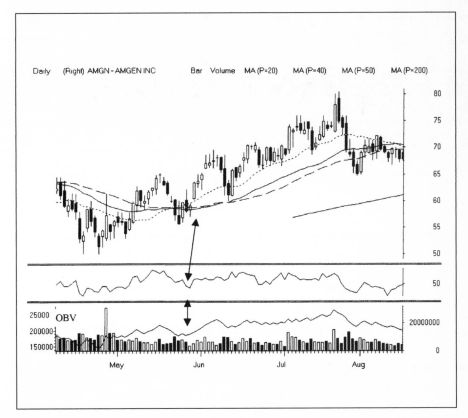

Figure 9-5.

This daily chart of Amgen, Inc., (AMGN) shows how a chart can have a convergence of signals. Look at the first set of arrows. The 20-day MA crosses over the slower MAs. The RSI moves up early in a bullish divergence. At the same time, the OBV has made a small double bottom and is starting up. Notice how the OBV stays in an uptrend for the entire time that AMGN stays in an uptrend.

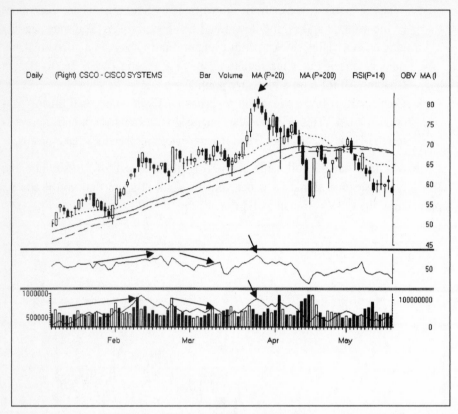

Figure 9-6.

On this volatile chart of Cisco Systems, note how the OBV moves in an orderly uptrend through January and half of February Interestingly enough, CSCO continued to drift up through the midpoint of March, while the OBV and RSI declined. CSCO made its last gasp to the upside (for a while to come) on March 27. Note that the RSI and OBV made slightly earlier tops. Then it was Crash City for the tech giant and most of its siblings. The OBV went into a downtrend, tried to recover in May, then headed back down again as money flowed out of the stock.

BOLLINGER BANDS: WHAT THEY ARE, HOW TO READ THEM

Bollinger Bands come to us courtesy of John Bollinger. They are displayed as an upper and lower band plotted above and below the equity's price pattern, and are calculated at standard deviation levels.

Are you scratching your head? Standard deviation equals a measure of volatility. High standard deviation levels occur when prices change dramatically (think: roller coaster). Low standard deviation values translate into quiet price movement (think: consolidation).

The operative theory behind Bollinger Bands is that *the price pattern tends to fluctuate within the upper and lower band. Further, when the price rises (or falls) to touch the boundary of one band, it will then reverse and fall (or rise) to the opposite band.*

What you need to know when using Bollinger Bands:

◆ When the price moves to touch one band, it usually reverses and heads all the way to the other band (good for projecting price targets).
◆ When the bands tighten because volatility lessens, look for a sharp price change to occur. Hey, same action as a breakout from a consolidation pattern—right? Right!
◆ When the price pokes through and moves outside the band, that implies strength in that direction—or a trend continuation.

Check out the following chart, Figure 9-7, to see how Bollinger Bands can be incorporated into a price pattern to give added information.

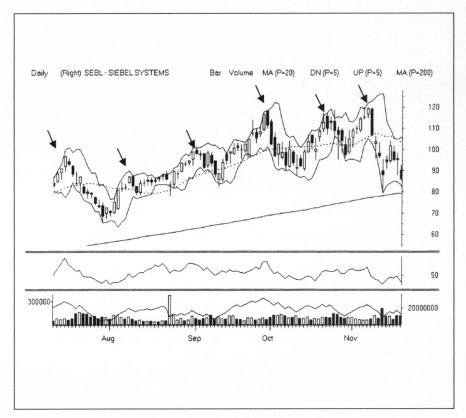

Figure 9-7.

This daily chart of the volatile Siebel Systems (SEBL) illustrates how Bollinger Bands work. Again, the major theme of these bands is that when a stock moves to the boundaries of the upper envelope, it will then reverse and head for the lower envelope and vice-versa (arrows). Also note how the bands tighten as SEBL consolidates or trades in a relatively tight range and how the bands widen when SEBL's daily range expands. (The 40- and 50-day MAs were deleted to avoid confusion. Only the 20- and 200-day MAs remain.)

Hot Tip

Say you go to dinner in a New York City diner. Typically, the waitress presents you with a menu as thick as a phone book that lists a zillion entrees. Your taste buds freak out in confusion—you can't make a choice. Similarly, beware of the "paralysis of analysis." If you overlay too many indicators and oscillators on your charts, you may end up with conflicting signals. So, limit your indicators and oscillators to a manageable number.

While Bollinger Bands are a useful tool for any trading scenario, I use them most often when selling short. Therefore, you'll bump into them again in Chapter 12, when we discuss shorting techniques.

FIBONACCI RETRACEMENTS: WHAT THEY ARE, HOW YOU READ THEM

We owe a debt of gratitude to the Italian mathematician Leonardo Pisano (1170–1250). Best known by his nickname, Fibonacci (he also went by "Bigollo," which may have meant "wandering good-for-nothing"), he wrote the famous book, *Liber abaci* (1202). In it, he introduced to Europe the Hindu-Arabic place-valued decimal system and Arabic. He also discussed mathematical problems that resulted in what we now call *the Fibonacci summation sequence* and the ratios derived from it. Here's one of the most important problems Pisano posed, and the result. Although the question sounds lighthearted, the answer has produced serious resolutions.

"If one places a rabbit couple in an enclosed place, how many rabbits would one obtain after a certain time assuming they reproduce once per month, and that those born can reproduce at the age of a month?" The following infinite progression (now called Fibonacci numbers), results: 1, 1, 2, 3, 5, 8, 13, 21, 34, 55, 89, and 144, after each month.

You'll notice that Fibonacci numbers run in a sequence. Each successive number equals the sum of the two previous numbers: 1, 1, 2, 3, 5, 8, 13, 21, 34, 55, 89, and so forth. The interrelationships between these numbers are intriguing. First, starting with the number five, any of these numbers equals approximately 1.618 times the preceding number. Second, any number equals approximately 0.618 times the subsequent number. Cool, huh?

It's remarkable that so many objects formed in Fibonacci proportions occur throughout nature, including butterflies, sea shells, and spiral galaxies. The pentagram, Christian crucifix, and Pythagorean triangles also contain these proportions, as well as the art pieces of Leonardo da Vinci and Michelangelo.

The four popular Fibonacci studies used by traders include arcs, fans, retracements, and time zones. Most charting software programs include Fibonacci retracements. Some of the more advanced programs utilize arcs, fans, and time zones. For now, we'll look at retracements.

What you need to know about Fibonacci retracements:

+ Fibonacci ratios are gauged at 38.2 percent, 50.0 percent, and 61.8 percent, and are considered a leading indicator (predicting possible future price action).
+ Your job is to draw an uptrend (or downtrend) line, connecting a major peak and trough. Then, activate your charting software's Fibonacci retracement option. Start at the bottom of the trendline and drag your cursor to the top of the trend. (Fancy charting programs will include a 23.6 percent line.) You'll see five horizontal lines, representing 0.0 percent, then 38.2, 50, 61.8, and 100 percent of the entire move, or trend.
+ These levels act as support and resistance areas.

Since so many traders use Fibonacci retracement levels for guidance, some support/resistance action may be a self-fulfilling prophecy. Still, it's positively uncanny how many times a stock in an uptrend will pull back to a Fibonacci level, then bounce. Or, a stock in a downtrend will rebound to a Fibonacci level, and then begin its fall anew.

Some traders use "Fib ratios" by placing their stop-loss points a quarter-point below a stock's 61.8 percent retracement level from the previous high.

Remember, though, that no indicator in this world predicts future price movement with absolute accuracy. Just because your stock happens to be heading for a Fibonacci retracement level is no guarantee it's going to halt there and bounce. It could just as easily slice right through it.

Indicators—no matter what flavor—are just that. They *indicate*. Please don't use them as an excuse to stay in a losing position!

While we're not going to use Fibonacci retracements for our buying criteria, they are a handy tool for you to have. Study Figure 9-8 to understand how price patterns use this indicator for support and resistance.

GAPS: A TRADER'S BLACK HOLE

Now that I've totally fried your brain with indicator/oscillator lore, let's wander into a place where no prices exist—gaps.

Surely, as you've studied the previous charts, you've noticed "holes" in the price patterns. In technical analysis, we call these "gaps." In candlestick terminology, they're called "windows."

Gaps are open spaces in price patterns created by an absence of trading at that price level. They mainly

Hot Tip

Stocks often retrace about 50 percent of their last major move up (or down). When the stock you're holding corrects more than 50 percent from its prior high, it may be weaker than you think. Consider taking profits.

occur when orders placed before the market opens (and/or after-hours trading) cause the specialists and market makers to set the price higher, or lower, than the previous days' close.

Example: Cranky Computers closed yesterday at 35.50. This morning it opens at 35, with no trades exchanging hands between the two prices. That causes a space to form on the chart, and we say the stock "gapped down."

Or, Bossy Bank closed yesterday at 51.85. This morning it opens at 53. Since the stock didn't trade at any price increment between 51.85 and 53, we say it "gapped up."

Many technicians insist that gaps, no matter how distant in time, *always* get filled. That means if a stock or index still has a gap that was created two years ago, the stock or index *will* return to that price to fill that gap. (Gulp!)

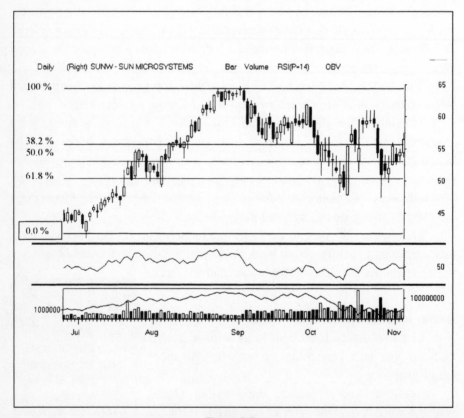

Figure 9-8.

This daily chart of Sun Microsystems (SUNW) displays Fibonacci retracement levels plotted from the bottom of the base to the rally peak. Note how SUNW uses these retracement levels as support while it rises, then as resistance when it falls and tries to rise again. Fibonacci retracement levels are great guidelines to add to your trader's tool kit.

Since I maintain that nothing *always* happens in the stock market, and since I happily celebrate getting through a week, or month, at a time with my profits, and my sanity, intact, I refuse to fret about a two-year-old gap until I see the whites of its eyes!

On the flip side of that, in-your-face gaps definitely need to be respected and studied.

Gaps come in three types: breakaway, exhaustion, and runaway. A *breakaway* gap usually occurs after the conclusion of a major price pattern, and presages the start of an important price move. An *exhaustion* gap takes place at the end of an extended uptrend, or downtrend, and signals the conclusion of that trend. Exhaustion gaps can be filled immediately. A *runaway*, or continuation, gap usually shows up about midway into a strong uptrend or downtrend. That means the price hops over one or more price levels, then continues in the direction it was headed.

Gaps can add a lot of excitement to your trading life! Of course, excitement arrives in different forms.

Say you're holding 500 shares long of Bargain Biotech, and it closed yesterday at 30. This morning Bargain opens at 33 and—praise the skies—you've banked a tidy $1,500 without any effort. That kind of excitement results in back-slapping "yeehaws" and, of course, comments to your friends about your incredible trading expertise.

On a different morning, you wake up innocently holding 500 shares of Bossy Bank. It closed quietly yesterday at 50. This morning it opens at 48 and goes into instant meltdown. You stare slack-jawed at the screen, then frantically grab your mouse and start clicking at the "sell" button. That sort of excitement produces sweaty palms, stomach churning, gulping noises, and graphic comments to your friends we aren't allowed to print here.

What do you do in either of the previous exciting situations?

1. You own the stock and it gaps up . . .

    ✦ *Swing traders*: If the stock has moved up for two to three days in a row, and you have a hefty profit, take some or all of your money off the table right at the open. *Do not wait a minute or two!* Most professional day traders will "fade the gap." That means they trade against the prevailing trend. In this case, they will short the stock *immediately* at the open. The result? Stock tanks! If the stock gapped open the past two mornings, take all money off the table. If you see the market is very strong, and your stock is also, wait until it trades .25 above the opening price—then buy it back.

    ✦ *Position traders*: Tighten your stop-loss.

2. You own the stock and it gaps down . . .

    ✦ *Swing traders*: Just as the pros fade gaps to the upside by shorting
      them, they sometimes fade gaps down by buying them. In this situa-
      tion, wait a few *moments* (especially in a positive market environment
      where there's no negative news about your stock or sector) to see if
      buying comes into your favor. Then, *sell* if your stock cannot close the
      gap to yesterday's close in the first half-hour, or less, of trading. If no
      buying comes in, and your stock shows signs of diving to depths
      unknown—go with the herd and *sell*. On the chance of a sudden
      reversal to the upside on favorable conditions, you can always buy the
      darn thing back.

    ✦ *Position traders*: Assess market and sector conditions, along with
      possible reasons as to your stock's fall. Bad news or a badly tanking
      market tells you to sell *immediately*. No news, and gap down is small
      and in context with pullback? No problem! Watch for signs of
      recovery with stop-loss firmly in place.

3. You *don't* own the stock, but you intended to open a position today if it
    traded over yesterday's high. Now, the silly stock gapped open *above*
    yesterday's high. Is it too late to enter the position?

    ✦ *Swing and position traders*: It's not too late if it per-
      forms in a certain way. Wait for the stock to trade for 30
      minutes after the open. When (if) it trades .25 over its
      high, and market conditions are favorable, *buy*!

      Now, a word about those ornery gaps up that
    reduce perfectly good traders to whimpering wusses.
    Exhaustion gaps. Please note: Exhaustion gaps are the
    exception to the above. If you get caught in one—GET
    OUT! Then you can calmly hold the door open for the
    screaming traders stampeding right behind you.

      What do they look like? Exhaustion gaps, as noted
    before, take place at the end of an extended uptrend or
    downtrend, and signal the conclusion of that trend.

      What to look for: A rocket stock that's shot straight
    up in a steep uptrend on a daily chart. (Hint: These
    stocks are usually overextended, trading high above
    their 20-day MA.) Yesterday may have been a jet
    propulsion day, meaning a huge price spike to the

> **Hot Tip**
>
> Monitor gap size in
> comparison to price per
> share and trading
> range. When a "muscle"
> tech stock that weighs
> in at $150 per share,
> and has an average
> daily trading range of
> 5-10 points, gaps up
> $2, that's no big deal. If
> a stock that trades at
> $10 per share, and has
> a range of 2 points per
> day, gaps up $2, that's a
> *very big deal!* Sell that
> baby immediately and
> take profits!

upside. Today, stock gaps open—*either up or down*—then tanks. It crashes through yesterday's close, and then streaks down toward the center of the earth.

> **Hot Tip**
>
> When a big price gap perches ominously above a stock's current price, know that the stock may have to struggle to climb back through it.

When you see the signs of an exhaustion gap in action, take profits fast. If you've targeted this stock for an entry to the long side for a swing or position trade, as they say in "New Yawk," "forgettaboudit."

A final word about gaps. Steve Nison, the candlestick guru, taught me this: Gaps, or "windows," as they are called in Japanese candlestick terminology, offer stock prices support and resistance. If a stock trades above (or below) a rising or falling window—even if that window remains weeks away—when the stock nears that window price zone, it may use it for support or resistance.

So, if your stock makes an unexpected U-turn, and you can't figure out why, check out the windows a few months back. As a wise trader, learn to check back on your stocks out of habit and note window price zones for this reason.

Okay, if your brain has gapped closed, don't worry about it. Just amble back to these charts (Figures 9-9 and 9-10) as soon as possible and absorb the awesome information about gaps.

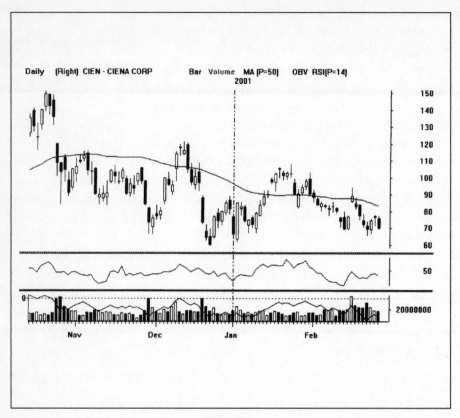

Figure 9-9.

On this gap-happy chart of Ciena Corp. (CIEN), the 50-day MA is the only one on the chart, so you can see the gaps more clearly. The big gap down during the last week of October 2000 was a negative for this tech stock, especially when it fell below its 50-day MA.

Now, go back over this chart, gap by gap. Study the price movement that took place each time CIEN gapped up or down. Remember, a gap up on a daily chart can be regarded as bullish, and a gap down, bearish. Note how many of CIEN's gaps formed resistance or support for subsequent price movement. Tip: The midpoint of a price gap will also act as resistance or support, depending whether a stock is trading under or over it.

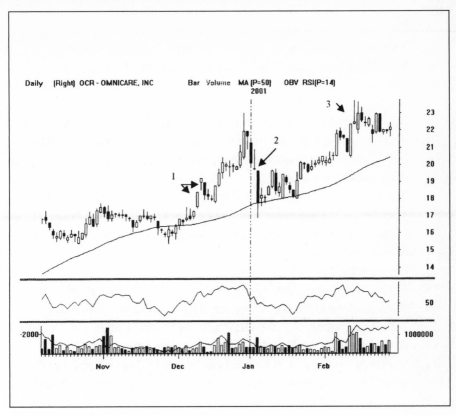

Figure 9-10.

This daily chart of Omnicare, Inc. (OCR) shows a healthcare stock in a dandy, tradable uptrend. 1. OCR gaps up two days in a row. If you're holding this as a long position in a swing trade, definitely take profits before the close of the second day gap-up. (Three days up total.) 2. Note gravestone doji on January 3, closing on the low of the day, right at support from the previous week. Swing traders and position traders holding this stock long need to take profits before the close of this day. The term "gravestone" is very accurate! Note how the stock gaps down the next day and falls all the way to its 50-day MA. The subsequent bounce off of the 50-day MA, however, tells you institutions may be accumulating this stock when it reaches this support area. 3. The shooting star pattern gapped up the day after this stock made an extremely high price move (for this stock). The star formation took place after the stock had made a nice, multi-week uptrend. Swing traders should take profits, although they might leave a little money on the table. Remember, the goal for swing traders is to take the sweet spot out of multi-day moves up.

QUIZ

1. Define an "oscillator."
2. What does "overbought" mean? What does "oversold" mean?
3. What does "RSI" stand for? What does it measure?
4. Say you're swing trading a stock and have been holding the position for five days. The stock price makes a new high but its RSI, which is in the overbought position, hooks down. What action will you consider taking?
5. When you're viewing the Stochastics Oscillator on a chart, readings _____ _____ are considered overbought, and readings _____ _____ are considered oversold.
6. You're using Stochastics as a decision support tool for entry into a long position. At the moment, both lines are below 20 and are hooked to the upside. The faster %K line just crossed above the slower %D line. What does that tell you?
7. Describe the MACD.
8. How does the MACD-H (histogram) give buy and sell signals?
9. What does the On-Balance Volume (OBV) indicator synthesize?
10. What information does the OBV tell you in an instant?
11. How should the OBV look when indicating a buying signal?
12. If a stock's price bumps its head on the top Bollinger Band, but doesn't poke through it, where might you predict that price will travel next?
13. Many times, after experiencing a major move up or down, a stock will correct and use Fibonacci retracement levels for _____ and _____.
14. You've been holding a swing trade for three days. You've made 15 delicious points. The stock gapped up yesterday and the day before. Today, it gapped up again. Wow, you have the feeling it will rocket forever! What should you do?
15. Yesterday, you bought Bossy Bank before the market closed as a swing trade, buying 300 shares at 48. This morning banks tanked, dragging Bossy with them. The stock just opened on a gap down at 45. What action do you take?

ANSWERS

1. An oscillator is a technical indicator that tells whether a market, index, or equity currently trades in an "overbought" or "oversold" condition.

2. An *overbought* stock is trading at the upper extreme of its current price range and may soon pull back or move into a consolidation pattern. A stock that's *oversold* is trading at the bottom of its current price range and is due for a bounce.

3. RSI stands for Relative Strength Index. It's an oscillator that measures a stock's current relative strength as compared to its own price history.

4. When your stock makes a higher high, but its RSI diverges by hooking down or *not* making a higher high, you take profits.

5. Readings *above 80* are overbought, and readings *below 20* are oversold.

6. When Stochastics lines are below 20 and then hook up, and the faster %K line crosses above the slower %D line, it's a "buy" signal.

7. The MACD is a trend-following momentum indicator/oscillator that shows the relationship between the 26-day and 12-day exponential moving averages of an equity's price pattern. Also, a 9-day signal line may be used.

8. The MACD-H (histogram) gives buy and sell signals by crossing over its zero line. A buy signal is given when the MACD-H rises above its zero line. A sell signal is given when the MACD-H crosses below the zero line.

9. On-Balance Volume synthesizes, or integrates, volume with price change.

10. One glance tells you whether money's flowing into, or out of, a stock.

11. To give a buy signal, the OBV should hook up or be moving in an uptrend.

12. When a stock rises to the top of its upper band and stays within its boundary, it should then reverse and fall to the lower band.

13. Support and resistance.

14. Will it go up forever? (Chuckle) Not in your lifetime! 'Scuse me, but you say it's gapped up three days in a row, and you've made 15 points? What should you do? You're kidding, right? Sell *fast!*

15. Quickly assess overall market conditions. If they are bleak, and the bank index goes into a free-fall, give your stock a minute or two (not much more) to see if anyone fades (buys) the gap down. On the chance no buying comes in, sell and take the hit. Here's an old trader's saying: "Your first loss is your smallest loss."

✦ ✦ ✦

CENTER POINT

Often people attempt to live their lives backwards; they try to have more things, or more money, in order to do more of what they want, so they will be happier. The way it actually works is the reverse. You must first be who you really are, then do what you need to do, in order to have what you want.

—MARGARET YOUNG

You Are Perfect Right Now!

We tend to become mired in our hectic lives, where one challenge leads into the next. When we struggle and feel overwhelmed with deadlines and formidable tasks, instead of coming to the world from an inner state of joy and harmony, we arrive each day from a place of fear. We fear missing opportunities, flubbing deadlines, disappointing those with whom we have relationships. So, we struggle, we push, we "keep our noses to the grindstone."

How can we change this? How can we free up energy we use to struggle and strain, and channel it to flow freely so we can accomplish more with less effort? By rewiring our mental and emotional circuits so that we come from a position of strength, empowerment, and joy!

Let's start with acceptance. We accept ourselves as perfect, right where we are. We accept what we've got, where we're starting from. We realize that the present moment is taking place because every thought, feeling, and action we created in our past brought us to this moment. We (not someone else!) created our perspective and chose the way we feel about the people, places, and situations in our lives. Knowing this, we can accept our life for what it is, with pure objectivity.

Next, we can take responsibility for our life's circumstances and recognize that a seed of opportunity lies in each one. Every event, every person in our lives touches us for a reason. Let's make a game out of tuning into conditions from a mindset (and heart-set) of love and empowerment. As our perspective changes, it's astonishing how it manifests itself in events and relationships! It's even more amazing how easily our energy flows, and how our toughest challenges turn into opportunities.

Let's remember that our lives are perfect at this very moment. Once we accept that, we take responsibility for approaching each day from a core essence of love and harmony. Our energy flows spontaneously and effortlessly, and we live in concert with our highest potential!

✦ ✦ ✦

CHAPTER 10

It's Showtime!

But my greatest discovery was that a man must study general conditions, to size them so as to be able to anticipate probabilities. In short, I had learned that I had to work for my money.

—JESSE LIVERMORE

As you start this chapter, I'm sure you're muttering something like this . . . "Hel-looo! I've opened my account and waded through financial Web sites. I learned where to find fundamental information. I've studied discipline techniques, candlestick formations, all the doggoned stages, and how stocks act in each one. I can draw a trendline in my sleep. My brain is stuffed with theories of greed and fear, supply and demand, support and resistance. I know when volume spikes should stick up, and when they should shrink, and I've got indicators and oscillators coming out of my ears. Now, pul-lease tell me when I can buy the gol-durned stock! Will it be in my lifetime?"

Patience, grasshopper. And the answer is "yes." Very soon, in fact.

But first you need to learn how to identify basic chart patterns. 'Scuse me, did I hear a groan? Trust me, this knowledge can make you—and save you—big bucks.

Case in point: In March and April 2000, both Nasdaq indexes (the Composite and 100) made double tops. Double tops equal lethal warnings. *If you were holding tech stocks in your portfolio, as most Americans were, and you identified that top, you could have sold and kept your profits intact instead of giving them back—and then some.*

Yet another double top reared its ominous head in August and September. The ability to recognize a simple pattern and its prediction would have saved traders and investors millions of dollars.

CONTINUATION AND REVERSAL PATTERNS: WHAT THEY ARE

Basically, price patterns fall into two categories: continuation and reversal. *Continuation* patterns indicate an interlude in a trend where the stock pauses or "rests." In other words, it pulls back, or consolidates, before breaking out and resuming its prior trend. As swing and position traders, we thrive on buying the breakouts that these patterns produce. We're going to scan for the most common of these patterns, which are flags, pennants, and triangles.

Reversal patterns, on the other hand, mean just that: they are price patterns that usually forecast an upcoming trend reversal. We'll check out the most prominent of the group: head-and-shoulders, cup-with-a-handle, and double tops and bottoms.

Continuation Patterns: How to Spot Them in the Making

Okay, back to the drawing board. (Don't worry, I won't give up trading to pursue a career as an artist!)

First, we'll check out the continuation pattern known as the "flag." You already know what it looks like. It's simply a tight consolidation pattern in the context of an uptrend (think: parallelogram). Traditionally, a flag lasts three days to three weeks and drifts down against the prevailing trend. When it completes its action, the stock resumes its previous trend.

The flag's colleague is the "pennant." The pennant resembles the flag, except that it moves horizontally in the shape of a small, symmetrical triangle. It, too, lasts from a few days to just weeks.

Figure 10-1 gives you an idea of how these patterns look when they appear in uptrends. Naturally, in downtrends they draw the same pattern, flipped upside down.

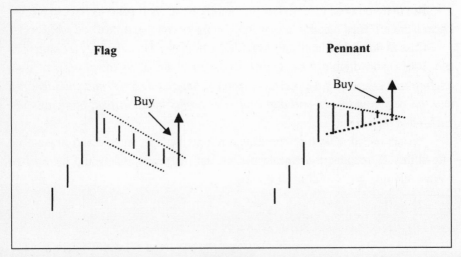

Figure 10-1.
Continuation patterns: flag and pennant.

Remember the analogy in Chapter 8 that compared consolidation patterns to a pressure cooker? Continuation patterns simply give these consolidation patterns a name. Besides, it makes impressive cocktail party conversation to tell someone you "played the breakout from the pennant."

A variation on the above theme is the continuation pattern known as the "triangle." Triangles come in three flavors: ascending, descending, and symmetrical. The *ascending* triangle consolidates sideways between converging trendlines, with the upper line staying relatively horizontal, and the lower line rising. The ascending triangle equals bullish. Why? Because each

> **Hot Tip**
>
> As tempting as it is to take an anticipatory jump into a stock that's experiencing a triangle, *don't*. While they are called "continuation" patterns, there are no absolute guarantees that the trend will continue. Always wait for confirmation.

consecutive day makes a higher low. The *descending* triangle forms the same way, only upside down. The converging trendlines involve the upper line sloping down (each candlestick makes lower highs) while the lower line travels horizontally. This continuation pattern is generally found in downtrends and is regarded as bearish.

As you can guess, the *symmetrical* triangle formed as a consolidation pattern begins with a wide price range that gets squished from the bottom and the top (even buying and selling pressure) into a tighter and tighter range. The top trendline declines, and the bottom line rises. Although this occurs as a continuation pattern, know that the stock can erupt either way out of this pattern.

Figure 10-2 illustrates the triangles described above.

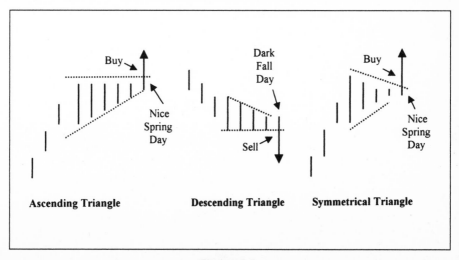

Figure 10-2.

Additional continuation patterns.

Now, here's some *mega-important information*: Revisit the drawings above. Take special note of how the trendlines are drawn *right through* the arrows. I did that on purpose. Those arrows represent the day (on a daily chart) during which the uptrend (downtrend) resumes.

Assuming all other buying criteria are in place (list follows soon), when the stock price (represented in the drawings by an arrow) shoots out of the consolidation pattern and trades .25 above the previous day's high, that's where you buy, or sell short. (To review the 1-2-3 buying signals, turn back to Chapter 7.)

In my previous book, *A Beginner's Guide to Day Trading Online,* I called the buying day "a nice spring day." "Spring" has a connotation of release, and that's exactly what happens when price breaks out of a consolidation pattern—the pressure is released. Naturally, we also associate "spring" with new growth.

In the descending triangle, which is the bearish pattern used for selling short, I called the break down from consolidation a "dark fall day." Obviously, the candlestick that breaks down out of this pattern will be black, or dark. (And, we associate the fall season with the onset of winter bleakness.)

Yes, I'm waxing picturesque. But when you need a quick mental image of how your target stock should look to take action, you want these images to come swiftly to mind. The charts in Figures 10-3 through 10-7 show continuation patterns in action.

REVERSAL PATTERNS: WHAT THEY LOOK LIKE

As mentioned earlier in this chapter, reversal chart patterns indicate that a change or trend reversal is about to occur. While you'll see continuation patterns develop on a chart as part of a broader pattern, such as an uptrend or downtrend, and while these patterns mature over the time frame of days to three weeks at the max, reversal patterns tend to evolve as important paradigms in their own right.

> **Hot Tip**
>
> Continuation and reversal patterns show up on charts of all time frames, be they weekly, daily, or intra-day.

You've surely heard the most popular reversal patterns mentioned in trader conversation: double top, double bottom, head-and-shoulders, reverse (upside-down) head-and-shoulders, and cup-with-a-handle.

These patterns, aside from forecasting predictive price moves, make great money management tools. When you see one in the making, you can take early profits or start monitoring for an entry point.

Figure 10-3.

On this daily chart of Extreme Networks (EXTR), you can see three continuation patterns in the form of "flags." Note how a flag drifts against the trend (in this case, an uptrend). You could also describe these flags simply as "pullbacks." And remember, if you're playing a stock in an uptrend, it's best if these flags, or pullbacks, take place on decreased volume. A high-volume pullback may turn into a major correction!

RealTick graphics used with permission of Townsend Analytics, Ltd. ©1986–2002. All rights reserved.

Double Top

Here are the key points:

✦ What to look for: When completed, it looks like an "M."
✦ Indication: bearish.
✦ How it happens: The stock is in an uptrend. It may become overextended at the zenith of first top (of eventual double top). The price pulls back, and then resumes its uptrend. When it reaches the resistance established by the first peak, buyers refuse to pay higher prices. The price starts retracing to previous pivot low, or middle of "M."

✦ Completion: A double top concludes when the price completes final retracement to middle pivot low of "M." (Think: an entire "M" is formed.)

✦ Forecast: If the price falls below consolidation support, it will sink lower.

✦ What you do: When you're holding a long position in a stock that's approaching the second peak in an extended uptrend, monitor market/industry (where your stock resides) conditions for weakness. Get ready to take profits. Also, if the stock is overextended, trading high above its 20-day MA, take profits as soon as you recognize this. To sell short, wait until the stock drops below the support zone formed by the pivot lows, and then enter. This will be a "dark fall day."

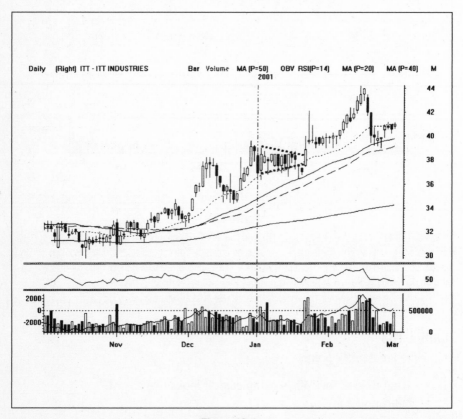

Figure 10-4.

This daily chart of ITT Industries (ITT) displays a pennant that formed as a continuation during the first two-and-a-half weeks of January. A pennant moves in a more horizontal line than a flag and may act as future support during the last week of February. Also, check how ITT fell *down* a fraction of a point when it exited the pennant, before it continued in an uptrend. For this reason, please don't "jump the gun" and buy before you see definite confirmation to the upside. In this case, if you bought early, you would have probably gotten stopped-out, and then the stock would have rocketed to the upside without you!

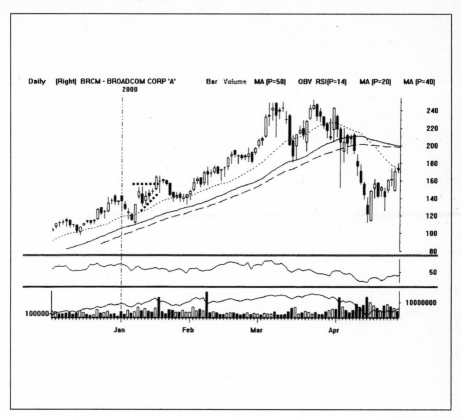

Figure 10-5.

On this daily chart of Broadcom Corp. (BRCM), an ascending triangle forms during the second week of January. It's important to realize that the candlesticks aren't going to fully cooperate by forming *perfect* highs and lows for you to draw trendlines. A shadow here or there will certainly misbehave and poke up, or dangle down, through the trendlines. Please realize that it's more important you grasp the big picture, than it is for you to worry about one errant candlestick shadow. Additional continuation patterns appear on this chart. Can you find them? One more point: Note how mannerly and orderly BRCM acts as it moves through its uptrend. When it rolls over into a Stage Three in early March, however, it becomes disorderly and volatile. That's why we closely monitor stocks experiencing this part of a cycle!

Also, remember that technology stocks tend to sell off in the spring and head lower into the summer months. September and October are usually net negative months in the market as a whole, as institutions sell losing positions and rebalance portfolios. November and December typically become more positive, especially if a "Santa rally" leads the market into a new burst of buying in January, called the "January effect."

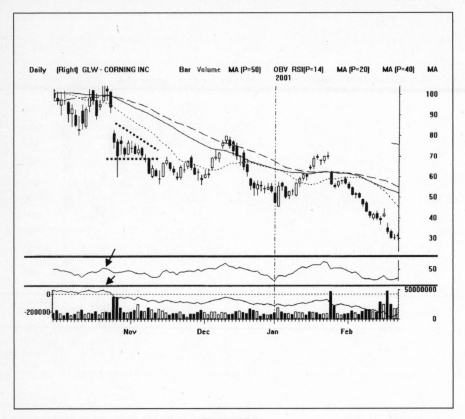

Figure 10-6.

Except for one dangling shadow that we won't pay any attention to, this daily chart of Corning Inc. (GLW) shows the stock in a downtrend that includes a good example of a descending triangle (late October, early November). On November 17, GLW broke down out of the triangle; at the moment of the breakdown, a perfect shorting signal was given for a two- to five-day swing trade. Notice the abrupt downturn in the RSI and OBV (arrows) *before* GLW fell like a sack of rocks!

Double Bottom

The key points:

+ What to look for: When completed, it looks like a "W."
+ Indication: bullish.
+ How it happens: The stock is basing after experiencing a downtrend. It possibly bounces off previous support and rallies to establish the middle peak of "W." It pulls back to the last pivot low (which becomes first pivot of double bottom), and then bounces off that price support. (Buyers recognize a second chance to "bottom fish.")

✦ Completion: A double bottom is completed when the price rises to the middle peak of the "W."

✦ Forecast: Price will initiate an uptrend. Typically, though, it will consolidate for days or weeks before that rise. The longer it consolidates, the more powerful the breakout to the upside may be.

✦ What you do: Monitor bases for double bottoms. When you see one forming in a target stock, get ready for buy criteria to be met so you can pounce! (This will be a "nice spring day.")

Figures 10-8 and 10-9 show a double top and double bottom. Study the pattern so you can learn to recognize it instantly.

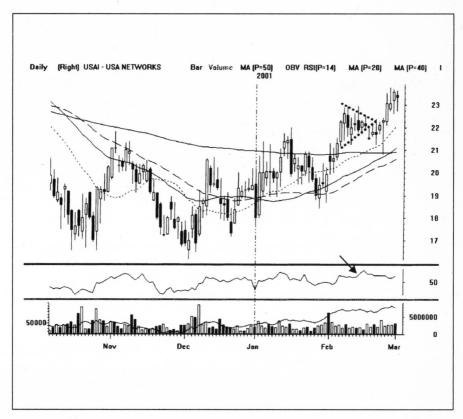

Figure 10-7.

This daily chart of USA Networks (USAI) displays a symmetrical triangle that took place in the context of an uptrend during the first part of February. As you can see, the first breakout from this continuation pattern took place to the downside, and although the actual drop from (arrow) the February 15 closing price to the February 16 open was barely over a half-point drop, it's another great reason to wait for confirmation of price direction before buying. Also, note the bullish divergence in the RSI (arrow) before the stock resumed its climb.

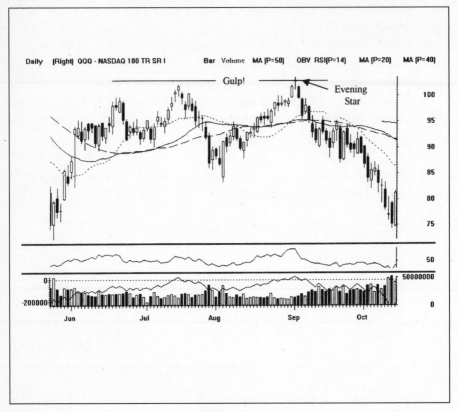

Figure 10-8.

This daily chart of the QQQ, which trades on the Amex and represents the Nasdaq 100, clearly shows a double top formation that took place in July and September of 2000. Note that each time the QQQ rose high above the 20-day MA, it soon returned again. The evening star candlestick formation on September 1 sounded a particularly ominous note when "the Qs," as traders call this stock, foretold a double top in the making for the Nasdaq. Also, had the top formed in June been a bit higher, this would have ended up as a triple top!

Hot Tip

Triple tops and bottoms embody the same characteristics as double tops and bottoms, except they have an extra pivot point. They are more rare, and their signals are even more powerful!

Head-and-Shoulders

The "head-and-shoulders" and "head-and-shoulders reversal" patterns show up less often than double tops and bottoms. Sometimes, it takes a trained eye to detect them. In a volatile market, recognizing a head-and-shoulders can resemble those old coloring book games, where you had to identify a monkey in a tangled jungle maze. Still, with a little practice, you'll learn to locate this important pattern.

The head-and-shoulders shape looks just like its name: left "hump," or shoulder, middle and much higher hump, or the head, and right hump, or shoulder. Figure 10-10 gives you an idea of the form a price pattern would take when completing a head-and-shoulders. Check out the "neckline," as that represents a very important component of this pattern.

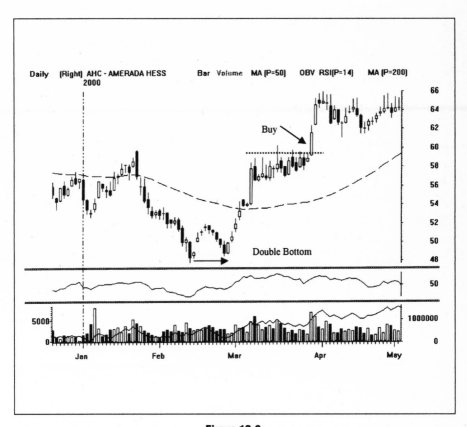

Figure 10-9.

This daily chart of oil company Amerada Hess (AHC) draws a perfect double bottom in a basing pattern. Only the 50-day MA is left on the chart, so you can clearly see the pattern. Notice how AHC drops to its low in February, and then rises near previous resistance from the consolidation area formed in early February. It drops to make a second pivot of the double bottom, falling just short of retesting the prior low. A higher retest of the lows is bullish! Then it moves up to complete the formation, consolidates sideways in a tidy pennant and rockets to the upside on March 29. Note the "buy" signal shown where AHC rises above resistance at 59.50. Signals: Market conditions are favorable. Stock breaks out of basing pattern over resistance on strong volume. It's trading over the 50-day MA and both RSI and OBV are trending up. Time to go shopping! (You'll soon learn about all Buy Triggers in detail.)

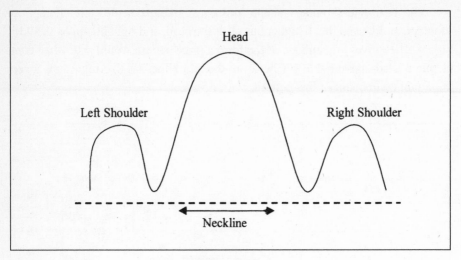

Figure 10-10.

Head and shoulders reversal pattern.

The key points are:

+ What to look for: It usually forms at the culmination of an uptrend and creates a Stage Three.
+ Indication: bearish.
+ How it develops: A stock in an uptrend rolls over and forms the first shoulder, which looks innocent enough. Then it rises to form the head, which at first glance appears as a bullish new high. The caution light blinks when the stock returns to support, provided by the pivot established by the first shoulder, at the soon-to-be "neckline." When the price rises and rolls over at the resistance high of the left shoulder, then falls back to the neckline to complete that shoulder, the signal is future gloom and doom. The stock cannot make a higher high, and the uptrend is broken.
+ Completion: A head-and-shoulders is completed when the right shoulder is concluded by the price falling to the neckline support.
+ Forecast: If the weak stock tumbles through support formed by the neckline, it will probably initiate a downtrend.
+ What you do: Obviously, you've sold your long position by now! Right? Right! If you're targeting this stock to sell short, enter the trade when the stock trades .25 of a point below the neckline support. This will be a "dark fall day."

Reverse Head-and-Shoulders

What you should know:

+ Look for: a mirror image, or "upside down" head-and-shoulders.
+ Indication: bullish.
+ How it develops: Like a double bottom, this pattern occurs in the context of a base.
+ Completion: When the price draws the left shoulder, head, and right shoulder, and then returns to resistance at the neckline, it is completed. Typically, the stock will now travel sideways in a consolidation pattern until it breaks out above neckline resistance and initiates an uptrend.
+ What you do: Monitor target stocks in basing mode for this pattern. When the pattern is complete, watch consolidation for a breakout above resistance. This will be a "nice spring day."

Figures 10-11 and 10-12 show charts of a head-and-shoulders and reverse head-and-shoulders. Outlines of the forms are drawn into the price pattern to make them more easily recognizable.

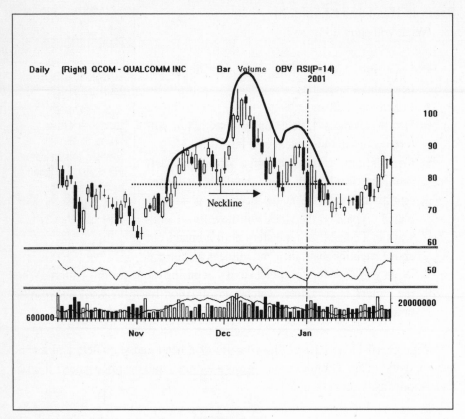

Figure 10-11.

On this daily chart of Qualcomm Inc. (QCOM), all moving averages are deleted so you can more clearly see the outline of the head-and-shoulders pattern. Poor QCOM fell through the neckline, and then struggled back up, but could not climb any higher than the last candlesticks you see on the "hard right edge." (Note: The "hard right edge" of a chart is just that—the far right side of the chart where it ends.) By March 2001, QCOM fell to 50!

Now, locate the long, dark candle QCOM made on January 1st. That was the break of the neckline, and you could have sold QCOM short as it tumbled through support. January 2nd was the day Fed Chairman Alan Greenspan surprised us by making an unscheduled cut in interest rates. Note how that day resulted in a long, clear, engulfing candle to the upside. While the stock market quickly shrugged the rate cut off, and QCOM subsequently fell to new lows, the surprise move should strengthen your resolve to set automatic stop-loss orders whenever possible.

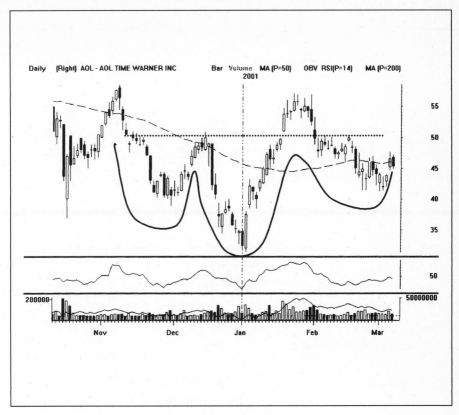

Figure 10-12.

This daily chart of AOL Time Warner (AOL) shows a nearly finished head-and-shoulders. If AOL can rise to 50, to the neckline, the pattern will be complete. (Only the 50-day MA is included on this chart, so you can more clearly see the pattern.) AOL did not move above the neckline in mid-January but returned to support of the left shoulder established in November–December. The point is that you recognize the pattern enough to see that AOL is now resting (hard right edge) on support from December and ready perhaps to rise over the neckline at 50. Remember, a head-and-shoulders is bearish, and reverse head-and-shoulders is bullish.

William O'Neil, founder of *Investment Business Daily,* receives the credit for naming the cup-with-a-handle reversal pattern. This bullish pattern appears on a chart looking just like it sounds, usually in the context of a base. Figure 10-13 illustrates the basic cup-with-a-handle pattern.

The cup-with-handle is a great bullish basing pattern, and you'll want to monitor high-quality stocks in this mode for an entry setup.

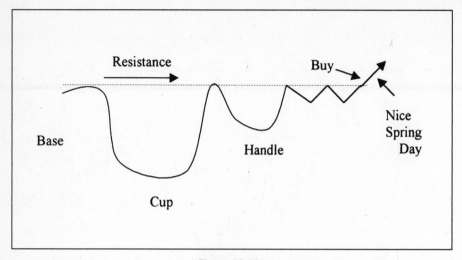

Figure 10-13.
Cup-with-handle reversal pattern.

Cup-with-Handle

What you need to know:

✦ Look for: A stock moving sideways in a Stage One base dips to previous support making a scoop (cup), then gradually rises to previous resistance. It dips again—flushing out "weak hands," or scared sellers—then returns again to resistance (handle). Then it moves sideways in a tight consolidation range, until high volume and other bullish market conditions propel it into an uptrend.

✦ Indication: bullish.

✦ Completion: When it concludes the handle by rising to the resistance line, it has reached completion.

✦ What you do: Monitor stock for completion of the pattern, and then enter .25 over breakout of consolidation, on a "nice spring day."

Figure 10-14 shows a chart displaying a cup-with-handle formation.

TRADING REVERSAL PATTERNS IN NON-TRENDING MARKETS

Generally speaking, position traders need solid uptrends and downtrends to take profits from the market. When the market moves sideways in a languid trading range, position trades are not effective. Short-term swing trades, well executed, present a lower risk opportunity. (In cases of volatile back-to-back days, when the market rises one day and falls the next, with no follow-through, it's a day traders' market. Holding positions overnight can be bad for one's wealth.)

With the last caveat in mind, if you wish to participate on the long side in a non-trending market, you can enter two to three day trades as long as you remain aware of the heightened risks involved. Using the reversal patterns you just learned, plan to enter with precision and establish tight stop-loss points. Once your stock moves up, move your stop-loss up with it as a "trailing stop." (The next chapter discusses the placement of stop-loss points in more detail.)

✦ Enter while a stock is still in a narrow base, with high potential to the upside (see "Buy Trigger List" in next section). When upside momentum is anticipated (the RSI may make a bullish divergence), take a small position *as the stock begins to break out of its base on strong volume*. Make sure your risk/reward ratio is 1:3, and adjust your stop-loss point accordingly. As it moves over resistance successfully, you may add to the position and tighten your stop-loss. Check the previous high for the next resistance area and your possible profit target.

✦ Double bottom. Buy as stock reverses from second pivot low off support, as it rises over the high of the previous "low day," on strong volume. In other words, as stock breaks into the final leg of the "W," buy when it trades .25 above the high of the reversal day. Place your stop-loss no lower than .25 or .50 below the low of the low day, adjusting to keep your 1:3 risk/reward ratio. Your target price will probably be the previous high, or mid-point of the "W."

✦ Buy the bottom of the cup-with-handle. Your target stock falls on high volume to a basing, support area. As selling volume dries up, it moves sideways in an extremely tight price pattern, forming the bottom curve of the "cup." Suddenly, you see the volume begin to increase, and the RSI hooks up (from under 30) in a bullish divergence. Buy as it breaks up from the bottom of the cup, on strong volume. Establish a trailing stop-loss, and target the previous high to take profits. Again, make sure your initial risk/reward is 3:1. Note: When a stock completes the "cup" pattern by rising to the previous high, it usually retraces quickly to start forming the "handle." Depending on market conditions, the handle may or may not form. I suggest taking profits as the cup pattern completes, then waiting to see if the handle and subsequent consolidation area develop in an orderly fashion. If they do, and all other signals say "go," then you can buy the breakout over resistance from the consolidation area, as previously discussed.

LET'S TAKE IT FROM THE TOP!

Are you ready? This is the moment you've been waiting for! This is where you pull your chair up to the playing table, stack your chips into neat piles, cock one eyebrow, and assess the other players with a steely gaze. When conditions become perfect, with rock-like discipline and quiet confidence born of study and planning, you'll deftly slide your money to the center of the table.

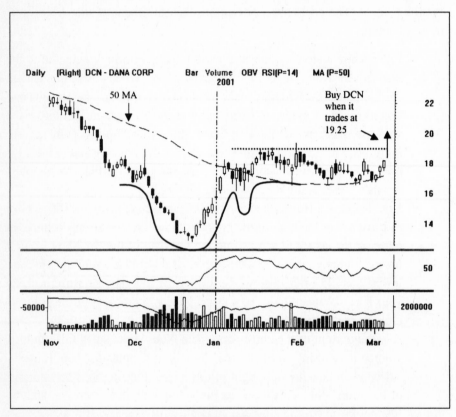

Figure 10-14.

It doesn't get any better than this! On this daily chart of Dana Corp. (DCN), the cup-with-handle formation is clear enough to be drawn by an artist. After the pattern became complete, DCN started moving sideways in an orderly consolidation movement along its 50-day MA. This is a pattern you scan for, then wait like a stealth trader(!) for it to break out over resistance on high volume. In this case, resistance is at 19. When all other conditions are "go," DCN is a buy at 19.25 for both swing and position traders.

BIG PICTURE DYNAMICS

When you go to the doctor, she takes your blood pressure and your temperature, and listens to your heart and lungs to determine your overall health before she zeroes in on your sore throat. Before a horse race, a jockey walks the track, observes the weather, and examines his horse to get a sense of how to end up in the winner's circle. The best burglars "case the joint" before they break into a mansion. They learn the entire layout of the estate beforehand to eliminate such surprises as snarling Dobermans and noisy alarms. No matter what the situation, evaluating the overall picture before taking action lessens risk and heightens the chance of success.

As astute traders, we always evaluate the overall market before we commit to a trade. It makes no sense at all to enter a long trade—even if your price target is hit—on a day when the markets feel ornery and perverse. Your stock may hover in positive territory for a while, but overall negative market conditions tend to erode price surges of even the most stalwart stocks. When you enter a trade, you want all possible odds in your corner.

In "trader heaven," the Dow Jones Industrial Average and the Nasdaq Composite move in tandem, drawing spiffy uptrends on daily and intra-day charts. Ever-increasing volatility, however, has assigned trader heaven to "special occasion" (think: *rare*) status.

Therefore, if your target stock is a listed stock, make sure the Dow is moving up on the day. When you're monitoring a Nasdaq stock, be sure the Nasdaq indexes (100 and Composite) trade in positive territory.

So, in summary, here's the first guideline to head the list of your Buy Trigger List: *Market conditions, Dow and/or Nasdaq, are positive.*

CHOOSE A LEADING STOCK IN A LEADING INDUSTRY

Say you're the captain of your neighborhood softball team. When you pick players, you select the strongest and most experienced to join your team, not the guy with a clumsy arm, or the girl who runs like a snail.

Just so, when entering the market on the long side, choose a leading stock in an industry sector that's a current market leader—not a market laggard.

You can accomplish this in one of two ways. The first is to choose the industry sector, then study the charts and fundamentals of that sector's leading stocks. For example, you see the semiconductor industry group currently serves as a Nasdaq leader. So, you target the cream of semiconductor stocks, such as Intel Corp. (INTC), Applied Materials (AMAT), and Micron Technology,

> **Hot Tip**
>
> One way to initiate a watch list of the strongest stocks in several industries: go to *www.holdrs.com.* Click on "HOLDRS Outstanding." "HOLDRS" are stocks traded on the Amex that designate industry groups. HOLDRS contains the top stocks in that industry, and those stocks are listed under separate HOLDRS. Example: WMH = Wireless HOLDRS. Top weighted companies (as of this writing) = Motorola Inc. (MOT), Sprint Corp. (PCS), and Verizon (VZ).

Hot Tip

When a basing stock dips to the low of its base in a double bottom, reverse head-and-shoulders, or cup-with-handle, "weak hands" (scared investors) flee and others decide to ignore it. Buyers who come in as the stock turns up and completes the pattern are more likely to hold, so a strong foundation develops.

Inc. (MU). Conduct a quick once-over of their fundamentals (see Chapter 4) to get a sense of each company's internal health. Then, bring up a weekly chart (for a "big picture" view of the stock's health) and daily chart of each of these stocks to determine which one you wish to focus on for an entry.

Build a complete list of industry sectors. Some of your entries may include the banking industry ($BKX.X), pharmaceutical industry ($DRG.X), biotechnology ($BTK.X), oil and oil services ($XOI.X and $OSX.X), semiconductors ($SOX.X), computer box-makers ($BMX.X), networking index ($NWX.X), retailers ($RLX.X), gold and silver index ($XAU.X), and so forth. *One of the most valuable money-making projects you can undertake is to do yourself this favor early in your trading career.*

Next, make a list of the prominent stocks in each of these industry groups. If possible, place these stocks in an online "watch" portfolio that stays updated in real-time. Now, when you want to know which stocks are advancing, and which are weak, the information is at your fingertips.

The second way of choosing leading stocks in leading industries is to select those you'd like to target and evaluate their charts. When you narrow your choice down to those with good setups in the offing, make sure they reside in industries currently in favor and poised to lead the market in the present environment. Check the *IBD* proprietary ranking (discussed in Chapter 4), "Industry Group Relative Strength."

Finally, go to my Web site, *www.toniturner.com*. Click on the "Sectors & Stocks" page—you will find a selection of industry groups and sectors, along with foremost companies that reside in each one.

Therefore, the second guideline for your Buy Trigger List: *Target stock is a leading company in a leading industry.*

CHECK OUT THE FUNDAMENTALS

Now that you've buttonholed stocks that you're going to monitor for optimal setups, complete your due diligence on their fundamentals. Again, this step was detailed in Chapter 4, where we talked about appraising a company's fundamentals in *IBD*.

Why do we check a company's fundamentals if the chart looks golden? Because we aren't day traders. Fundamentals don't mean a rat's patootie to a trader who intends to hold a stock for only minutes to hours.

Checking a company's fundamental health *does* make sense when the intent is to hold a position from days to weeks. Money is more likely to flow into a stock on a continuing basis—especially by institutions—if that company is blessed with admirable fundamental rankings.

Another reason to appraise fundamentals is because "surprises happen." Say you're an office manager. You place trades before work, during lunch, and on breaks. Today, you place a trade, and then abruptly get called into a meeting before you can set your automatic stop-loss with your online broker. By the time you run out of the meeting and check your new position, it has done a belly flop past today's low. Rats! If you decide to hold it for a bit longer, it may have a better chance of recovery if it has good fundamentals. Translation: If you accidentally get stuck in a crashing stock, make darn sure it's not a fundamental "dog."

Here's something to consider doing. Refer back to Chapter 4 and create a list of the *IBD* rankings and the minimum standards outlined; create columns underneath. In columns to the left, jot down the date, each stock symbol and related industry group or sector, and then its *IBD* rankings. Now you've started a watch list of high-quality stocks you can trade, or keep on hold, until the proper setup appears.

So, Buy Trigger number three is when *company fundamentals meet or exceed* IBD *standards.*

THE INDUSTRY GROUP OR SECTOR SHOWS IMMEDIATE STRENGTH

Are you opening your mouth to advise me I've gone addle-brained, because we just discussed this point? Hold on. Let's narrow the point further.

You can target a leading stock in a leading industry, which is perfect. Still, that industry could be correcting and moving down on your "nice spring day." If that's the case, and your stock represents a leader in that industry or sector, chances are it will correct along with its industry group.

What you *don't* want to do is buy a stock that sinks below your buying price the day you buy it. *One of your initial goals is to have a gain, no matter how small, the first day you enter a trade.* This gives you a comfortable profit pillow to start with (along with peace of mind). One of the best methods of assuring this is to enter a trade when your stock's industry or sector is trending up on the day.

Therefore, the fourth Buy Trigger: *Industry/sector is in an uptrend and positive on the day.*

INDICATORS: ALL SYSTEMS ARE GO!

If your final target stock's chart looked good, the next triggers are almost a given.
Still, it's better to be safe and lock this information into place.

+ Stock has formed a base or is in an uptrend on a daily chart. It's ready to break out of a consolidation or pullback to support.
+ Strong volume on the break above resistance (yesterday's high).
+ Stock is bouncing off of, or is near, the 20-, 40-, or 50-day MA, and it is trading over the 50-day MA.
+ RSI is below 30 and hooking to the upside, or is drawing an uptrend. (It is not overbought.)
+ The OBV is rising or is in an uptrend.

THE URGE TO FUDGE

Say it's a "nice spring day." Your stock is perched, ready to break out, so the indicators listed should automatically fit into the picture. But what if one of them doesn't match up?

All indicators I listed are important. Still, if I had to choose *one* that didn't match the Buy Triggers, I'd nominate the RSI, or your chosen oscillator. (Caveat: If it showed a reading over 80 and it hooked down, I wouldn't take the trade.) But if all other systems were "go," and the RSI was nudging its nose into overbought position, or just looking neutral, I might (the operative word here is "might") enter the position.

As always, use common sense.

GET READY TO PULL THE TRIGGER: THE BUY SETUP

Now, zoom in on your stock.

Let's assume that, it's midmorning in the trading day. You've been monitoring the market and have checked off the first four triggers on your list. The Dow and Nasdaq are happy. Your target stock is a leader in a favored industry. Today, the industry is rocketing to the upside. Ah, trader heaven!

If you're planning a swing trade, you're monitoring a stock that's due to break out of its base, *or* due to resume an uptrend from a pullback or consolidation. Today promises to be that "nice spring day." The stock is trading above its opening price and moving up.

Primed and ready, you're waiting for the setup: the stock has to trade .25 point above yesterday's high. Then you'll pounce, issuing a "buy" order, followed by a stop-loss order. (You'll learn where to place stop-loss orders in Chapter 11.)

If you're planning a position trade, you also observe your stock moving up, forming a "nice spring day." You wait patiently for it to break out of its base, above resistance. Like the swing trader, when the stock trades .25 point over yesterday's high (which should equate with resistance), you issue a "buy" order. (After you buy, you place your stop-loss order.)

When the time is right, remove the safety and squeeze the trigger! Here's number five on the Buy Trigger List: *Target stock is trading above its opening price and moving up on the day. Buy signal: It trades .25 point over yesterday's high.*

If you think the Buy Trigger List is involved or complicated, or too much to think about, know that with practice and experience—as long as you've done your homework—you'll learn to assess current market/industry/stock conditions in a few nanoseconds!

BUY TRIGGER LIST

To review, here's your complete Buy Trigger List. You may want to copy it onto a regular sheet of paper to keep at your elbow when you trade.

1. Market conditions, Dow and/or Nasdaq, are positive.
2. Target stock is a leading company in a leading industry.
3. Company fundamentals meet or exceed "IBD" standards.
4. Industry/sector is in an uptrend and positive on the day of your trade.
5. Stock has formed a base, or is in the context of an uptrend on a daily chart. It's ready to break out of a consolidation or pullback to support.
6. Strong volume on the break above resistance (yesterday's high).
7. Stock is bouncing off of, or is near, the 20-, 40-, or 50-day MA, and it is trading over the 50-day MA.
8. RSI is below 30 and hooking to the upside, or is making an uptrend. (It is not overbought.)
9. The OBV is rising or is in an uptrend.
10. Target stock is trading above its opening price and moving up on the day. Buy signal: It trades .25 of a point over yesterday's high.

Even though you have the necessary information to pull the trigger and enter a long position, you'd be wise to wait until you study Chapter 11 before you jump into a trade. In that chapter, you'll learn money-management techniques that will help you achieve your goal of consistent wins in the stock market!

QUIZ

1. Name two general categories of price patterns.
2. Give a brief explanation of each of the two categories above.
3. Briefly describe an ascending triangle. What category of pattern is it?
4. What is a double top? What does it predict?
5. Describe a double bottom. Where does it mostly occur? How do you play it?
6. Why do you monitor market conditions as a whole, including the Dow and/or Nasdaq, just to play a single stock?
7. Why is it important that the industry group or sector that a stock resides in represent a current market leader?
8. True or false? One of your initial goals is to have a gain, no matter how small, the first day you enter a trade.
9. Name three Buy Triggers that describe optimum indicator positioning on a chart.
10. Define the final moment you "pull the trigger," meaning issue a "buy" order.

ANSWERS

1. Continuation and reversal.
2. Continuation patterns indicate an interlude in a trend where the stock pulls back or consolidates, before breaking out and resuming its prior trend. Reversal patterns forecast a trend reversal.
3. An ascending triangle usually forms in the context of an uptrend. During this time period from days to three weeks, or so, the stock trades in a tight consolidation pattern between converging trendlines; the top trendline is horizontal, the bottom rises as the stock makes higher lows. The indication is bullish and the stock should break out and resume its uptrend.
4. A double top takes place (usually) after a stock has made an extended uptrend. It reaches a new high, then pulls back to support, but when it rises to the previous high, buyers refuse to pay more and the stock starts to drop, forming the shape of an "M." When the stock price reaches support of the "M's" middle pivot, the pattern is completed. If it falls below this support, the signal is very bearish, and the stock may fall into a downtrend.
5. Double bottoms, when fully formed, are the mirror image of a double top, and resemble a "W." The form occurs mostly in stocks basing in a Stage One. You play a double bottom by monitoring it as it completes its pattern, and then moves in a sideways consolidation pattern. When it breaks above resistance of the consolidation pattern, if all other Buy Triggers are in place, you buy.
6. By the end of the day and perhaps sooner, a depressed Dow or Nasdaq will take the majority of stocks down with it. Your goal is to enter on a day when all conditions are positive.
7. It's best to choose stocks from industry groups that presently lead the market because that gives the stock extra propulsion! A sector in disfavor puts a damper on the stocks that reside within it, no matter how strong they are.
8. Positively, absolutely true!
9. Breakout above resistance on strong volume, stock pulling back or consolidating into the 20-, 40-, or 50-day MA, OBV turned up or in a definite uptrend.
10. Issue the buy order when all Buy Triggers are in place, and the stock trades .25 point over the previous day's high.

✦ ✦ ✦

CENTER POINT

Do not weep; do not wax indignant. Understand.

—BARUCH SPINOZA

Awaken to Forgiveness

Many times, we establish our vision in our heart and our minds. We declare what we want to feel and define the life we want to live. We may strive for a fulfilling career, loving relationships, vigorous health, spiritual awareness, or all of those goals.

Suddenly, though, we find ourselves "stuck." We sense an invisible roadblock in our path that we cannot identify. No matter how we strive to push past it and resume our journey, we remain transfixed. What's holding us back?

Chances are good that if we become quiet and reflect, we'll find a situation or person (including ourselves) in our past that we need to forgive.

It's like we've left a bag of rotten potatoes in our refrigerator. Oh, how sour that bag of moldy potatoes smells! We go to the store and buy a new supply of fresh fruit and vegetables. Arriving home, we open the refrigerator and fill it with the fresh food, but we leave the bag of potatoes on the shelf. Can the newly introduced fresh food overcome the rotting potato smell, or stop the potatoes from molding? No! The potatoes continue to decay, exuding the nasty odor that rapidly seeps into the fresh food.

Just so, we haul old grudges and anger into our new lives, and then wonder why we get stuck. Consider this: When we hold resentment in our heart toward someone whom we think wronged us, we actually give our power to that person.

Also consider that *the way we feel about a situation is our choice.* Unfortunately, when we choose to feel anger and betrayal, we end up hurting ourselves!

Could it be that the person who acted badly toward us did it because that was all they could have done, given the conditions of their lives? Or, could it be that it was easier to blame someone for a situation than to take responsibility for it ourselves? Moreover, did a life lesson permeate the event? Were we so busy judging that we overlooked what could be learned from it?

When we insist on dragging around heavy, moldy bags of potatoes filled with past grudges and blame, they weigh us down. The minute we realize how those sacks act as roadblocks and obstacles (think: negative energy) that stop us from reaching our goals, we can toss those sacks away . . . we can forgive.

Forgiveness causes the obstacles in our path to dissolve. We are filled with a delicious sense of lightness and freedom, and we step back on the road to happiness!

✦ ✦ ✦

CHAPTER 11

Where the Rubber Meets the Road: Money-Management Techniques

People who look for easy money invariably pay for the privilege of proving conclusively that it cannot be found on this . . . earth.
—JESSE LIVERMORE

It's easy to buy a stock . . . a walk in the park. All you need is some cash and a brokerage account. One mouse click, or one phone call, and voilà! You own shares in a company!

What separates the men from the boys, and the women from the girls—or more accurately, the winners from the crash-and-burn losers—is the ability to manage a position and the savvy to take consistent profits out of the market.

The initial action step for this is to haul out your discipline. You're going to need it! Consider rereading Chapter 3 to review how emotions affect your trading techniques.

Remember, your goal is to place trades with the calm confidence that comes with a well-thought-out plan. You also want to make the inner declaration that *the market only hurts you when you allow it to*. Now, let's get on with money-management strategies that will give you the edge as a consistently winning trader.

PLAN YOUR TRADE AND TRADE YOUR PLAN

First, let's create a trading log and an optional worksheet. I say "optional" because you can enter all the necessary information on one, comprehensive log or split it into two entities. Your choice.

Your trading log will be in spreadsheet form, with headings and columns underneath. The following details a basic records log. Naturally, you can alter it to fit your own needs.

Whatever form it takes, just make sure it's in a special place near your computer, where you can see it at all times. Please don't misplace it in a pile of bills or papers. You'll find yourself in Panic City if you lose your trading log with your stop-loss numbers at the moment the market screeches in a lightning U-turn.

It's wise to develop a basic log that includes the headings and columns detailed in Figure 11-1.

DATE	STOCK SYMBOL	BOUGHT OR SOLD SHORT	SHARE SIZE	PRICE	STOP-LOSS	CLOSING DATE	PRICE	PROFIT/LOSS (INCL. COMM.)
3/07	BBT	Bought	500	37.15	36.25	3/12	45.50	+ 4,175

Figure 11-1.
Basic log format.

The sample entry on this log shows a complete trade involving Bargain Biotech. The trade was 500 shares bought at $37.15 on March 7. The stop-loss point, which may be updated to a current trailing stop-loss, was $36.25. The trade was closed out five days after it was entered, at the price of $45.50 per share. Commissions of $10, each way, were factored in. If you plan to scale in and out of positions, remember to leave extra spaces under the initial trade information to enter the additional shares.

This is the simplest log you can use. Some traders like to include columns that list the actual dollar amount of the entry, in this case, $18,575, including a $10 commission. They also add the proceeds, which would have totaled $22,740, again minus a $10 commission. (These figures should be available to you from your broker in a running total on your account screen.)

Now, let's look at additional information that it's best to keep in front of you when you have an open trade. These numbers can be added to the basic log in Figure 11-1, or can made into a separate worksheet.

Personally, I prefer worksheets on yellow legal pads. Hey, trivia buffs: Know why legal pads are yellow? Because yellow is known to vitalize and stimulate the brain.

Let's say you just bought Bargain Biotech, so it's an "open trade." You've set your stop-loss point, and entered it. Now, on your worksheet or trading log, jot down major support and resistance areas currently pertinent to your stock, as seen on a daily chart. The next resistance area is particularly important, as that may be the target price to take profits. (More on this soon.)

You may also want to check a daily chart of the related industry group or sector, and note its support and resistance zones. To add to the fun, bring up weekly charts of your stock and sector. Then jot down price zones created by gaps

over the last few months. As you become more experienced, you'll be amazed how gap zones can cause a
stock to hop unexpectedly—one way or the other!

PIECE OF THE PIE

Say you want to buy even more Bargain Biotech. In fact,
it's moving up so strong and fast, why not max out your
account with this baby? Not!

*Commit no more than 33⅓ percent, or one-third of
the capital in your account, to a single equity.*

That means, if you have $25,000 in your account,
spend no more than $7,507, total, on Bargain Biotech
shares. Figure this out *before* you jump into the trade.
So, $7,507 divided by the current price of Bargain
Biotech, which is $37.13, means you can buy 202, or
200 shares of the stock. (Some brokerage houses don't
accept orders for odd lots.)

As you have guessed, your goal is to diversify your
portfolio, so you don't get caught with your entire
account maxed-out in a diving stock.

> **Hot Tip**
>
> An event that adds
> special excitement to
> anyone's trading day is
> to get caught holding an
> open position in a stock
> that *halts trading.* That
> means the company
> experiences incredible
> news—nice or nasty—
> and market officials halt
> trading in the stock until
> the news is sorted out or
> confirmed. This limbo
> condition can last from
> minutes to days, and the
> stock generally opens at
> a much different price
> than it closed (halted).
> What a great reason to
> diversify holdings in
> your account!

RISK/REWARD RATIO: WHAT IT MEANS, HOW TO CALCULATE IT

You're out of beer. It's 7:00 P.M. on a Friday night, and you've worked hard all
week. You deserve a beer, doggone it, but a quick scan of the refrigerator reveals
a definite absence of a tall bottle of golden brewski.

No problem. You'll jump into the car, drive to the store, and grab a six-pack.
Because you've done it a thousand times before, and you're familiar with the situation, you don't weigh the risk/reward ratio.

But what if you had to? It might look something like this:

Risk, or possible odds, to the downside: Since it's a party night, the store could
sell out of beer by the time you arrive. Long lines at the cash register may await
you. Friday night means heavy traffic. Your car could get a flat tire, or suffer
an unexpected mechanical problem, causing a delay. Or, you could, conceiv-
ably, be involved in a fender bender, which would cause an even greater delay.

Reward, or odds, to the upside: You can easily afford to buy beer. Your car is
filled with gas, and you take good care of it with frequent servicing, so
mechanical problems rarely crop up. You're a careful driver; you wear your
seatbelt and have never had an accident. Besides, the store is only a ten-minute

drive from home. If your favorite beer is sold out, no problem. More than one brand can wet your whistle. You expect a long line at the cash register, so you'll shrug it off. Besides, you may run into a friend who will want to go out to dinner or the movies over the weekend. Finally, the reward occurs the delicious moment you settle onto the sofa, and sip the icy, golden liquid.

Risk? Low. Reward? High.

We unconsciously weigh risk before we do anything, including speaking to a stranger or putting our hand on a hot stove burner.

Learning how to plan risk/reward ratios when you trade is worth every moment you spend, and is essential for trading success.

Here's a general rule to implement: *Whenever you plan a trade, please make sure your profit target—reward—is at least two, and preferably three, times greater than your possible loss, or risk (stop-loss).*

The following represent high-risk scenarios. Learn to recognize them, so you can avoid them.

You follow the 1-2 portion of the buy setups for a swing/position trade with Bossy Bank: You bought on a breakout from a base (1), and then added to your position on the "nice spring day" (2). Swing traders may have taken profits from the first upswing. So far, all Buy Triggers have cooperated. Setups 1 and 2 are complete and now your stock, Bossy Bank, is moving up from the first pullback and heading for the previous high established last week. Mother Market is happy, the financial index looks serene, and you're itchy to pull the trigger and add to your position *before* Bossy pokes through 35. See Figure 11-2 for illustration.

Why is this a high-risk play? Because when you buy a stock that's trading a point or less than a point away from a recent previous high, you're taking a big chance.

✦ First, where is your stop-loss point? Technically, it will be several points away, which is unacceptable to apply to shares added here. (We'll discuss stop-loss points in the next section.)

✦ Second, know that resistance (supply) will cause most stocks to retrace when they reach, or almost reach, a prior high. What if Bossy Bank (Figure 11-2) can't climb through 35 and trade above it? In that case, you should be taking quick profits from your 1 and 2 entries (*not buying more*). If Bossy stops short of 35 and drops back—it may etch a double top pattern! Your entry at 34 will be history—and you'll get caught in a downdraft. You may have to chase Bossy down to get out of your entry at 34, and instead of taking home tidy profits from your earlier entries, you'll give them all back in a hurry!

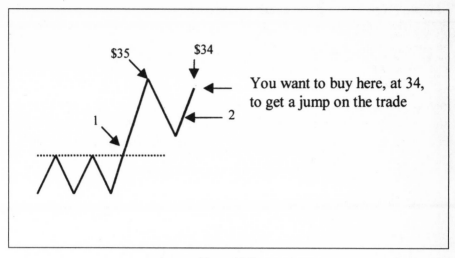

Figure 11-2.
Is this trade a good choice?

The moral of the story is, don't buy until your stock trades at the proper entry point. An early entry equals high risk/low reward.

Here's another scenario to consider. I will rarely buy a stock that's moving up for the third day in a row. Stocks tend to trade up or down in Fibonacci numbers. That means they may rise for three days, then pull back for two; or, they may rise for five days and retrace for three. When a stock rockets for three days in a row, it becomes a profit-taking target. As someone said, "Those who buy on the first day up are geniuses. Those who buy on the second day up are late. And those who buy on the third day up are fools." Remember, whether you're focusing on a double bottom, cup-with-handle, plain vanilla base, or the second swing in an uptrend, *you buy the breakout from consolidation or pullback. If you miss the proper entry point, walk away. Don't wander in one or two days late.* Wait for the stock to complete the next move up and subsequent retracement. Then enter at the proper point, with Buy Triggers in place.

With a smorgasbord of approximately 9,000 equities to choose from, there's no need to chase a stock. You have 8,999 more to pick from, one of which will offer a low risk/high reward entry.

Remember, when you enter a trade early, you're entering on "hope." As discussed in Chapter 3, hope and optimism are gratifying traits to evoke in your everyday life, but *leave them out of your trading.* Hope and optimism will get you slapped hard in the stock market!

WHERE TO PLACE YOUR STOP-LOSS ORDERS

An ancient saying goes, "Never test the depth of the water with both feet." Stop-losses equal water wings. They keep one foot on the shore, and save your account from drowning!

From this moment on, the very first question you ask yourself before you enter a trade is: "Where's my stop-loss point?" Decide your risk point, or your stop-loss point, *before your enter the trade.* If you find your stop-loss point is too far away from your entry point, or creates a risk (in points) equal to or larger than your profit target, don't enter the trade!

Stop-loss points can be set in many different ways. Find the way that best suits your trading style—and account balance—then stick with it. Whether you set a technical stop, a percentage stop, or a dollar-amount stop, the important thing is—set it and adhere to it. No excuses allowed. Period.

My old commodities coach used to say, "Where you set your stop-loss depends on your tolerance for pain." Let's see if we can refine that and give it a more positive spin. Here are options for setting stop-loss points:

✦ When you initiate a swing or position trade, place your stop-loss one-quarter point, or .25, under the low of the day (which should be a "nice spring day") you entered the trade. Some traders set it .25 under the low of the entry day, or the previous day's low, whichever is lower. (I prefer tight stop-losses, so I stay with the entry-day stop.)

✦ Never put more than 2 percent of your total account at risk in any one trade. In other words, say your account total is $20,000. Two percent of that equals $400. That means if you buy 400 shares of Bossy Bank at $33, you can lose *one point* on the trade. You'd set your stop-loss point at $32. If you determined that stop-loss point was too tight, and you wanted to allow Bossy to fall two points before you jumped out of the trade (stop-loss set at $31), you could only buy 200 shares. So, no matter what size position you take, you figure your *maximum* loss at no more than $400.

✦ Some traders set stop-losses at 7 to 8 percent of the cost of the stock. Say you buy Bossy Bank at $33 per share. Seven percent of 33 is 2.31. So you set your stop-loss at $30.69.

✦ A "trailing stop," as we call it, means that the stop-loss tags along behind the price rise like a shadow. Position traders use these the most; wise swing traders also apply them. You can keep your trailing stop as tight as you like, but here's one option: Your stock rises in the initial upswing, then pulls back or consolidates. Next, it bounces off price support, or moving average support (think: buy setup two) and starts to move up, again. *Reset your stop-loss point to .25 point under the low of the pullback or consolidation.* After all, if your stock retests the lows of the pullback or consolidation, then crashes through them, the trend is broken. You don't want that stock for sure!

Once you enter a trade, your next action is to set your stop-loss point. Don't wait. *Do it immediately!* If you trade with an online broker, enter the stop as a GTC, which means "good till cancelled." On the chance that your stop-loss price is touched, your pending order will turn into a market order, and you'll be filled at the next available price. Many level-II brokers now allow stop-loss orders to be entered. Some last only for the current day, or a "day order," and you have to reset it each morning. The important thing is to *do it.* As soon as you enter the order, write it into your trading log.

If you cannot set an automatic sell-stop (stop-loss) with your broker, you'll have to monitor the stock. When I set a "mental stop," I not only enter it on my trading log—I circle it. For some reason, the act of circling the stop-loss price declares it law. Is this circle-the-stop ploy a head-game? Absolutely. Do I care? Nope. If it makes me exit a trade when I should, thus saving me money, I'll happily play along.

Why am I rattling on about setting stop-loss points? Because ignoring these exits, while clinging to "the need to be right," has lost more traders more money than any other action. Think I'm bonkers? Ask an ex-trader the truth about why he or she crashed and burned. The standard answer is, "I held onto losing positions." In this market, with its ever-increasing volatility, hanging onto losers will blow out your account in a heartbeat.

Hey, I'm no stranger to this scene. Early in my trading career, I ignored or lowered my stop-losses. Sometimes, I didn't even set them. The result? Ugly, ugly losses. And, hard experience taught me it takes a lot longer to make the money back, than it does to lose it!

So, please raise your right hand. Say the following words out loud and with gusto:

"From this day forward, I, (your name), do solemnly swear on my mouse pad to adhere to all stop-losses. I shall never, ever, lower a stop-loss. I shall never ignore one. As soon as said stop is touched, I shall exit the trade."

Good. Got that done! If you keep your word, you'll be laps ahead of 99 percent of the traders and investors in this world. And if someone asks you if you're *really* that tall, you can reply, "No. I'm standing on my wallet!"

NOW THAT YOU'VE GOT IT, WHAT DO YOU DO WITH IT?

Planning your price target before you enter a trade is almost as important as entering your stop-loss. Plotting these two components of your trade form a large part of your risk/reward ratio. Figure it this way: If you don't know where you're going, how are you going to get there?

Note that most of the following pertains to swing trading techniques. As you know, in a position trade, you buy the breakout out of the base and stay in the trade until the current trend is broken or until your stop-loss is hit.

Say you're waiting for Stealthy Software to complete its pullback and to begin the second leg up of its uptrend. Today may be the last day of the pullback. Market conditions improved this afternoon, and the software index gained legs. Tomorrow may well turn into a "nice spring day" for this stock.

On a daily chart, look for Stealthy's most recent high. When was it? What was the price? Write that on your worksheet or log. If Stealthy is breaking out of a base, the most recent high could be weeks or months away. Fantastic! Remember, the further away resistance (in the form of a previous high) is, the less important it is.

On the other hand, what if the most recent high that preceded the pullback was three days ago? No problem, but if you're swing trading, that may be your profit target. (Since position traders stay in a stock for the duration of the trend, nearby highs aren't *as* important to them.) Check out Figure 11-3 to see what I'm talking about.

You enter this trade on a "nice spring day" as Stealthy shoots out of the pullback or retracement low of 42. You buy at 43. You set your stop-loss at 41.75. Your first possible price target is 55, the most recent high. So, that's where Stealthy is most likely to run into resistance (supply).

So, the risk equals 1.25 point; the reward equals 7 points (possibly more).

One strategy is to sell one-half of your Stealthy position when it reaches 54–54.50. Another, which we've discussed, is to monitor market conditions as the stock approaches 55. If it jets to the upside and trades .25 point over 55, you can add to the position if you wish. Now, raise your stop-loss to protect profits. And, *look for the next possible resistance area.* That's your new price target.

Congratulations on learning how to plan your trade! Using these methods and sticking to them will raise you to the ranks of the pros and will help you stay a consistent winner.

With that pat on the back, though, comes a "heads up." Just because you have a price target on Stealthy Software of 55, *doesn't mean it's going to go there.* Sure, it could rocket to 55, zoom right through it, and shoot like a ballistic missile to 75 before you can catch your breath. It can also crawl up to 44, hiccup, sputter, then sink below 42, past your stop-loss, and finally stop at 20.

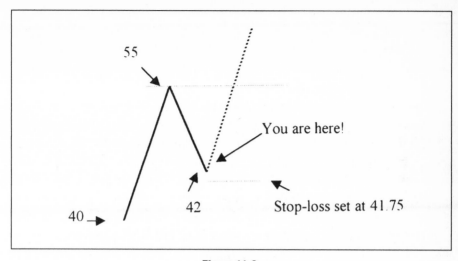

Figure 11-3.
Daily chart of Stealthy Software.

A zillion times during the past few years I've heard full-of-themselves traders—who ought to know better—make calls that novice traders take as gospel. Big-Shot trader spouts, "Worldwide Wireless is trading at 60. It'll be 85 by next Friday!"

Novice Trader yells, "Wow, I'm in!" He loads the truck with Worldwide, then bewildered, watches it tank to 50. Novice ignored his stop-loss, because Big-Shot *said* the stock was going to the moon.

The absolute truth: *No one on earth knows where the stock market, or a stock, will move to next. No one.*

Your goal is to plan your trade precisely, with as little emotion as possible. You follow your plan. While you can and should study the methods of market professionals, strive to become proficient in your own right. Make your own decisions based on your own discipline, knowledge, and experience. Take responsibility for those decisions. Then you've arrived at the gates of success.

INTRA-DAY REVERSAL PERIODS: WHAT THEY ARE, WHAT THEY MEAN TO YOU

In the course of a trading day, market dynamics cause "reversal periods" to occur. If you watch the stock market during trading hours, you've probably observed an ebb and flow—time-wise—that repeats itself each day. While active traders become highly tuned to market rhythms, you—particularly as a swing trader—

may want to be aware of them. Then you'll know why stocks act the way they do, during certain time slots.

Since the discussion refers to Eastern Standard Time (EST), translate them into your time zone.

The market opens at 9:30 A.M.

(Note: the following times are approximate.)

The first reversal period takes place from approximately 9:50 A.M. to 10:10 A.M. This means that if the market has moved up since the open at 9:30, as a whole, it will start to retrace or "come in" at 9:50, and will continue to drift down until 10:10. One reason this happens is that market makers and specialists often take the opposite side of your trade. They will "bring the stocks in" to adjust their positions (think: make profits). At 10:10 on a positive day, the market resumes the upswing.

The next reversal takes place at 10:25 (yes, just fifteen minutes later), but only lasts five minutes or so. I would call it more of a "shift" than a reversal. You may not notice it.

By 11:30, the lunchtime moody blues edge in. Traders start taking profits before lunch, and institutional managers leave for a break, so buying subsides. Stocks start to drift down. Conversely, sometimes on a bearish day, stocks will rally at noon. Short-covering may be responsible for some of the pop up. Whatever the direction on the day, most stocks move sideways during lunchtime.

From 1:30 to 2:30 P.M., fresh action permeates the market. On a positive day, strong stocks may break out. I've also seen the market dive hard and fast in this time span.

The next reversal begins at 3:00 P.M., when Treasury bonds close. Now, unfettered by its connection with the bonds, the market moves with added lust. At 3:30, institutional managers adjust their positions for the following day. Traders who "go home flat" also exit their positions. That's why the last half-hour can be highly volatile. It's not unusual to see a strong stock fall at this time. On the heels of the traders are the short-sellers, who are closing out their positions. Their short-covering causes stocks to rise. No wonder the last half-hour can turn into such a circus!

Know this: Just because the market trended up all morning, doesn't mean it automatically resumes that uptrend in the afternoon. It might. It might not. *The only absolute in the stock market is change.*

MARKET ORDERS, LIMIT ORDERS, AND MORE

You buy or sell stocks using the following methods: market orders, limit orders, buy stops, and sell-stops.

Market Orders

When you buy or sell a stock "at the market," you're giving the specialist or market maker carte blanche. That person chooses what price you pay, or receive, for your stock. Yes, you're supposed to receive the inside bid or offer when your order reaches them. But "bad fills" are commonplace when you issue a market order. (This is a form of "slippage" discussed in Chapter 2.) If you must buy or sell in a hurry, use a market order. Otherwise, don't. Use limit orders instead.

Limit Orders

When you place a limit order, you give instructions to buy or sell a specified number of shares of stock, at a specified price. You issue a limit order to buy at a price *lower* than the posted inside offer. Or, you place a limit order to sell *above* the posted inside bid. *The specialist or market maker will only fill your limit order when the stock's price touches your specified price, or better.* Issue a limit order to specify a price when you want to buy a stock at a price between the bid and the ask, or offer. Say Awesome Airlines is trading at 35 × 35.25. You issue a limit order to buy 300 shares at 35.15. Your order will only be filled if a market maker (or specialist on the NYSE) decides to sell it to you at that price. If Awesome moves up quickly, you may not get filled with that limit order. In that case, only you can decide if you want to cancel your limit order and raise it (translation: chase the stock). Of course, you can leave the order in place for the rest of the day (not longer).

The same procedure takes place with a sell order. If you own a stock and want to sell it at a higher price than is currently posted, issue a limit order to sell your shares at a price *above* the posted price (example: Sell 300 Awesome at 36). Again, your order may be filled, but if the stock doesn't trade at your specified price, your order may not get filled. Limit orders can be either "day orders," or GTC ("good 'till cancelled"). You may also have the choice designated AON. AON means "all or nothing." If you issue an AON order, you instruct the specialist or market maker to fill the total number of shares you request, or not at all. So, if you put in a limit order for 500 shares at a certain price AON, and they can only give you 350 shares at that price, it tells them to ignore the order.

Buy Stops

When you place a buy stop, it means you specify a number of shares you want to buy at a certain price *above* the stock's posted price. Say Awesome Airlines is trading at $35.50, which is key resistance. If it breaks *above* $35.50, that's the perfect entry point. You're sure, however, that when (if) Awesome trades over $35.50, every trader in captivity will try to buy Awesome, and the price will rocket. How do you get an edge? You place a buy stop order for the number of shares you want at $35.75. Then you wait. If Awesome doesn't trade at $35.75, your order will not be filled.

The drawback is that *buy stops are filled when the stock trades at your specified price, or the next highest price.* If you place a buy stop with your online broker for 300 shares of Awesome at 35.75 *before* the market opens, then the bell rings and Awesome gaps open three points higher than yesterday's close of 35.50, *that's* where you get filled, at $38.50. *Gulp!* The lesson here is don't issue buy orders before the market opens. Once the market opens and you're unable to watch your stock if it reaches the perfect entry, that's good use of a buy stop order.

Sell-Stops

Sell-stops are many times called stop-loss orders. When you're holding a NYSE stock long, you can place a sell-stop, or stop-loss, *under* the stock's current posted price. If the stock trades at that price, your stop-loss reverts into a market order, and your position is liquidated. The Nasdaq doesn't grant stop-losses. Most online and level-II brokers, however, provide stop-losses on Nasdaq stocks as a customer service. You place a sell-stop for the number of shares you own at a specified price. When the stock trades at that price, the sell-stop reverts to a market order, and your position is sold. Because your order reverts to a market order when your designated price is touched, depending how fast the stock moves, you may be filled a fraction of a point or more away from your specified price.

IN TIMES OF CRISES

As I write, the United States—indeed, the world—struggles to restore a sense of calmness in the aftermath of the acts of terrorism directed at our Pentagon and World Trade Center on Tuesday, September 11, 2001. The stock market opening was wisely cancelled on that horrific morning, and it remained closed for the following three days.

Many traders and investors waited for the markets to open on the following Monday, September 17, with mixed feelings of relief and trepidation. Would the stock market—which had been weak for months before—gap down with no support and continue down in freefall? Would entire accounts be wiped out as swiftly as our beloved World Trade Center?

Fortunately, the worst did not materialize. On September 10, the day before the "Attack on America," the Dow Jones Industrial Average closed at 9,605. It opened on September 17 at 9,580, fell to 8,976 during the first hour of trading, and finally closed the day at 8,920. The fall was dramatic, and even heartbreaking, after the events of the previous week. Still, the day's trading proceeded in an orderly fashion, allowing those who wanted to exit positions to do so.

In the event of a crisis, wait a few moments before acting. Don't place a market order to sell right at the opening bell, unless absolutely necessary. Check the next support level on a daily chart, or intra-day chart if you prefer, then issue a stop-loss order a fraction of a point beneath that level. On slow-moving stocks, place limit orders to sell at the inside bid price. The most important action you can take is to stay calm and clear-headed. Panicked selling benefits no one. Also, avoid taking on new positions during extreme volatility. Explosive price swings coupled with overloaded order systems reduce your chances of accurate fills, to say the least. Cut your losses in a composed, professional manner, then step to the side-lines. Remember, in times like these, a single, unexpected news announcement may send the market into excessive fluctuations. So once in cash, stay in cash until stability returns.

CONCLUSION

There's a lot of material to absorb in this chapter, but I promise you, if you go slowly and weave these money-management techniques into your trades, you'll keep your losses small and your gains high.

And, congratulations. You're well on your way to becoming a conscientious, profitable trader!

QUIZ

1. What is the maximum amount of capital in your trading account that you should commit to a single equity?
2. What is the general rule for risk/reward ratio?
3. True or false? As long as the market looks favorable, it's a good idea to get an early start on a swing trade by buying before the stock moves above resistance.
4. What's the most important question to ask yourself immediately before entering a trade?
5. True or false? Buying a stock on the third consecutive day of an upswing is a high-risk play.
6. Describe three possible methods for setting an initial stop-loss.
7. True or false? Once in a while, it's perfectly fine to lower your established stop-loss point because of market rhythms.
8. When you're planning a swing trade, what do you look for to find your price target for an exit?
9. What's a "reversal period"? When does the first one occur after the market opens?
10. Define "limit order."

ANSWERS

1. A commitment to a single equity should be no more than one-third of the account.

2. The profit target, or reward, is at least two times greater than my possible loss, or risk (stop-loss).

3. False. While you may get away with this move occasionally, it raises your risk ratio. You may end up giving back previously earned profits if the stock suddenly decides it cannot trade over the resistance area.

4. "Where's my stop-loss point?"

5. True, true, true! You want to buy a stock that's moving up on the *first* day out of consolidation or pullback.

6. Three methods for setting initial stop-losses: (1) Place stop-loss .25 point below the low of the entry day. (2) Calculate 2 percent of account total and adjust share size and stop-loss amount to fit. (3) Set stop-loss at 7 percent of the value of the stock price.

7. False, false, false, false, false, false!!!!

8. To find your profit price target, look for the most recent high. That price will form possible resistance and an exit point to consider taking profits.

9. Various market dynamics cause "reversal periods" to occur. When the market is trending up on the day, stocks pull back, or drift down, during reversal periods. On a bearish day, stocks typically move up during reversal periods. The first reversal period takes place from 9:50 A.M. to 10:10 A.M. Eastern Standard Time.

10. When you place a limit order, you give instructions that you wish to buy or sell a specified number of shares of stock at a specified price.

✦ ✦ ✦

CENTER POINT

In fact, the easiest way to get what you want is to help others get what they want.
—DEEPAK CHOPRA

The Circle of Giving

Dynamic energy moves in a constant state of harmony—a circle of giving and receiving. In fact, giving and receiving is a law of the universe.

Because each of us acts as a vital part of this universe, it is inherent in our nature to give and receive. When we stop giving, we stop contributing to ourselves and to those around us. Imagine a stream bubbling down a mountainside, nourishing and replenishing life as it flows. If the stream is blocked, the dammed water grows stagnant. The bed below becomes cracked and dried.

Just so, when we stop the flow of positive energy to any area of our lives, it cuts off the natural return of positive energy that would have come back to us. Money is referred to as "currency," which means "to flow." Therefore, if we hoard our money and never share with others, that action blocks and strangles the return of more money to us.

Try maintaining a stern, unsmiling countenance one day. Observe what you receive in return. The next day, smile with genuine happiness and notice the difference in return greetings!

The law of giving and receiving is clear: *Give what you want to receive.* Do you want to receive more love in your life? Then give love. Would you like more joy and happiness? Then become a purveyor of authentic joy and serenity. Do you wish for more attention and appreciation? Give your attention and appreciation to those around you. Would you like additional abundance to manifest in your life? You can have more by helping others acquire abundance.

Remember, you must give with pure intention to put this law into action. Your gifts—be they smiles, hugs, appreciation, or money—must be offered to provide for the good of others. If you feel that by giving you have less, the energy behind the giving diminishes the gift and the return.

The life forces that empower giving and receiving are among the most important in the universe. The more you give with freedom and joy, the more it will return to you multiplied!

✦ ✦ ✦

CHAPTER 12

Winning Strategies for Selling Short

As I said before, a man does not have to marry one side of the market till death do them part.

—JESSE LIVERMORE

On any bearish market day, ask a roomful of traders to raise their hands if they sold stocks short. Only a smattering of hands will shoot up, if any.

Why does selling short earn such a bum rap? For openers, it has to do with the American psyche. We are a land of optimists. We like our glasses half-full, not half-empty. We insist our books and movies end happily. We won't kick the underdog; in fact, we'll usually cheer him on, even defend him. Our parents raised us to help those less fortunate than ourselves. We learn that nice people don't benefit from another's sorrow or misfortune. So, it makes sense that we avoid selling stock in a company suffering from financial blues.

Besides, the process of selling short seems downright weird. In "real life," whether it's stocks, cars, or houses, we buy an item and then sell it. When we sell short, however, we sell a stock we've never owned . . . cross our fingers that it falls like a rock . . . buy it back when it hits the skids . . . then return it to its previous owner. No wonder selling short resembles wandering a strange planet with no tour book in hand, armed only with warnings that the natives are unfriendly.

And *if* the trade goes against us—unlike a trade to the long side, where the most we can lose is the initial investment—when we short a stock, theoretically, it can go against us to infinity. That's a groan, if ever there was one!

The first time I sold a stock short, I relived the same feelings I experienced while attending competition car racing school. Picture this: *Moroso Race Track, West Palm Beach, Florida.* I sat wide-eyed, tightly strapped by gigantic seat belts into the open cockpit of a low-slung, rumbling Formula Ford. I felt like I was driving a rocket with pedals.

My instructor knelt next to me, explaining that when I reached the sharp bend in the track, I was to take the curve's radius *fast*. My tires should squeal as loud as possible to assure they worked at the outside level of their adhesion. *Whatever you do,* the instructor told me, *don't hit the brakes.* Sure. No problem. (Gulp!)

Jaw set, I threw the car into gear and roared down the open stretch toward the bend. As I skidded around the curve, tires screaming and pulse pounding in my ears, instincts from 30 years of driving on city streets took over.

I panicked and jammed my foot on the brake.

Instantly, the car careened off the track and spun like a top. The sky churned, the landscape whirled around me in a blur. Grass and sand funneled overhead, then rained on my helmet and down the front of my jumpsuit. Finally, the car ground to a stop. The engine sputtered and died into silence. When I divined I was still alive, I exhaled and spit the sand out of my mouth. Whe-eew! Some days you're the bug, some days you're the windshield.

And, yes . . . I finally learned how to go around a corner at Mach 2 with my hair on fire, gas pedal to the metal, tires shrieking like banshees. But it took practice to overcome years of traditional driving habits.

The same self-preservation instinct that presses our foot on the brake when we drive around a corner, especially when we hear our tires squeal, insists selling short is unnatural. Yet, it really isn't. It's merely another mechanism tucked into our traders' tool kit that allows us to take profits from the market.

And guess what else? Stocks tend to move down *three times faster* than they rise. Why? Because panic can be three times more powerful than greed! Which means if you learn to sell short successfully, you can make tidy profits in a hurry.

OVERCOMING MENTAL AND EMOTIONAL ROADBLOCKS TO SELLING SHORT

Let's drag the mental roadblocks to selling short into the sunlight so we can remove them with logical explanations:

Nice people don't benefit from another's bad luck. Trading is not charity work. Besides, when you sell short, you add liquidity to the stock you're trading and help bolster its price when you buy it back. Feel better?

The market has an upside bias. "It moves up more than it moves down," you continue smugly. "Even taking bear markets into account, both the Dow and the Nasdaq have risen thousands of points since their inception." Absolutely. But even bull markets move down at least one-third of the time.

A stock in a short trade can make a U-turn and go against you ad infinitum. It's possible to lose more than your initial investment. You got that right! But to you, as an astute trader with a plan etched in stone, a large loss is not even a remote consideration. Just as you set a sell-stop right after you enter a long trade, you enter an automatic "buy to cover" order right after you enter a short position. If your stop-loss is a mental one, you cover the position the moment that price is hit, just like any other trade. If, heaven help you, you allow the trade to get out of control, take your lumps fast, and then reassess if the trading life is really for you!

Because selling short seems like a backward process, it's easy to make mistakes. True enough. Humans are creatures of habitual reaction, especially when safety is an issue. It's quite common for new traders to accidentally *sell* shares when in a panic to exit the trade. Then, instead of closing the trade, they actually double their short position. (Laugh if you like, but as a new trader, I've done that!) You can overcome this panic move by paper trading before you sell short. It helps you become accustomed to selling *first* and buying *second*.

When you're new to selling short, minimize risk and assure a positive experience by trading small lot sizes, say 50 to 100 shares. Next choose a slow-moving stock—perhaps a NYSE stock—that's highly liquid (high volume). That way, you tame your terror, and a door (seller) always remains in sight, if you decide to beat a hasty retreat.

SELLING SHORT: THE RULES

Before you start selling short, you'll need to understand shorting rules:

+ All stocks are not shortable. Your broker may issue a "short list" before the market opens each day. If not, when you place your order, your broker will advise you if your stock's shortable or not. The larger the broker, the larger the short list.
+ You can only sell short from a margin account.
+ Uptick Rule: Established by the exchanges to prevent selloffs like the 1929 Crash, the uptick rule (which may soon be repealed) says you can sell short only on an uptick or a zero-plus tick. You cannot sell short on a downtick. If you place your order to sell short with your online broker, you don't have to worry about the downtick rule, but you should know that on a fast-falling stock where no uptick may take place for several points, a limit order may not get filled. When you place your order on a level-II screen, it must be a penny higher than the inside bid. If not, it will be cancelled.

Ticks

+ Uptick: When a stock trades an increment higher than the previous trade.
+ Downtick: When a stock trades an increment lower than the previous trade.
+ Zero-plus tick: When a stock trades on an uptick, then the following trade goes off at the same price.
+ A NYSE uptick must appear on the Time & Sales screen (usually attached to your level-II screen).
+ A Nasdaq uptick is considered in place when the inside bid is raised by a cent. Yes, you can create your own uptick by entering your order at that price. It may, or may not, be filled.

HERE'S THE PROCESS

Here's a brief description of the shorting process.

Say you enter a limit order with your online broker to sell short 300 shares of Awesome Airlines, at 40. Your broker takes Awesome out of his own inventory or another client's account. If he obtains it from a client's account, he leaves an IOU that guarantees the stock's return on demand. Then he removes $12,000 from your account, plus his commission, and tucks it away as a security deposit so you can return the stock if need be. Next, the broker sells the borrowed 300 shares of Awesome Airlines in the market for $40 per share. He puts the $12,000 away for safekeeping.

During the next two days, Awesome falls to support at $35. You issue an order to buy it back, known as "covering your short." Your broker takes $10,500 out of the safekeeping account, goes to the market, and buys 300 shares of Awesome at $35 per share, the current price. He returns those shares to his inventory, or the other client's account. Next, he tears up the IOU.

> **Hot Tip**
>
> Avoid issuing "market orders" to sell short. If no uptick takes place for several points, your order may get filled far away from your original entry price.

Now your broker returns to you the $12,000 security deposit he took from your account, plus the $1,500 leftover when he bought the stock back, minus a commission. Your original $12,000 investment yields nearly $1,500 profit. Nifty, huh?

WHAT MAKES YOUR SHORTS FALL DOWN

One or more of the factors in the following list may contribute to a stock's drop in price:

+ Overall bearish market conditions
+ Anticipation of interest rate hike by FOMC (Federal Open Market Committee)

+ Industry group/sector labors under institutional disfavor, or is downgraded by analysts
+ Weak company fundamentals
+ Company announces bad news or earnings. An "accounting irregularities" announcement almost always ensures that the stock's price will take a pounding.
+ Fear and panic-driven selling
+ Disinterest by buyers

FUNDAMENTALS: WHAT TO LOOK FOR

On an overall basis, you choose target stocks to sell short differently in bull markets than you do in bear markets. If you're smack in the middle of a raging bull market, look for lagging stocks in lagging industries to short. Typically, gold and oil stocks drag when broader markets thrive.

If, however, you're slogging through the muck and mire of a bear market, industry or sector leaders can tumble like bricks, as money pours out of them and into second-tier stocks, bonds, and money market funds. (When investors sell stocks to buy bonds, it's sometimes called "flight to safety.") The bottom line is that during a major market downslide, previous market leaders may make the best shorting targets.

After assessing market conditions, target stocks to short that have poor fundamentals. Use the same proprietary rankings in *IBD* as when you intend to buy. Now, though, instead of looking for winners, seek out the laggards, the puny, and the disfavored.

Optimum *IBD* Rankings for selling short:

+ *Composite:* 50 or lower
+ *Earnings per Share:* 50 or lower
+ *Relative Strength:* 50 or lower
+ *Industry Group Relative Strength:* C or lower
+ *Sales + Profit Margins + ROE (Return on Equity):* C or lower
+ *Accumulation/Distribution:* C or lower

What if most of the above ratings are negative, with one or two showing positive? Look at the big picture. Take overall market conditions into consideration, as well as the industry and stock daily chart. Then decide if the stock still looks like a good shorting target.

CHART PATTERNS AND SETUPS: WHAT TO LOOK FOR

Just as you look for stocks experiencing Stage One basing patterns for breakouts to the upside to buy, you monitor stocks moving sideways in a Stage Three pattern that may break to the downside to sell short.

As discussed in Chapter 10, look for reversal patterns that include double and triple top, head-and-shoulders. Some Stage Threes come in plain vanilla. That is, they don't draw a fancy reversal pattern. They simply move sideways in a frothy congestion pattern, alternating highs and lows. At some point, they retest the bottom of the congestion range, and buyers refuse to support them. As supply floods the market, they plunge into a Stage Four downtrend.

The position trader will sell short the stock when it begins a Stage Four downtrend (initiating lower highs and lower lows) and hold it until the stock breaks its downtrend by making a higher high.

The swing trader will short the stock as it falls into a downtrend, and then buy it back to cover, just before it drops the next support level on a daily chart. After the stock rebounds to previous resistance (think continuation patterns here, like descending triangle and pennant, or simple consolidation) and finally resumes its fall to the downside, the swing trader enters again.

While position traders essentially make two trades—one to sell short, then one to cover and close the trade—swing traders who sell short successfully have to stay nimble. As long as the uptick rule is in place, it's sometimes difficult to get filled when a stock is tumbling fast and no uptick occurs.

Imagine Bargain Biotech reports "accounting irregularities." Traders and investors dump Bargain's shares like crazy. Is anyone buying? Nope. And only buying creates upticks. So poor Bargain catapults into the basement, with few upticks occurring for many points. Will you, as a short seller, get your order filled quickly, if at all? Maybe. Maybe not.

> **Hot Tip**
>
> The steeper a stock's rise in a Stage Two uptrend, generally speaking, the steeper the fall in its Stage Four downtrend.

Solution: Anticipate a stock's fall early and pull the trigger *slightly* (slightly being a fraction of a point) faster than you would when trading to the long side. That means you may short a weak, fast-falling stock *as it falls through support*, rather than waiting for it to trade *below* support. To compensate for the added risk, keep initial buy-to-cover stops tight and monitor price movement until the stock drops into profitable territory.

Also, *only pull the trigger early when every odd possible is in your corner.* You want bad news on your stock or the industry it resides in. Examples are weak earnings guidance, weak earnings, falling sales or rising inventory reports, stock or industry downgrade.

For example, perhaps your stock is a market leader. Currently Cisco Systems (CSCO) is a Nasdaq benchmark. When the Nasdaq nosedives for several days at a time, technology chieftain CSCO usually falls as well. Similarly, banking giant J.P. Morgan (JPM) represents a top banking industry nabob. When the bank index ($BKX.X) plummets, count on JPM to dive with it.

Consider this: The biotech index ($BTK.X) is overextended, or rolling over in a Stage Three. Amgen (AMGN) and Biogen (BGEN) are biotech leaders. *Odds are*, if the biotechs fall, AMGN and BGEN will tank. Then check their charts for confirming weakness.

Now, review Chapter 10 and the head-and-shoulders pattern. Remember, on a daily chart showing a head-and-shoulders pattern (assuming all other odds are in your corner) you sell short a fraction of a point below support, or as the stock sinks through the neckline.

The next two charts, Figures 12-1 and 12-2, show stocks experiencing plain vanilla Stage Three rollovers into Stage Four downtrends.

> **Hot Tip**
>
> When you study the charts in this chapter, take a plain sheet of paper and cover up the right side of the chart, up to the entry point. Now you know what the setup should look like before you enter!

SHORTING INDICATORS: UGLY IS GOOD!

When you sell short, you want all indicators showing weakness, in fact "pig-ugly" is good! "Ugly" translates into declining moving averages and overbought oscillators. This means they'll be reversed from their earlier readings on long entries.

Volume

Do you recall that when you buy a breakout from consolidation or a pullback, you look for strong volume to assure the move upward? (Puh-lease say "yes.") When you sell short, it's best to enter on strong volume as well. Still, stocks also fall nicely with low volume. Low volume equals disinterest, which means buyers don't give a hoot, which equals lower prices.

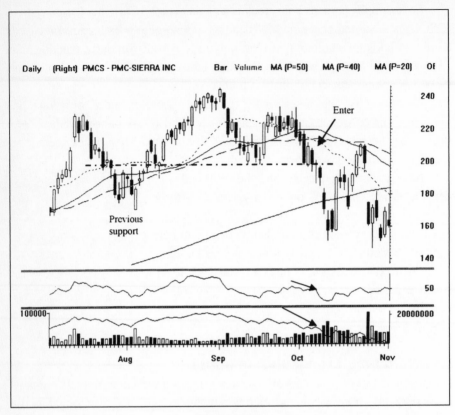

Figure 12-1.

On this wild and woolly daily chart of PMC Sierra Inc. (PMCS), you can see how this semiconductor networking systems company couldn't rise to make a higher high during the last weeks of September. When a stock can't make a higher high—whether it's on a weekly, daily, or intra-day chart—that's a sign of weakness and it bears watching. Also note the move up from August 11 to September 1, where PMCS moved from about $200 to $245. Then, from September 5 to September 13, it moved down from $243 to $198, erasing all gains from the prior rise. That tells you the stock has problems! It retraced approximately 50 percent of the move down, then consolidated and drifted down. That's when you can tell it's in a Stage Three. Notice how the 20-day MA falls down over the 40-day MA, then the 50-day MA, giving you an added shorting signal. The RSI started falling, as did the OBV.

On October 3, PMCS plunged through support established at 199, opening at 207 and closing at 198. Swing traders and position traders could have entered a short position as the stock traded below 199. Support lies in the 197 to 183 range would have to be monitored. As it turned out, poor PMCS found no support there and plunged to a low of 151.69 on October 11.

Please note that PMCS falls much faster than it rises, because fear and panic is stronger than greed. This characteristic is shown on many charts! Since this is a volatile stock, swing and position traders would exit with multi-point profits before or at the first sign of strength on October 13. Added signals for short exit: The stock is oversold and the RSI is making a bullish divergence. Time to take profits and run!

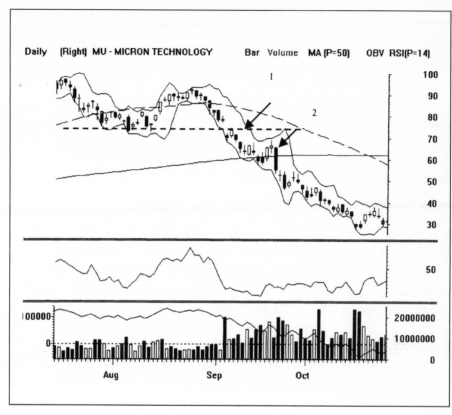

Figure 12-2.

On this daily chart of Micron Technology (MU), another semiconductor stock, Bollinger Bands have been added and only the 50- and 200-day MAs are on the chart for clarity. Use the 50-day MA as a guide to tell when stocks are rolling over. Notice how the 50-day MA was rising, and then flattened out toward the end of August. Plus, MU made a lower high at the same time. MU gapped down seven points (eeek!) through the support line drawn at 73, and opened at 71.25 on September 6. Know that gaps like to be filled, so entering a trade you intend to hold overnight on a big gap-down day can be a dicey play. The next day, September 7, MU moved up to 74.50, which may have taken out some short positions established the previous trading session. On September 8, MU opened at 71.50 and started falling, to a low of 68.19 and finally closing at 69. You could have shorted it when it sank through support at about 70 (1). Of course, you would be aware of the semiconductor index and Nasdaq Composite at the same time, looking for correlating weakness.

Once in the trade, the 200-day MA could offer strong support, so that would have to be monitored closely and partial or all profits possibly taken just above that area. A more definitive shorting opportunity also presented itself on September 21, when MU gapped down and fell through its 200-day MA and previous support of 57.50. From there, poor MU continued to tumble, until it finally hit a low of 28.50 (not shown).

Say you're selling bead necklaces on the beach. A woman walks by and you call out, "Want to buy a necklace for only $10?" No reply. "I'll lower the price!" She doesn't look back. "Hey!" you call out. "How about half-price?" No sale.

Other passersby show the same indifference. You reduce the price of the necklace with each averted gaze, each case of apathy.

See what I mean? While a selling frenzy causes a stock to plummet quickly, disinterest and apathy also push a stock downward, albeit with less excitement along the way.

Moving Averages

When you sell short, find stocks with major moving averages trending down *over* the stock's price. Just as MAs act as support when a stock pulls back while in an uptrend, MAs act as resistance when a stock rebounds in a downtrend. The overhead MA acts as a not-so-fragile glass ceiling.

Also, when a shorter time frame MA crosses down over a longer-term MA, it gives a bearish signal. For example, when the 20-day MA crosses over the 50-day MA and continues south, that's a big negative.

Relative Strength Index (RSI)

Ideally, the RSI should be above 70, showing an overbought position. A hook down adds confirmation. RSI bearish divergence means the stock is moving up, while the RSI is moving down. In this case, monitor stock price for signs of weakness.

On-Balance Volume (OBV)

The OBV should be trending down.

Bollinger Bands

Please turn back to Chapter 9 to review this handy tool. Use the premise that when stocks rise to their upper Bollinger Bands (if they actually pierce the band— don't short the stock—that's bullish), they are doomed to eventually drop to their lower band. When all other indicators look weak, apply Bollinger Bands. Keep in mind that they give the most accurate signals on overextended (trading high above their 20-day MA) stocks. Stocks in sharp downtrends tend to stumble down to their lower Bollinger Band, thus emitting a weak signal.

HOW TO PLACE YOUR ORDER

Enter your order to sell short when your target stock breaks a fraction of a point below support. For fast-moving stocks, enter your order *as* the stock falls through support.

Online Broker

If stock is falling slowly, place a limit order .01 to .05 above bid. If stock is dropping rapidly, place a limit order to sell short .25 to .30 below the bid.

Level II Platform

Watch arrow (green up, red down) to determine uptick. If the stock is drifting slowly, place your limit order to sell short at the inside offer price. For rapidly sinking stocks, place your limit order .01 to .05 above inside bid. Hit the "sell short" button the second the green arrow flashes an uptick. (An arrow near the top of the level-II screen will flash green for an uptick, red for a downtick.) Most level-II systems automatically cancel shorting orders placed at the inside bid price on a red downtick arrow.

Set Your Buy-Cover Stop-Loss Immediately

Next, place your automatic buy-to-cover stop-loss .25 to .50 above the day's high. (Or place a point or percentage stop-loss as discussed in Chapter 10.)

SHORTING STRATEGY: THE OVEREXTENDED STOCK

We just discussed the most traditional shorting strategy: You initiate a short position when a stock falls from a Stage Three into a Stage Four. Position traders hold until the stock breaks the downtrend, and then exit. Swing traders may trade the entire downtrend, selling short each time the stock rebounds to resistance and continues its fall. Wise traders cover the short and exit the position after no more than two to three days down, and no more than one to two points before the next support level.

Now, for adrenaline junkies, and those with a bit more experience under their mouse, let's look at overextended stocks as targets for selling short. This is a swing trading strategy and is a high-risk setup! Only traders who can closely monitor their trades and issue automatic, buy-to-cover stops with their broker should enter these trades.

Setup: Look for a stock screaming skyward in Stage Two uptrend soaring high (several points) above its 20-day MA on a daily chart. (Note: This is *not* the same as shorting a stock in the middle of a healthy uptrend.) The steeper the angle of the uptrend, the better! For confirmation that the stock is overextended, scan the stock's price pattern for the last six months or more. How high, point-wise, can it rise over its 20-day MA before it falls back to the 20-day MA? (Remember, major moving averages act as a magnet.) Is it *at least* as overextended now, point-wise, as it has been in the past? The more overextended, the better!

Check out the industry group, or sector, where the stock resides. The best setups take place when the industry/sector is also overextended and ready to correct.

Now wait for the first sign of weakness. When you see it, get ready to pounce. An ideal setup takes place when yesterday's candlestick developed into a long, wide-range real-body to the upside. Today, the stock gaps down at the open in an exhaustion gap on high volume.

Candlestick alternative: Although stock price rose sharply in the uptrend, yesterday's candlestick results in a doji, indicating indecision, and buyers' reluctance to pay higher prices. Figure 12-3 shows the two basic candlestick patterns just described.

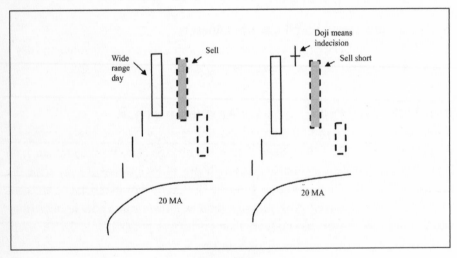

Figure 12-3.
Two shorting setups for overextended stocks.

To enter, wait for the stock to trade for a few minutes after the market opens, to ensure it won't immediately gain strength and fill the gap. With weakness confirmed, sell short with a limit order. (More details on gap entries follow.)

Because you're dealing with a highly volatile stock in this technique, plan to cover this short quickly. Buy to cover when:

+ It nears previous support.
+ It has tumbled for two to three days *max*.
+ You have a multiple-point profit. There's nothing wrong with closing a position in a single day if you've made big bucks!

Since you're dealing with an explosive situation, you may take profits early, only to find you left mucho money on the table. My advice? Get over it! Leaving money on the table beats getting caught in a short squeeze.

Indicators

+ *Volume*: As previously explained, volume may vary on falling stocks, but in this setup, high volume (panicky selling) squashes the stock faster, giving you a multiple-point profit in a short time period
+ *Moving averages*: Stock will be trading high above 20-day MA and all other major MAs
+ *RSI*: Oversold
+ *OBV*: Falling
+ *Bollinger Bands*: Stock touching or approaching upper band, but unable to penetrate it

SHORTING STRATEGY: THE OVEREXTENDED DOUBLE TOP

Shorting the rally to resistance that *may* develop into a double-top reversal pattern represents virtually the same setup as the overextended stock.

Again, target a stock that's soared in a moonshot uptrend, thus becoming highly overextended. You may even have spotted the stock when it made its first overextended high. It returns to support, then bounces, forming the middle pivot point. Then it resumes its upward thrust. The previous high acts as resistance (supply), and buyers once again refuse to pay higher prices.

At the first sign of weakness—assuming all other signals flash "go"—sell short and set your buy-to-cover stop-loss as previously discussed. Indicator readings remain the same as for the overextended top setup.

The next three charts, Figures 12-4, 12-5, and 12-6 illustrate the overextended shorting setup and the double top shorting setup.

> **Hot Tip**
>
> Don't hang onto a crashing stock for too long a time period. When you have a multiple-point profit—and hear yourself making oinking noises—take your money and run!

Remember, since double tops are reversal patterns, you don't have to sell short the tops or pivots. A viable setup may occur for swing/position trades when the final move down to support (to the middle pivot of the "M") can't hold, and the stock catapults into a downtrend.

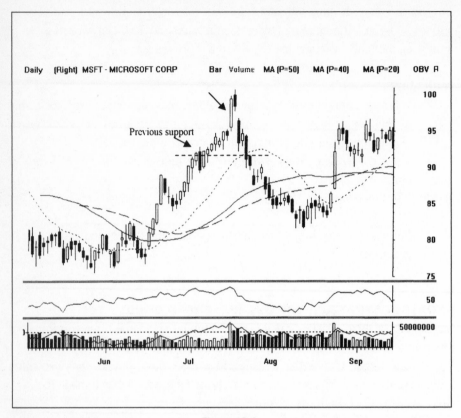

Figure 12-4.

On this daily chart of Microsoft Corp. (MSFT), notice how this tech stock moved almost straight up from mid-June to mid-July. On July 16, MSFT gapped open one point, at 95.50, and climbed on climactic volume to a high of 100. Look how it soared nearly ten points over its 20-day MA (arrow)! When you are watching a stock that's this overextended, wait for weakness to enter. The next trading day, July 19, MSFT opened at 100, rose to 100.75, and then started falling to a low of 97.75. When it fell below the previous day's close, 99.50, short-sellers could have entered for a swing trade with a tight stop-loss at 101. The next day, July 20, MSFT gapped down two points and fell to a low of 96.50, plunging through its 20-day MA. Watch for previous support from early July, in the area of 92. MSFT finally fell to a low of 81.63 by August 10. Then it started to recover.

As an aside, there's a lesson on Figure 12-4 pertinent to those holding MSFT on the long side. Say you bought MSFT in mid-June, when it broke into an uptrend. On July 16, it flew to the new high on climactic volume and traded in nosebleed territory far above its 20 MA. That's your signal to take profits. First, things that go straight up, come straight down. Second, the price of 100 is a huge psychological target. Stocks that hover above 100, then soon drop back below it, tend to trend lower for the short-term, and maybe longer.

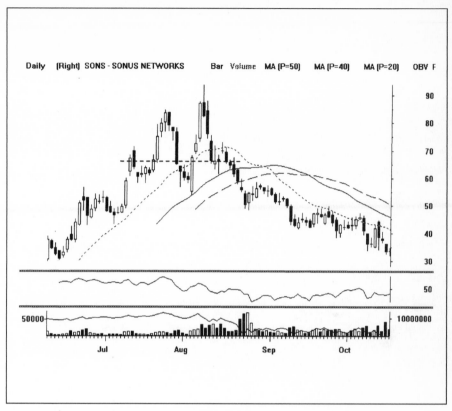

Figure 12-5.

On this daily chart of Sonus Networks (SONS), note the double top. The first top took place on July 25, as SONS hit a high of 85, trading 17 points above its 20-day MA! On August 8, it shot to a high of 94, trading 14 points over its 20-day MA. That day presented a good shorting opportunity, as SONS continued to fall for three days in a row—the maximum amount of time I recommend holding a short swing trade. By the end of the day on August 10, beaten-up SONS fell to a low of 65.33, nearing previous support and a multiple-point profit. Time to take your gains and run!

Of course, there were more shorting opportunities during this stock's downtrend for savvy short-sellers. Can you identify them?

SELL SHORT TRIGGER LIST

Here's a Sell Short Trigger List. Some of the points on it may appear redundant. Still, variables abound when you're selling short, so this will act also as a summary. While every single item on the list may not apply when you enter the trade, try to check off as many as possible. Remember, the more odds you corral into your corner before you pull the trigger, the lower your risk and the fatter your wallet.

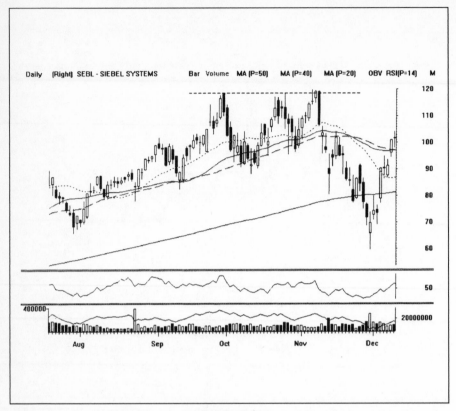

Figure 12-6.

This daily chart of volatile tech stock Siebel Systems (SEBL) shows a dandy triple top, with all three tops overextended. Poor SEBL subsequently fell 50 percent from those highs. If a double-top pattern formation is negative, a triple top can be lethal! Notice how up until the final top occurred in November, SEBL neatly walked up its 50-day MA. Once it fell through that moving average, however, the party was over. The fall was a volatile one, which brings up a lesson: Downtrends are usually more volatile and disorderly than uptrends. If you sell short a volatile stock like SEBL, stay in only a brief period of time, so you don't get caught in a short squeeze.

On the third topping formation, once SEBL made it clear it couldn't establish a new high, short-sellers could have entered right below the previous day's low of 119.31 with a tight stop-loss at 120.

Here it is:

1. Market conditions, Dow and/or Nasdaq, are negative.
2. Target stock is a lagging company in a depressed industry. (Exception: In bear markets, leading stocks may fall fastest.)
3. Poor company fundamentals.
4. Industry/sector is in a downtrend and negative on entry day.

5. Stock has formed a Stage Three rollover and is cracking support, or is experiencing a downtrend on a daily chart. Or, it is highly overextended and suffering an exhaustion gap or breakdown.

6. Strong volume on the breakdown is best, but not always absolutely necessary.

7. Stock is trading under major moving averages, and cannot penetrate them. Or, stock is overextended, trading high over 20-day MA (swing trade only).

8. RSI is above 70, and hooking down, or is etching a downtrend. (It is not oversold.)

9. The OBV is falling, or in a downtrend.

10. Target stock is trading below its opening price and moving down on the day. General sell-short signal: stock trades .25 to .50 below support, or yesterday's low.

SHORTING TIPS: FAQS (FREQUENTLY ASKED QUESTIONS)

What if my target stock gaps down at the market open, taking out my entry price? When a stock you're waiting to short gaps down more than .50 at the open, wait 15–30 minutes before you sell it short to make sure it won't fill that gap and move higher. Then short .25, or so (don't chase!), below the first 30-minute low.

Can we short the pullbacks of a stock climbing in an uptrend? Sure. If you get your jollies burning adrenaline by the gallon. I don't, however, recommend shorting strong stocks. Major reason: short squeeze.

Definition of a short squeeze: Say you're short Stealthy Software. The Nasdaq is weak, the computer software sector is weak, and Stealthy falls obligingly. Suddenly, the Nasdaq makes a U-turn and rockets upward. Stealthy screeches to a halt, finds support, then shoots up. Short sellers buy frantically, attempting to cover their positions.

Now, buyers are buying. Short sellers are buying. With little supply on the market (sell orders) to slow its ascent, the stock screams straight up. Short sellers who fail to recognize early warning signs of the stock's reversal give back profits and/or lose money, as they chase the stock up multiple price levels to cover, thus getting "squeezed."

So, while getting squeezed by your honey is fun, getting caught in a short squeeze is no fun at all. And that's most likely to happen when you short a stock in an uptrend, where the stock is strong and its overall bias is to the upside.

Can we hedge our account by selling short? You betcha. There's lots of ways to hedge, but here's a simple one. Go to *www.holdrs.com*. HOLDRS are stocks traded on the Amex, and each represents a basket of stocks in a certain sector. A dandy feature of the HOLDRS is that they can be sold short on a downtick.

Now, click on "HLDRS Outstanding" and check out the sectors. Say you are long a position trade of 300 shares of Comverse Technology, Inc. (CMVT), a broadband stock. The stock is nowhere near your stop-loss point. Still, the broadband sector is pulling back and looks like it may continue down for a few days. You can sell short the BDH (broadband HOLDRS) for the duration of the pullback, then cover the short at the first signs of sector recovery. That way, you haven't lost money during the correction, and in fact, you've added to your profits! (Caveat: Some HOLDRS trade on small volume. Only trade those with volume of one million shares a day or more, to keep risk low.)

Other index stocks you can short on a downtick:

+ DIA (Diamonds Trust Series 1 Index) represents the Dow Jones Industrial Index.
+ SPY (Standard & Poor's Depositary Receipts) represents the S&P 500 Index.
+ QQQ (Nasdaq 100 Trust Series 1 Index) represents the Nasdaq 100.

As you can see, you don't have to target a single sector. You can sell short the SPY (called "Spiders" by traders), which represents a broad index, in this case the S&P 500.

I hope you've enjoyed this selling short learning marathon. In the next chapter, you'll experience an actual trade, step-by-step. And congratulate yourself. You're well on the way to becoming a knowledgeable trader!

QUIZ

1. Why do stocks tend to move down three times faster than they rise?
2. When you're new to selling short, what two preventatives can help you avoid bleeding ulcers?
3. Define the uptick rule.
4. What's a "downtick"?
5. True or false? All stocks traded on the major exchanges can be sold short.
6. When you issue an order to sell short, you are selling a stock you don't own. Where do the shares come from?
7. Give one reason a stock might serve as a good shorting candidate.
8. When targeting a fast-falling stock that may not experience an uptick for several points, how can you raise the odds of getting your order filled?
9. When scanning for a stock to short for a position trade, or initial swing trade, name one pattern to identify.

10. As a position trader who entered a short trade when the stock initiated a downtrend, where is the most likely place you will cover the short and take profits?
11. When scanning for an overextended stock to sell short, what are some of the first signs to recognize?
12. Assuming all signals for a shorting setup are in place, when do you enter your order to sell short a stock experiencing a double top?
13. What should the RSI reading be for the ideal shorting setup?
14. In the best shorting setup, where should the OBV be heading?

ANSWERS

1. Stocks move down faster than they rise because fear and panic are stronger than greed.
2. When new at shorting, trade small lot sizes, such as 50–100 shares, and only trade slow-moving, high-volume stocks. NYSE stocks can be ideal candidates.
3. The uptick rule states that you can sell short only on an uptick or zero-plus tick. You cannot sell short on a downtick.
4. A stock creates a downtick when it trades an increment lower than the previous trade.
5. False.
6. To sell a stock short, you borrow the shares from your broker.
7. The company announces bad news or earnings.
8. You can short a weak, fast-falling stock *as it falls through support*, rather than waiting for it to trade below support.
9. Look for a stock experiencing a Stage Three rollover and ready to fall into a Stage Four downtrend. A head-and-shoulders pattern is ideal.
10. When the stock breaks the downtrend by making a higher high.
11. Enter your order to sell short when your target stock slides a fraction of a point below support. For fast-moving stocks, enter your order *as* the stock falls through support.
12. The best overextended shorting candidates should be: experiencing a *steep* uptrend; trading *high* above their 20-day MAs on a daily chart; correlate with their industry group or sector as being very overbought.
13. For the best shorting setup, the RSI should read over 70, and/or be hooking down (not in oversold territory, under 30).
14. Down, down, down.

✦ ✦ ✦

CENTER POINT

Our deepest fear is not that we are inadequate. Our deepest fear is that we are powerful beyond measure.

—MARIANNE WILLIAMSON

Banish Fear and Let Your Light Shine

In Western civilization, we are taught almost from birth to disown our unique talents. Our culture dictates that people who "blow their own horns" are cocky and conceited. They are "egotists" with "big heads."

We take the admonition to heart. Not only do we deny praise when we receive it, we discount and depress our God-given talents, even to ourselves. Over and over, we play our personal mind-tape that reminds us that we're not as good, smart, or attractive as others. No wonder we're so reluctant to put our visions in motion. We constantly come from, dwell in, and paint our perspectives with fear.

Fear is a state of mind that stops us from revealing our unique, authentic selves. It handcuffs us to our trumped-up limitations and thwarts us from touching, tasting, and learning from all the exciting possibilities available to us.

Our fear encompasses anyone, and anything, outside our comfort zone. We strap blinders around our own eyes, avoid risk, say "ain't it awful" to anyone who will listen and agree, and set out to prove why the circumstances in our lives detain us—even stop us—from realizing our dreams.

Somewhere along the way, we've forgotten that *we choose how the world treats us.* We create our own canvas. We can paint our lives with brushstrokes full of angst and fear—or joy, love, and fulfillment. Either way, we'll experience what we've chosen!

How can we climb out of this mental and emotional morass of fear? Charles Dubois says, "The important thing is to be able at any moment to sacrifice what you are for what you could become."

We must surrender our old ways of seeing and experiencing ourselves. The moment "I can't do that" escapes our thoughts and/or our lips, try replacing it with, "*I can do that*, and wow—is it ever going to be fun!"

Let's banish fear, and focus on the truth of our being: We are bright lights evolving and unfolding toward our highest potentiality. Our talents give us the tools to reach that potentiality. Let's polish them, and then shine them on every area of our lives!

✦ ✦ ✦

CHAPTER 13

Anatomy of a Trade

> *When a man makes his play in a . . . market, he must not permit himself set opinions. He must have an open mind and flexibility.*
>
> —JESSE LIVERMORE

When you read a trading book or take a class, it's easy for the instructor, myself included, to point to a chart and say, "If you'd been trading this stock, you would have bought here, at this setup, and sold it here." Sounds easy, yet many times the actual journey from the entry to exit feels far less effortless!

From the moment you buy to the moment you sell (or vice versa), your stock, its sector, and the market thrashes around. You weigh a zillion options in your mind.

"Heck, my stock's going down. So is its industry group. But the market's going up. What should I do?"

"Wow, my stock just flew through resistance! Maybe I'll take half my profits here. Or, maybe I should take them all. If I do, I might leave a ton of money on the table." (Quick glance toward the heavens.) "What should I *do*?"

"Yee-ooow. My stock's tanking! In another half-point, it's going to hit my sell-stop. And I can't find any bad news on the stock—so what's wrong with it? Should I wait for it to hit my stop, or get out now and save a half-point? Help!"

Maybe you sustain a small loss, or maybe you take home a chunky profit. Either way, you made lots of choices on the journey from start to finish.

In this chapter, you're going to experience a swing trading journey. Using actual charts, I'll show you the thoughts and the actions they triggered. You see the actual charts ahead of time. The written journal details each day's thoughts and actions and tells you what I would do in certain situations. Keep in mind that my style—my musings and decisions—will differ from yours, and from every other trader on the planet. Use them as guidelines.

FIND AN INDUSTRY GROUP OR SECTOR TO TARGET

Let's start with the assumption that you know the current mood of the market, including the NYSE and the Nasdaq. Financial television networks and other information sources will keep you updated on industry groups and sectors in the forefront of the market with statements such as, "Oil stocks and pharmaceuticals have taken center stage lately, while techs lagged."

So, pinpoint the industry group you want to target, and remember to use *if/then* logic to zero in on it. Then study each group's chart to find one that looks optimal. As mentioned earlier in the book, you'll want to have a list of industry groups and sectors assembled on a "watch list," with five or more leading stocks in each.

One simple way to start your watch list is to use the HOLDRS Trusts mentioned in Chapter 12. Again, go to *www.holdrs.com*. Click on "HOLDRS Outstanding." You'll see a list of HOLDRS stocks, traded on the Amex, that represent sectors. When you click on each HOLDRS, you will find its component stocks listed. Sectors include software, telecom, Internet architecture, pharmaceuticals, biotechs, regional banks, oil services, and more.

On Fridays, *IBD* publishes "Weekend Review," a list of top-performing stocks listed by Industry Group Relative Strength Ratings, providing another great source from which to start and maintain your watch list. In addition, some end-of-day charting software programs offer leading stocks in leading sectors.

Finally, go to my Web site, *www.toniturner.com*, and click on "Sectors + Stocks." You will find a regularly updated roster of sectors and leading stocks that reside in them. This is a complimentary service for my readers. Enjoy!

THE PREPARATION

Now, let's take a specific example:

Trading time span: January 20 to February 22 (2000). (The actual dates of this trade are unimportant. What *is* important are price patterns, interaction of the stock and related indexes, and the actions taken to keep losses small and gains high.)

Sector: Networking. The index we'll watch in conjunction with stock movement is the $NWX.X, the Networking Index.

Stock: Juniper Networks, Inc. (JNPR), a company that provides Internet infrastructure solutions (routers) for ISPs (Internet Service Providers) and other telecommunications providers. Since we'll be looking at the time frame in January–February 2000, and those fundamentals from *IBD* are past, we'll assume JNPR's rankings were propitious.

The reason I chose this sector and stock is that the $NWX.X and JNPR rose in a shallow, yet steady and orderly uptrend in the months previous to these trades. (An orderly basing pattern would have been optimal as well.) The Nasdaq 100 Index also rose in a healthy uptrend, with no signs of slowing, the perfect environment for swing and position trading. Figures 13-1, 13-2, and 13-3 show the $NWX.X, JNPR, and the Nasdaq 100 Index during the overall time period in which the trades occurred.

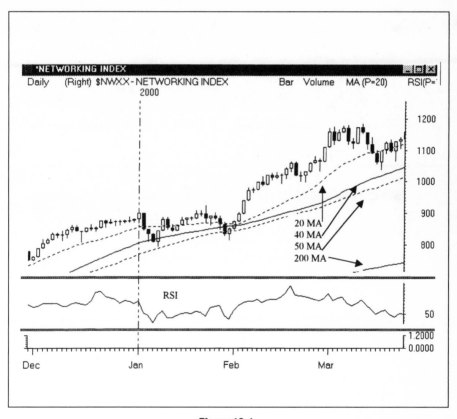

Figure 13-1.

As you can see on this daily chart of the NWX, it rose in a gentle uptrend in the months previous to the trade we're considering, corrected during the first part of January to its 50-day MA. It rose to resistance during mid-January, and then once again fell to retest support at the 50-day MA.Then it took off with the rest of the Nasdaq to soar through February. Notice how the RSI starts falling in mid-February, heading lower as the index soars higher—a bearish divergence. As a savvy trader, you would have seen this happen and by the end of February, you would have sat safely on the sidelines. The RSI eventually proved correct.

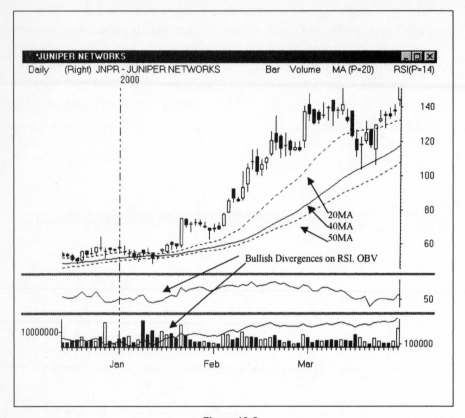

Figure 13-2.

This daily chart of Juniper Networks, Inc. (JNPR) shows it to be stronger than the NWX (where it resides), during the correlating time period. Notice the tight base coming into January—an optimum, flat base. "Flat" bases usually don't form reversal patterns, such as double bottoms or cup-with-handles. They simply move sideways, fluctuating no more than 10 to 15 percent. Compact bases such as these create awesome opportunities for swing and position traders. Notice the increased volume during the second and third week of January, while the stock stayed relatively flat. That volume rise signals accumulation. Also check out the bullish divergence on the RSI and OBV during the same time period. These converging signals all scream, "Pay attention. We're going to party hearty soon!" (JNPR had no 200-day MA during this time period, as the stock had not been on the market for long enough to establish this moving average.)

THE JOURNEY

January 18. It finally happened! After watching the Networking Index move up nicely for the past couple of months, I've targeted Juniper Networks, Inc. (JNPR), which has crept sideways in a tight base. Today the stock penetrated resistance. The recent high of the base is approximately 58.90, so I set my entry point at $59. The NWX (Networking Index) surged as well, showing strength in that sector and closing at the high of the day, 885. The Nasdaq 100 Index also closed near the highs of the day, at 3705 (all indexes are rounded to the closest whole number).

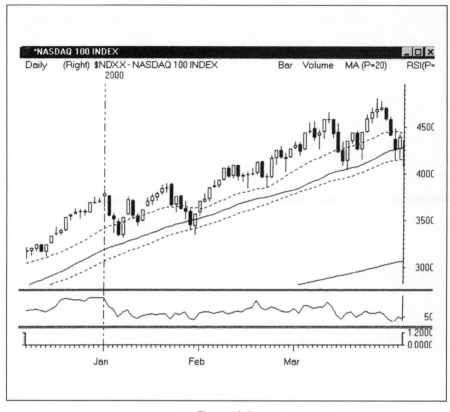

Figure 13-3.

Notice the similarities between this chart of the Nasdaq 100 Index and Figure 13-1, the chart of the Networking Index. Here, the NDX also neatly walks up its moving averages, moving back to the 50-day MA when it dips. Until March, when the index shows signs of shooting into overextended territory (notice the bearish divergence of the RSI in March: While the NDX makes new highs, the RSI falls—a BIG warning to traders/investors), the NDX climbs in a neat and orderly uptrend. This provides a dandy climate for swing and position trading.

Soon after the stock rose through resistance on high volume, I bought 300 shares of JNPR at $59.15. I placed my temporary stop-loss order at 56.50, below yesterday's *close* of 57.15. That gives it enough room to wiggle, and I'll move the stop up tomorrow, as soon as (if) JNPR moves higher. JNPR is a volatile stock, so setting the stop-loss *too* close invites getting stopped out. Also, these days, market makers enjoy pushing stocks *way* below round numbers. They know a truckload of stop-losses wait just under those numbers a quarter of a point or so. (After the market makers buy the stock from the "weak hands" who get flushed out, the stock can bounce again. Then the market makers sell it to players at higher prices, pocketing the spread).

JNPR's next resistance is a high set on December 28 at 64.06.

Rise/reward ratio: Risk–2 points (59.15 minus 57.15). Possible reward: nearly 5 points (64.06 minus 59.15). So ratio equals 1:2.50.

Once 64.06 is penetrated, there's nothing but blue sky above! Plus, the daily chart looks awesome. The stock's sitting on the 20-day MA, and breaking out of a dandy base. The RSI etched a recent bullish divergence, and the OBV is moving up nicely on increased volume. JNPR closes near the high of the day at 59.38, a good sign.

See Figures 13-4, 13-5, and 13-6 for close-ups of current action.

Each set of arrows points to a single trade. The first arrow points to the day I bought JNPR. The second arrow points to the day I sold it.

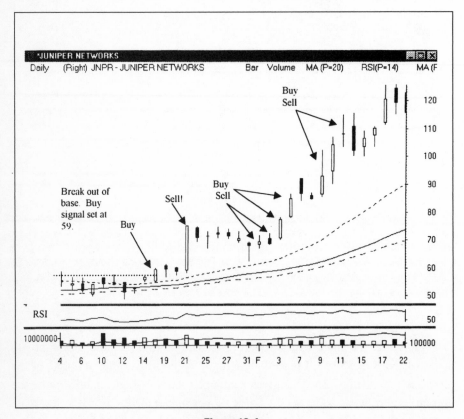

Figure 13-4.

When you're watching a base for an entry point, draw a horizontal trendline over the tops of the highs. Then, assuming all other trigger signals are "go," set your buy price .13 to .25 over the resistance high. (This is number 1 in the 1-2-3 setup.) To see how the chart looks on the entry day, just cover the right side of this chart with a blank piece of paper, up to January 18. Then move it a day at a time, to see how the progression takes place.

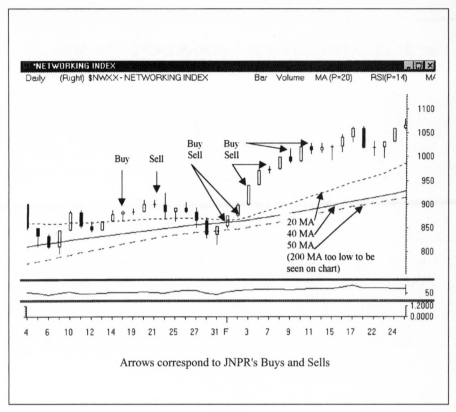

Figure 13-5.

This close-up of the daily of the Networking Index chart shows a double bottom. Do you see it? (Hint: Check out pivot points on January 7 and 31.) Notice how the NWX is sitting on its 20-day MA the day of the buy signal, appearing ready to shoot through resistance. Although the 20-day MA is moving sideways on that day, the 40- and 50-day MAs were rising, which is a positive sign. From January 31 through February 11, when we close our trades, the NWX rose nicely, and then became overextended.

January 19. JNPR gaps open to 60.88. The NWX opens even with yesterday's close, and the Nasdaq 100 Index gaps open big-time, some 36 points. JNPR rises to 61.25, and I'm about to raise my stop-loss higher, when it falls to 56.82. I admit to holding my breath. By the end of the day, the NWX forms a doji, which is neutral in the sideways move it's making. The Nasdaq 100 Index is again positive on the day. JNPR bounces off its daily low to close at 59.50. My trade is still in positive territory. I exhale.

January 20. JNPR opens at 60.25, gapping open .75. The NWX opens even, then starts drawing an uptrend on the day. The Nasdaq 100 Index gaps open and also trends to the upside.

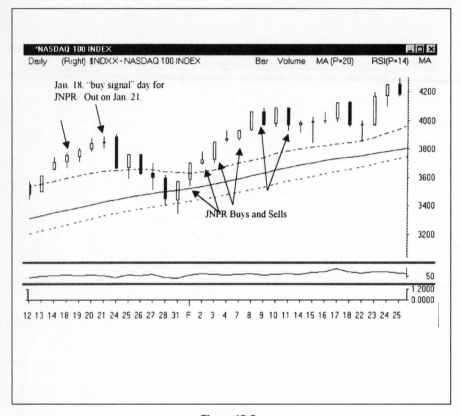

Figure 13-6.

The Nasdaq 100 Index is healthy on January 18, the day we bought a position in Juniper Networks, Inc. (JNPR). It closed near the high of the day, a positive sign. By the time the Nasdaq closed with a near-doji on January 21, it was time to take profits on JNPR. Good thing, because on January 24, the Nasdaq fell. JNPR, however, didn't fall as violently—a sign of possible future strength. From January 31 through the remainder of our trades, the Nasdaq 100 Index rose in an orderly uptrend, providing a great trading environment.

C'mon, JNPR, *move.* I decide to raise my stop-loss to 57. Seconds later, the stock falls to 57.44. Wince. Trading is a real character-builder!

JNPR closes at 58.47, just a little more than .50 away from my buy point. I'm not a happy camper, but my stop-loss is higher. If tomorrow looks dicey, even if JNPR *doesn't* hit my stop-loss, I may take my profits and go elsewhere.

January 21. JNPR gaps open again, this time to 59.07. The NWX opens almost even, then heads up. The Nasdaq 100 opens even and heads up as well. However, the perverse JNPR slides down to close the gap down to yesterday's close, and a little more. Oooh, boy. When the stock finally *does* bounce at 58.25, I decide I've built enough character. With the NWX and Nasdaq 100 Index moving up on the day, this doggoned stock may struggle back to my buy price. Then, I'll happily provide some of that "supply" we traders talk about.

JNPR cooperates and crawls up to its open. Just as I'm ready to pull the plug, the stock laughs and shoots skyward. Up, up, and away, it scrambles past 59.50, to 60, to 65. I raise my stop-loss to 60. I'm not giving these profits back. No way, José! Obviously JNPR issued good news.

I'll check a news Web site in a moment, but first, I take a quick look at the daily chart. On its biggest days to date, JNPR trades in a five-point range. More than that is a big deal, so this move is *huge*. The RSI jabs into serious overbought territory. I didn't just fall off the turnip truck. I'll take profits before the close.

By the end of the day, moon-shot JNPR soars to an all-time high of 75.09. As the market close approaches, I take my profits, exiting at 74.30. Once the trade is closed, I pull out my calculator: $4,540 profit after commissions.

I know better, however, than to confuse brains with a rocketing stock. Sure, I entered at the proper point, and all signals were "go." And, yes, I always stick to my stop-loss point. But I've traded enough to know how fast stocks rocket, then crash, with little or no warning. Today, Mother Market smiled on me.

January 24. It's Monday, and I'm curious to see how JNPR will treat the new week after the glorious run-up on Friday. I'm going to monitor the stock's likely pull-back. Maybe another entry point will show up in a few days, although JNPR's now overextended and will have to come in quite a few points to present a good setup.

The stock opens at 74.32, struggles to a high of 74.88, then falls to a low of 69.41 before closing at 70.69. Hmm. After Friday's huge run-up, I imagined it would fall harder. Looking at Friday's long candlestick reminds me that *many time stocks find support (or resistance) in the middle of extended real bodies*. Quick calculations reveal the candlesticks' midpoint at about 66.

I note the NWX makes a run up, penetrating resistance and the high for the (calendar) year of 900.79, but closes lower on the day, as does the Nasdaq 100 Index.

January 25. My mid-candlestick calculations worked well. JNPR traded sideways on the day, closing in a near doji (indecision). Guess what the low of the day was? Yup, 67. Neat trick, huh?

January 26, 27, and 28. I wait for the remainder of the week for JNPR to sink back to its 20-day MA, but no dice. Instead, it consolidates, moving sideways and forming a flag. What a strong stock! Still, JNPR's way overextended and no setup appears, so I rein in my impatience and wait. By Friday, January 28, it drifts lower. Finally. By next week another money-making opportunity should present itself with this powerhouse networking stock. (If not, I have others in my sights.)

January 31. All ri-ight! JNPR cracks to the downside, dipping to nearly touch the 20-day MA. The Nasdaq 100 Index retraced quite a bit the week before and today tumbles past its 50-day MA. That's not a good thing. Let's see if it bounces. The NWX falls a bit less, but still below its 50-day MA, where institutional buyers should step in.

The NWX ends the day with a low of 815, nearing support of the last low of 797 formed on January 7. Tomorrow will be crucial. End-of-day chart shows JNPR finished in a hammer. That's bullish. If the NWX and Nasdaq 100 Index bounce tomorrow, I'll enter JNPR in a swing trade if she moves over today's high of 69.32, on strong volume. Entry: 69.50.

February 1. JNPR opens at 68.19. The RSI started making a bullish divergence a couple of days ago. The OBV is trending up. The NWX gapped open and started trending higher. The Nasdaq 100 Index is positive on the day. I have to leave for an appointment, so I enter a "buy stop" with my online broker to buy 400 shares of JNPR at $69.50. I'll check with the broker later to see if my order gets filled. If it does, I'll set my stop-loss just under the low of the day.

I realize JNPR has resistance from the gaps down, or "falling windows." The first resistance zone it has to penetrate formed from the close of January 28 of 70.38, to yesterday's open of 69. The next waits just a bit higher, from the close of January 27 at 71.22, to the open of January 28 at 69.50, which is smaller and less than a point. Finally, JNPR will have to penetrate resistance of recent (all-time) highs in the 75 area to once again find blue skies.

That day, my order to buy JNPR was filled at 69.55. The low of the day remains relatively close at 67.10, so I place my stop-loss at 66.50.

February 2. JNPR gaps open to 70.50, an auspicious beginning. The NWX opens even, dips slightly, then powers up. The Nasdaq 100 follows suit. Yeessss! It's gonna be another awesome day.

As I watch, however, strong volume doesn't come into JNPR. And, low volume equals failed breakouts. It starts trading lower, dropping to 68.50. Oh, boy. Here comes another character-building trade.

When it becomes evident JNPR intends to close at the low of the day, which many times portends a gap down the following morning (that may stop me out). I sell my position with only seconds left to the closing bell. Out at 68.58. That's a loss of .93 per share, or approximately $392, including commissions. Rats.

Why did I sell? With the NWX moving up today, JNPR should have risen as well. The Nasdaq 100 Index moved up a bit, but also weakened to close barely above the low of the day. Not good.

Yesterday, when I bought JNPR, the stock looked strong, but by the end of the day, volume tapered off. Another negative sign. I've adhered to the old trader saying, "When in doubt, get out." If the stock rebounds, and the new setup meets my Buy Triggers, I'll buy it back.

February 3. The bell rings and I smile wryly, mildly amused that JNPR rockets out of the open by gapping up two-and-a-half points, to open at 70.57—

without me, of course. The NWX opens and screams straight up. The Nasdaq 100 Index gaps to the upside, dips a little, then flies!

Under my breath, I mumble, "Double rats."

Stop. Wrong mindset. I quickly brush off the regret at selling the day before. I made best decision possible given the information at hand, a decision that involved protecting my principal. Besides, regret colors perception. I quickly shift gears to a clear, sharp mentality fueled by positive energy.

I wait to see if JNPR fills the gap up, but it only dips one-quarter point before surging up on extremely strong volume. I wait until it passes yesterday's high of 72.41, then buy 400 shares at 72.50. (An alternative buy point occurred when JNPR traded above its first 30-minute high, a gap-open tactic; see Chapter 9.) I set my stop-loss just under the day's low of 70.25 at 69.50.

As the day unfolds, JNPR races through all recent resistance, breaking to new highs. The NWX follows suit. All indexes, including the Dow, S&P 500 Index, Nasdaq 100, and Nasdaq Composite soar. JNPR's RSI and OBV continue to sail up on the daily chart. What a party!

When the stock torpedoes past its previous all-time high of 75.09, I add 200 additional shares to my position, fill price: 75.30.

JNPR's volume ends the day at nearly nine-million shares, more than double the average daily volume. I move my stop-loss to previous support of 75, and the stock closes out the day at 77.47. There's one thing for sure about trading. It's never, ever dull!

February 4. JNPR gaps up a half-point at the open and never looks back. I tow my stop-loss up behind the giddy—and powerful—stock. The NWX shoots up for most of the day, pulling back slightly at the close. Encountering resistance from January, the Nasdaq 100 Index trends up on the day, yet penetrates 3,874.

As the market nears the close, JNPR again hits a new high, 86.47. Although the stock is still screaming to the upside, I decide to close the trade and sell at 85.

Reasons to exit (besides hefty gains): JNPR *and* the NWX are overextended on their daily charts. As I mentioned before, the Nasdaq 100 Index bumped into resistance, a high of 3,905 established on January 24. Intra-day, the burly Nasdaq index popped to 3,929, but is closing the day near its lows. That resistance could easily push it lower, tomorrow.

Also, JNPR has gapped up three days in a row. Volume dropped off a bit from yesterday. It will surely gap open to the upside Monday morning, as it closed near the high of the day today, on good volume. I may leave some money on the table, but we know what happens to little piggies who go to market!

Current trade profit, minus commissions: $6,900. I'm a happy camper.

February 7. Talk about leaving money on the table! JNPR leers at me, and then flies out of the open, gapping up seven points to 92.07. I itch to buy more, but my discipline won't allow me to place the order. I've learned the hard way: Careless trades shrink profits. I shut down my computer and head for the beach.

February 9. JNPR pulled back the last two days. On February 7, it moved down on the day, and yesterday it gapped down and finished in a narrow-range day—a sign of market participants' indecision.

Today it gaps open a little more than a point, to 86.25. Although the stock is still overextended, it looks muscular after its rest. The RSI is rising, as is the OBV, on good volume. All moving averages surge upward. The NWX looks strong on the day, and heads for a new high early on. The Nasdaq 100 doesn't look quite as hearty, but it's holding.

When JNPR passes yesterday's high of 87.07, I buy a limited lot of 200 shares, entering at 87.30. I set a tight stop-loss at 85.50, just under the day's low. The tech stock shows no fear, shooting to another new high of 102.35. By the day's close, however, it pulls back to 93. The NWX loses vitality, and the Nasdaq 100 Index closes near the lows of the day. Strong stock or not, I'm glad to be holding only a minimal position.

February 10. JNPR gaps open a point-and-a-half to the upside, at 94.50. It drops to 90.32, filling the gap, then zooms, missile-like, to 107. I raise my stop-loss to 100 (if it drops back through 100, it may fall hard), then watch in awe. The NWX hurtles to a new, all-time high of 1,021, just topping the previous day's high of 1,016. The Nasdaq 100 Index also makes a new record high of 4,090. Life is good. Maybe too good. A few minutes before the close, I sell half my position, 100 shares, at 104.

February 11. JNPR gaps up at the open to 108.03. It's the third day to gap up in a row—again!—and I'm taking no chances. The NWX is struggling to hold ground, and the Nasdaq 100 looks dicey. I issue an order to sell my 100 remaining shares, and I'm out at 107.50.

I exit for these reasons: On the NWX and Nasdaq 100 Index daily charts, the RSI shows a slight curl to the downside, the possible beginning of a bearish divergence. Both indexes are overextended. JNPR is also overextended and highly overbought, with the RSI pushing 90. I'd rather sell when everyone's still buying, than get flattened in a stampede of sellers. Even with my small share size, I reap profits of $4,370, after commissions.

Undaunted, JNPR flies up to 115, making yet another new high. By the end of the day, though, JNPR closes in a doji, a sure sign that indecision has set in. I'm doubly glad I decided to sell. The stock also traded as much as 32 points above its 20-day MA. Surely JNPR will get a nosebleed from trading at such heights, and soon!

I'll consider entering JNPR again, when it pulls back to its 20-day MA, and not sooner. In the meantime, I'll search for another stock just breaking out of its base.

THE REST OF THE STORY . . .

Juniper Networks, Inc. (JNPR) finally topped out during the week of October 15, 2000, at 244.50! Soon after, the mighty tech stock suffered a much more violent malaise than a nosebleed. It tumbled into a volatile downtrend with the rest of the market.

Figure 13-7 shows a weekly chart of JNPR. You can see how the stock crashed to its lows (as of this writing) during the week of April 1, 2001. The price? $28.60, just a few dollars above its initial offering price of 20.99 in June 1998!

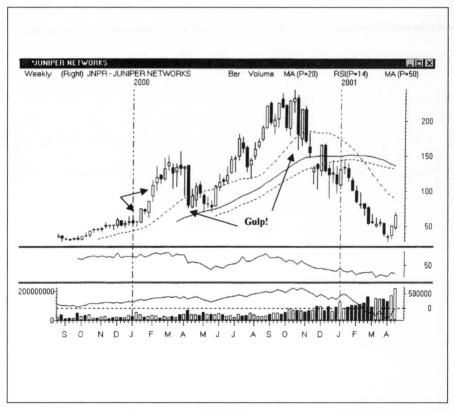

Figure 13-7.

This weekly chart of Juniper Networks, Inc. (JNPR) shows a stock that made a complete cycle, while it took traders for a roller coaster ride! Our swing trades took place between the arrows. After that, the fires blazed hotter! Look at the week of April 9, where JNPR fell from a high of 137 to a low of 76. And check out the week of October 22, when it crumbled from 237 to 160. Talk about heart-stopping!

The lesson here is this: As the bear market of 2001 has taught us, stocks don't rise forever. In these roller coaster markets that show no signs of quieting, while it's good to recognize the proper entry for a position, it's more important to know when to get out. Can you imagine being an investor who bought JNPR at the high, then held to its low?

The JNPR trade used as an example profited from a steep uptrend. As you know, *most stocks do not soar so high, so fast, delivering such gargantuan profits.*

My goal was for you to witness extreme volatility, and observe how to weigh the actions of relative indexes with stock movement.

Surely, skilled traders who participated in JNPR's uptrend as we did took home hefty profits. Those who continued to trade JNPR as it gyrated through February and March, however, would have gotten stopped out several times over and given back a portion of the gains. During that time, the stock's uptrend changed character from accommodating to acrimonious. When a stock changes character—and they all do—seek profits elsewhere.

A QUICK LOOK AT INTRA-DAY CHARTS

While we're looking at the anatomy of a trade, this brief section is included for those who wish to maintain a closer watch on their positions and see how intra-day charts appear in comparison to daily charts.

Figure 13-8 shows a daily chart of Corning, Inc (GLW). Figure 13-9 zooms in for a close-up of the most recent 33 days on that chart. Figure 13-10 puts the most recent 19 days under a microscope, using an intra-day, 60-minute chart. Intra-day charts reveal how a stock moves through its trading range during the course of a day.

Some swing and position traders prefer using intra-day charts, such as the 60-minute (or even a briefer time frame) to enter and exit trades.

While entering and exiting using intra-day signals presents a valid trading technique, since you may enter trades earlier, the risk is higher. It's best to have experience under your belt when you attempt this exercise.

Savvy traders new to this scene "paper trade" for several trades before they plunk real cash on the line.

Because of the nature of the text in this chapter, there is no quiz to close it out. Before you get *too* comfortable, though, know that the quiz in the next chapter is a doozy!

Figure 13-8.

On this daily chart of Corning, Inc. (GLW), you can see how it fell in a downtrend, from a yearly high of 72.19 in January to a low of 18.19 in April. There, it etched a saucer, or rounded bottom, a bullish pattern. Note how it climbed over previous resistance to leave its base behind during the last three days of the month. This is a buy.

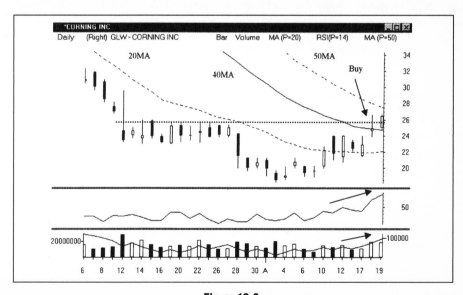

Figure 13-9.

This chart displays a close-up of the last thirty-three days of GLW's chart in Figure 13-8. Now it's easy to see the saucer formation that occurred the last of March and into April. You can also see the exact place where GLW gapped up and out of its base. Note the rising RSI and OBV and breakout on strong volume. Even though the stock's moving averages trend down from overhead, lots of market players recognized it as a buy.

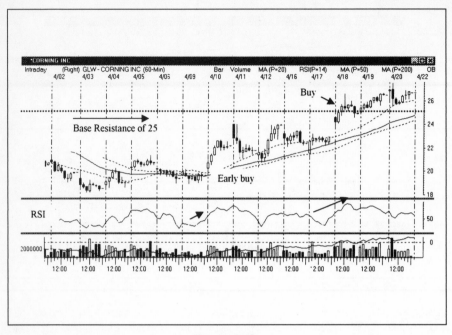

Figure 13-10.

This sixty-minute chart of GLW shows an "x-ray" of the most recent fourteen days of price action. (Remember, each candlestick represents an hour in the trading day.) Traders who use intra-day charts to enter swing and position trades might have been ready to pounce on GLW a bit earlier than those who use daily charts exclusively. Note how all the moving averages (20-, 40-, and 50-day) converge on April 6 and 9, and then the faster MAs (20- and 40-day) cross over the 50-day MA, a bullish signal. Also note the bullish divergence of the RSI on April 9, giving a clue that the stock may be ready to pop. The stock does just that on April 10. On April 11, it gaps up and tanks (note diving RSI) then gaps down slightly on April 12, and rises back to resistance of 24 from the day before. Note that once GLW rose over its moving averages, it only barely penetrated the 20-day MA to fall to the 40-day MA on April 12, and the 50-day MA on April 17. It bounced in both instances, a good sign. Check out how GLW gapped open on April 18 on this intra-day chart, then compare the same gap on the previous daily charts. Interesting, isn't it?

✦ ✦ ✦

CENTER POINT

And in our willingness to step into the unknown, the field of all possibilities, we surrender ourselves to the creative mind that orchestrates the dance of the universe.

—DEEPAK CHOPRA

Detachment Brings New Possibilities

One of the most exciting and rewarding concepts that leads to success in all areas of life remains one of the most challenging to understand: the theory of detachment.

Western civilization teaches us to attach ourselves to everything in our circle of existence. By attaching ourselves to people, places, and things, we supposedly attain an important goal: security. Trouble is, if these things disappear—and they often do—we are left with feelings of emptiness. Our so-called "security" is only smoke and mirrors.

As a consumer-driven, materialistic society, we Americans put great worth in the attainment of fancy cars, large homes, and impressive financial portfolios. While it may be fun to acquire these symbols of success, the problem arrives when we attach our sense of self-worth, our feelings of security, to these items.

We also attach feelings of security to the outcome of certain situations. In the financial markets, this can be disastrous in that it fosters the "need to be right." In other fields of endeavor, it can lead to noncreative, stagnant mindsets. Surely you've heard someone say, "We can't do it that way. We've never done it that way before." That attitude cancels other options that might result in a more effective course of action.

In practicing detachment, we become free, realizing *our security lies within each one of us.* As empowered spirits, we know innately how to fulfill every need. We also understand that cars, homes, and portfolios represent the manifestations of our desires.

When we become detached to the outcome of situations, we work with a vision in mind. Yet we stay open to new options and ideas that could produce greater outcomes than we, ourselves, envisioned.

Your security lies within you. Tune into the exhilaration that occurs when you're secure in your personal inner power, you step into a world of infinite possibilities.

✦ ✦ ✦

CHAPTER 14

You, the Wizard of Odds

But I can tell you after the market began to go my way I felt for the first time in my life that I had allies—the strongest and truest in the world: underlying conditions.

—JESSE LIVERMORE

In this chapter, we'll talk about big picture dynamics. You've learned from previous chapters how important it is to take overall market conditions into consideration when you plunk your money on the line. Now we'll define certain circumstances that take place regularly. You'll learn how to use them to your advantage and increase your skills as a successful trader.

BACK UP AND LOOK AT THE BIG PICTURE

When I was new to trading, I took a course from a crusty commodities trader who bellowed regularly, "Back up! Back up and look at the big picture!"

Maybe his delivery lacked charm, but it packed a verbal punch I've never forgotten. And, boy, was he right! You can find the perfect setup, enter at the perfect point, smile like a cat-in-cream while your stock heads for the stars, and then *whap!* You get blindsided. Something happens, like Fed Chairman Alan Greenspan appears on the financial networks and announces inflation lurking around the corner. *Eeeeuuuu klaboooooom!* (That's the sound of the financial markets crashing like a boulder off a cliff.)

Now, you, as an astute trader, had a trailing stop-loss set on your positions. Perhaps you read or heard that Mr. Greenspan was due to speak. You tightened your stop-losses to guard against any such reactions to his comments. If so, great—that's "big picture" thinking. Here are more ways to align your mindset so you profit from market dynamics.

THE "IF, THEN" MINDSET

In my previous book, *A Beginner's Guide to Day Trading Online,* I talked about cultivating an "if, then," mindset as it pertains to overall market conditions. That way of thinking is so important to your success as a trader it bears repeating.

Think: *"If* this happens, *then* that happens." Example: If Alan Greenspan comments that "inflation lies around the corner," it means the Federal Open Market Committee (FOMC) may consider raising interest rates at their next meeting to hold inflation in check. Simply put, higher interest rates mean companies pay more to borrow money. That lowers their earnings, which means lower stock valuations.

Additional "if, then" scenarios follow, tagged with this caveat: *remember that nothing "always" happens in the stock market.* While it's usually true that the price of gold and gold mining shares rise when stocks fall, it doesn't *always* happen, at least in the short-term. So consider the following as guidelines:

+ Gold and the U.S. dollar have an inverse relationship, which means the gold market figures importantly into inflationary environments and may act as a leading indicator to inflation. *If* the stock market tops looks toppy and overextended, *then* gold mining shares may provide a profitable play.

+ *If* the dollar is strong, *then* American products sold overseas cost more, and some pharmaceutical companies, retailers, and techs that export to foreign countries suffer. Conversely, we Americans can buy imported goods cheaper, so stocks like Ericsson Telephone and Toyota head north.

+ The Treasury bond market usually leads the stock market. (When the price of bonds rise, their yield or accompanying interest rate falls. When bonds fall, interest rates rise.) *If* bonds rise, *then* stocks rise. *If* bond prices fall, *then* the stock market may follow along.

+ Treasury bonds and the CRB (Commodity Research Bureau) Index have an inverse relationship. Falling commodity (e.g., soybeans, grains, metals, livestock, oil, cotton, coffee, sugar, and cocoa) prices can mean higher bond prices. *If* commodity prices fall, *then* bond and stock prices may rise.

+ *If* the price of bonds fall, and interest rates rise, *then* money may flow into cyclical stocks. (Companies with cyclical earnings aren't as dependent on interest rates; they include paper, aluminum, automobiles, some technology, and retailers.)

+ *If* bonds rise and interest rates fall, *then* interest-sensitive stocks like financial institutions and homebuilders move up. Lower interest rates mean banks pay less to borrow money, so the spread between the money they borrow and the money they lend widens. And, as interest rates fall, people buy new homes and refinance existing ones.

✦ *If* oil prices rise, *then* transportation stocks fall, and vice-versa. Why? Because high oil prices cause companies to pay more to deliver goods; in the case of the airlines, higher fuel prices means it costs more to deliver passengers to their destinations.

ANALYZE THE BROADER MARKETS

Every day or so, analyze daily and weekly charts of the Dow Jones Industrial Average (DJIA), the S&P 500 (SPX), and the Nasdaq 100 Index (NDX) or Composite (COMP). If your charting source doesn't list these indexes, use the DIA for the Dow, SPY for the S&P 500, and QQQ for the Nasdaq 100 Index.

Check out the overall picture of each. How is Mother Market feeling? As I've said before, "When Mama ain't happy, ain't nobody happy." Conversely, when her exchanges feel perky, she can give generously of her wealth.

Look at the broad index charts the same way you would a stock chart. Are they in uptrends, downtrends, or moving sideways in Stage One or Stage Three modes? Where is support and resistance? Are they overextended? Overbought? Oversold?

Correlate major market trends with your buy/sell decisions. *If* you're long a leading Nasdaq tech stock, and the Nasdaq 100 just reached into overextended, overbought territory, *then* take profits! *If* you're long a big bank stock and the Dow also teeters precariously high, *then* grab your gains. Many times, financial stocks lead the Dow higher or lower.

Also, monitor other indexes for possible market tops and bottoms. Say the oil index (XOI) sits at a major low, on support. (Oil is a commodity, remember?) Betcha my duck slippers that the broader stock indexes hover at their highs. (*If* oil prices dip to lows, *then* stock prices may be toppy.) Wouldn't it be a cool move to grab your gains and get a good seat on the sidelines? Then you can watch all the yelling and arm waving, as market players who weren't as savvy as you scramble for any exit they can find!

LEARN TO ASSESS THE TRADING ENVIRONMENT

We'll summarize a point here that you already know: It's important to evaluate the market environment to determine whether it's conducive to your trading style. To trade like a professional, learn which environments offer high reward/low risk scenarios, and which should be avoided.

First, let's revisit ye olde trader saying, "The trend is your friend." While that oft-repeated statement advises you to trade with the prevailing trend, it also advocates trading with a *trend in place*. In other words, sideways patterns don't extend a hand in friendship. When you hold stocks overnight in whippy, choppy, sideways markets, you *will* get slapped—hard.

As you know, sideways markets exist during Stage Ones and Stage Threes. Say the Nasdaq is basing in a Stage One. Breakouts to the upside and downside usually fail. Stocks that feel strong and bullish one day, gap down and whimper at their lows, the next. Result? Holding a stock overnight can prove disastrous.

Who makes money in these choppy sideways zones? Active traders who close out their trades at the end of each trading day, and long-term investors who bottom fish, set a tight stop-loss orders, and wait out the pain!

Obviously, when the major exchanges experience a Stage Two uptrend, traders in all time frames who catch the upswings on the long side, make out like rich kids in a candy store.

Short-sellers of all time frames thrive in the downdrafts produced by Stage Four downtrends.

Important note: *It's okay to be in cash.* The biggest traders in financial captivity don't trade everyday. Nor do they always hold stock positions in their portfolios. As a smart trader, you'll follow their lead.

If the market is in basing mode, or experiencing a frothy top, take your marbles and go home. These periods mean it's time to take your vacation. Trust me, no matter how much money you spend on entertainment or recreation, it won't begin to total your losses if you stick around and trade. How do I know? Because I've been there, done that . . . more than once. Took pictures, bought the entire T-shirt factory. And, watched the market swallow my money.

The bottom line is that during whippy markets, you should take some time off. You'll return refreshed and with money jingling in your pockets!

THE ADVANCE/DECLINE LINE: MARKET NARRATOR IN A CAPSULE

Remember sneaking peeks at CliffsNotes in college—those nifty summaries of Shakespearean plays and classic books? If you want to know the market's mood and manner in "CliffsNotes style," check out the Advance/Decline, or A/D Line. You'll find it displayed in financial newspapers or on Web sites.

The A/D Line (NYSE, Amex, and Nasdaq) is a line chart that measures the breadth of a stock market's advance or decline. Swing traders will want to stay updated on this indicator every few days. Position traders can monitor it weekly.

The A/D works like this: Each day, or week, the number of advancing issues is compared to the number of declining issues. When the advancers outnumber decliners, the total is added to the previous, overall total. When decliners outnumber advancers, the difference is subtracted from the total.

Compare the correlating A/D Line to the Dow, for example, or the Nasdaq Composite. Typically, they trend in the same direction. When we're approaching a market bottom or top, however, they may diverge. Then, read the A/D Line the same way you do an overbought/oversold oscillator. When the market heads lower, while the A/D Line bottoms and hooks up, it indicates a trend reversal in stocks may soon occur.

A "HEADS UP" ON ECONOMIC AND EARNINGS REPORTS

Trading will never rank at the top of the "comfortable occupations list." Just when you think you're safely ensconced in a pillow of profits, and you decide to exhale, economic reports or earnings news pop onto the horizon. And you'd best pay attention.

On CNBC and other financial networks, pundits spend a lot of time spewing out acronyms such as the "CPI," "GDP," and "PPI." These reports represent indicators that relate the overall health of the American economy.

A host of economic indicators come out each month, some quarterly. A few, like Non-farm Payrolls and the Unemployment Rate, cause a quick and eruptive impact on the market. Stocks may sink or soar, depending on the numbers issued. In an explosive market, consider grabbing some or all of your profits the day *before* one of these reports are announced.

Check out *Barron's* weekly section, "Review and Preview," near the front of that periodical. You can see at a glance which reports are due out during the following week. The two-page section also shows consensus estimates, upcoming earnings numbers, and other important events.

Here is a partial list of economic indicators and a brief description of each:

✦ *Consumer Confidence Index (CCI)*. Figured by conducting a monthly survey that gauges consumer outlook concerning finances, the economy, employment, and plans to purchase expensive items. Since consumer optimism or negative perspective reflects in personal spending, which impacts the economy, this represents a leading indicator.

✦ *Consumer Price Index (CPI)*. Issued by the Bureau of Labor Statistics, this index indicates the change in prices on the consumer level. The CPI may influence salaries, social security payments, and pensions. It is a lagging indicator.

✦ *Durable Goods Orders Report*. Durable goods equals nonperishable goods that last for three years or more. Reported by the U.S. Department of Commerce, this report indicates whether businesses intend to invest capital for future needs. Since a shift in demand influences the need to purchase durable goods to expand capacity, it is regarded as a leading indicator.

✦ *Gross Domestic Product (GDP)*. Shows America's total output for a certain time period, taking into consideration all conclusive goods and services.

Reported quarterly, the GDP serves as the broadest indicator as to whether America's economy is expanding or contracting. It is a lagging indicator.

◆ *Housing Starts and Building Permits.* These numbers reflect new homes or units in a building for which a permit is issued. Historically, housing starts fall six months before the remainder of the economy, so this is considered a leading indicator.

◆ *Index of Leading Indicators.* Issued monthly by the U.S. Department of Commerce, this index consists of combined leading indicator statistics. It foretells the direction of the economy three to six months in the future.

◆ *National Association of Purchasing Managers Index (NAPM).* Based on a survey of purchasing managers from 300 companies, the monthly NAPM indicates economic direction three to six months in advance. When the index is above 50, the manufacturing sector indicates growth; a reading below 50 shows a decrease.

◆ *Non-farm Payrolls and Unemployment Rate.* The Bureau of Labor Statistics issues this report the first Friday of every month. It shows the number of non-farm jobs created in the U.S., subtracting jobs gained through attrition. The unemployment rate equals the number of unemployed workers who are unsuccessfully seeking jobs. Both Non-farm Payrolls and the Unemployment Rate influence the American public's confidence in the strength of the economy. Even though it is a lagging indicator, when these numbers come out, the stock market reacts emotionally.

◆ *Producer Price Index (PPI).* This index measures change in prices on the wholesale manufacturing level. The PPI comes out in the middle of the month, giving the previous month's data. The Bureau of Labor Statistics reports two numbers, the overall PPI and the core PPI, which excludes volatile food and energy prices. Because the PPI shows advance notice of price changes and thus inflationary pressures, it is a leading indicator.

Another "heads up" you'll want to remain aware of is earnings season. That's when publicly held companies issue quarterly earnings. Oh, boy, can earnings reports cause excitement!

Please do not hold a company overnight that's due to issue its earnings report after the closing bell rings. You may wake up to a stock that's gapped down big-time!

Further, if a giant bellwether is scheduled to announce, and you hold stock even remotely related to it, again close the position *before* the earnings announcement takes place. Why? Because in this age of volatility, when an industry leader so much as breathes funny, all related stocks faint in sympathy. Too many tech stocks depend on each other for integrated equipment and sales. When one gets woozy, they all get woozy. Smart traders take profits before the epidemic begins!

Another onerous market event that stymies new traders: A company reports good earnings. Result? The stock tanks. Rumors of good earnings sometimes leak out before the report becomes public. The stock may soar on the wings of that rumor for a few days leading up to the actual announcement. When the report comes out, since the stock's price has already factored in increased earnings, sellers take fast profits and the stock tumbles. Heed the trader adage, "Buy the rumor, sell the news."

OPTIONS EXPIRATION DAY—YOU'RE OUTTA' HERE!

Stock options contracts expire on the third Friday of every month. Also, on the third Friday of every third month (quarterly—March, June, September, and December), options expiration day is called "triple-witching day," because contracts expire on stocks, stock indexes, and futures.

On options expirations day, triple-witching or otherwise, avoid trading. You'll be glad you did. On this day—and sometimes a few days before—options players, arbitrageurs, and institutional managers shift their positions, causing erratic and irrational price moves. Breakouts/breakdowns fail and volatility reigns.

If you have open positions, check your automatic stop-losses, then take the day off. If you're in cash, you're worry-free.

FOMC REPORTS

Here's another opportunity to take the day off. Typically, the FOMC (Federal Open Market Committee) meets one day, then reports its decision to hike or lower interest rates two days later. On the day it reports, you may decide to take your account flat.

These days, "inflation" is on everyone's lips. Newscasts blare opinions galore of what Federal Reserve Chairman Alan Greenspan will do next, concerning interest rates. No wonder each time the Fed announcement comes out, the markets go bonkers!

I've seen the S&P futures crash on news of a rate *decrease*, taking stocks down with it. Now, we all know lower interest rates mean higher stock prices. So why would the market tank moments after a decrease in interest rates? Choose the *reason du jour,* depending on current sentiment. Whatever the rationale, you, as a savvy trader, will stand on the sidelines and let the bulls and bears duke it out. You can jump back in when the emotional frenzy subsides.

Before we leave this subject, let's talk briefly about inflation. This information gives you more ammunition for your "if, then" scenarios.

Inflation facts:

+ The top priority of each nation's central bank—ours is the Federal Reserve—is to keep inflation under control. As prices rise in a strong economy, each dollar earned becomes worth less because its power to purchase lessens. Without constant reigning in, inflation will strangle an economy.
+ The central bank controls inflation through monetary policy, meaning interest rates and money supply. Interest rates equate to the cost of borrowing money.
+ Stocks are vulnerable to inflation because (1) Each dollar earned by the underlying company buys less; (2) Rising interest rates means the company spends more money to borrow money; that adds higher costs to debt structure and affects future growth; (3) As interest rates rise, bond prices fall, attracting investors who want a safe, secure place to stow their money.

MOTHER MARKET'S CONTRARIAN INDICATORS

Few entities on the face of this earth are more moody and contrarian than the stock market. Seems she's never content with feeling too happy or too sad.

Still, with practice, you can anticipate her moods. All you have to do to in times of excessive euphoria or negativity is think backwards!

The next three indicators represent inverse sentiment. Translated, they suggest that excess optimism or excess pessimism in our markets eventually causes the opposite reaction. Keep an eye on them, especially when they shoot to extremes.

Bull/Bear Ratio

Investor's Intelligence in New Rochelle, New York, takes a weekly poll of investment advisers and publishes the Bull/Bear Ratio. CNBC routinely announces the Bull/Bear Ratio during market hours.

The poll scores how advisers feel about the stock market—bullish, bearish, or neutral. The ratio is calculated by dividing the number of bullish advisers by the number of bullish plus bearish advisers. (Neutral advisers don't count.)

Since it's a contrary indicator, the more bullish the advisers feel, the more bearish the indication. For example, *if* 55–60 percent of the advisers polled feel bullish, *then* that extreme optimism suggests the market is top-heavy and ready to fall. *If* the reading slides south to 40 percent showing extreme pessimism, *then* the Bull/Bear Ratio implies a bullish reversal is in the wind.

Bullish Consensus

These numbers, issued weekly, are based on a poll of newsletter writers published by Hadady Publications, in Pasadena, California. When 80 percent of newsletter writers wax bullish, the market is considered to be overbought and susceptible to a price decline. Readings below 30 percent imply an oversold market and are considered bullish.

CBOE (Chicago Board Options Exchange) Equity Put/Call Ratio

The CBOE Equity Put/Call Ratio tracks investors' trades in the options markets. It's calculated by dividing the volume of put options by the volume of call options. (Puts and calls are options contracts that give participant the right to sell—put—or buy—call—the underlying security at a specified price, during a specified time period.) Financial newspapers list the weekly ratios for the CBOE Equity Put/Call ratio. You'll also hear it mentioned on financial networks.

This also serves as a contrary sentiment indicator. The higher the options players' level of pessimism, the more bullish the outlook for the market. The lower the level of pessimism, the more bearish the outlook. For example, a reading in the Put/Call Ratio of .80 or higher is considered bullish. Bearish signals flash when the ratio reaches .30.

STAY TUNED TO CHANGING CONDITIONS

One of Steve Nison's favorite Japanese sayings goes, "To learn about the market, ask the market." It's important to stay updated on market conditions as they relate to world events. Know that a trading style that worked yesterday may not work tomorrow.

That's why many trading systems make profits for a while, then deliver a string of losses. Like our minds, they are programmed to react to certain stimulus and expect a certain result. When a different result takes place, the system tangles. (So do our brains.)

To succeed in this business, you must alter your trading techniques to fit the changing market. As a wise trader, you'll learn to keep an open mind on a 24/7 basis, and internalize market conditions. Sometimes you'll wander off-base. No problem. Before long, Mother Market will get your attention by smacking you upside the head!

As global markets become more and more connected to each other, the events that occur in one major economy influence others in a domino effect. Volatile situations cause our financial markets to roil. When a central bank, for example, fights to keep a country afloat, as Japan is doing right now, industry groups affected by our ties to Asia gyrate wildly, and traders find it difficult to stay on the right side of the market.

To bring this close to home, here's my personal rule: If I make two trades in a row that immediately go against me, I stop trading and re-evaluate market conditions. Then, I "get small." That's trader talk for reducing lot sizes, setting tight stops, and taking modest profits, to keep "green on the screen." When I feel once again tuned into market rhythms, I return to normal lot sizes.

A WORD ABOUT LOSSES

Everybody has losing streaks. Period. The trick is to recognize the symptoms, tie a tourniquet—fast—then learn from the experience.

Surely you've heard the definition of insanity: repeating the same actions over and over, while expecting different results!

So, again, when two trades in a row hand you losses, stop trading. Go to cash and take a couple of days vacation. Back up and look at overall market conditions. Try reading a financial newspaper or magazine outside of your usual reference area, to obtain a different viewpoint. The goal here is to refresh and rejuvenate. When you feel ready to return to the market scene, take baby steps and stay "small" for a while.

Along the same vein, if you've been on vacation, when you come back to trade, it's best to observe—without trading—for a few days. Soon you'll internalize current market rhythms, and you can fall back into step.

THE BEST GIFT TO GIVE YOURSELF: A TRADING JOURNAL

One of the best techniques to ensure your success as a trader is to keep a trading journal. I recommend this activity to everyone. It speeds you along the pathway to trading mastery by leaps and bounds.

Buy a high-quality bound notebook. Mine is green, the color of money. Record each trade (both winners and losers) in a short paragraph. Start with, "I entered this trade because . . . (glowing stock fundamentals, positive market and sector conditions, stock was oversold but bouncing off of 20-day MA, risk/reward ratio = one-point risk to five points reward, etc.)." Next, jot down the trade events briefly. Including when, and at what price you closed the trade, and why. Once a week, read over your journal entries. Does a common thread run through your trades?

Reward yourself for winning trades, no matter how small the profits (little profits add up to big profits). Next, evaluate the trades that went against you. What steps can you take if the same situation pops up? By learning from your mistakes, you turn your losers turn into winners!

LEVEL-II TRADING: IS IT FOR YOU?

Years ago, and before decimalization, the spread between the bid and ask on some stocks were wider than the Grand Canyon. It was not uncommon to see a point or more difference.

Novice active traders (myself included) found the bid yanked out from under us so fast it caused a lot of undue stress. (Imagine the chair you're sitting in right now suddenly jerked away so you fell to the floor—same feeling.)

In 1997, the availability of level-II quote screens and direct-access brokers brought transparency to the markets. Now individual traders could see how many participants lined up to buy the stock, how many shares they wanted, and at what price. Ditto for the sell side. Sure, the wide spreads still existed, but traders could evaluate the players, and sometimes, their intentions.

Now, traders could compete with specialists and market makers at their own game, entering orders to buy on the bid price and sell on the ask, which is the equivalent of buying at the wholesale price and selling at retail. And, since some active traders make from 100 to 2,000 trades per day—yes, you read that right— saving any increment of money adds up big-time for them!

Decimalization has changed the execution game. The ability to place orders in penny increments has lessened the spread between the bid and ask dramatically. Still, traders who use level-II order-entry systems offered by direct-access brokers, maintain more control over the entry and exit price of a trade than those who can only access level-I systems.

Direct-access systems with level-II quote screens are more complicated to use than the usual straightforward buy/sell screen with level-I quotes provided by online brokers. So, you guessed it—brokerages are in the process of developing hybrids. You'll soon issue buy/sell order for shares with ease, while enjoying the transparency afforded by the level-II screen.

Figure 14-1 displays a level-II screen. As you can see, those who want to buy Juniper Networks, Inc. (JNPR) line up in the left column. Those who want to sell wait on the right.

With the standard level I quote screen furnished by an online broker, the quotes for JNPR would read: 33.19 x 33.20. Typically, you'd place your order to buy at 33.20, which is the inside ask (offer) and the market price you'd receive if you get a fast fill.

With a direct-access account showing a level-II quote screen, however, you'd see that only 400 shares of JNPR are listed on the inside bid. The market maker Knight (NITE) is bidding to buy 100 shares (add two zeroes to "size" numbers) and Mayor Schweitzer (MASH) is bidding to buy 300 shares. In the ask (offer) column the Redibook ECN, Bloomberg ECN (BTRD), Island ECN (ISLD), and Instinet ECN (INCA) wait to sell 27,500 shares. That much selling pressure will surely lower JNPR's price in the short-term (seconds to minutes) to the next price level down on the bid, 33.15.

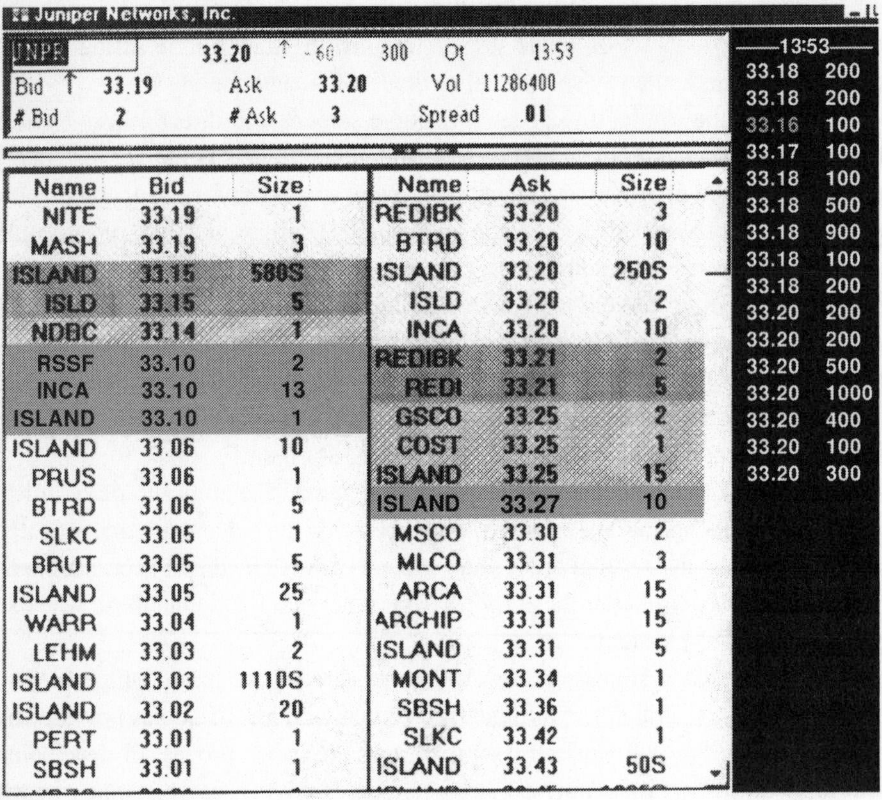

Figure 14-1.

Level-II screen, Juniper Networks, Inc. (JNPR).

RealTick graphics used with permission of Townsend Analytics, Ltd. ©1986–2002. All rights reserved.

At 33.15, the ECN Island waits to buy, with a large order of 58,000 shares. If it isn't offset by sellers on the ask (offer) side, that relatively large buy order should push JNPR's price higher, again on the short-term.

Bottom line, if you had a direct-access account with a level-II order-entry system, you could place your order to buy JNPR at 33.15, with a chance that your order would be filled .05 lower than the current inside ask (offer) of 33.20. That would save you .05 a share. On 1,000 shares, that's $50, which might cover the commissions.

Also, direct-access trading gives you the opportunity to exercise complete control over your entry and exit prices. Have you ever placed a limit order on your traditional online broker's order-entry screen, and not known for what seemed like a lifetime whether your order was filled or not? With direct-access order-entry screens, you watch your order get filled.

Consider your style of trading, and the number of trades you make per month. If you complete five trades or less, you may want to remain with your online broker's basic order-entry screen, using level I quotes. When/if you increase your trades to a higher number, check out the new hybrids of level I and direct-access (level II) order-entry systems that many brokers offer.

Congratulations! Now, I congratulate you. By absorbing this book in its entirety, you've come a long way in accomplishing your goal of becoming a consistently winning trader. Know that it takes guts and persistence to succeed in this field, but since you've made it this far, you'll surely make it the rest of the way!

Know that I'm with you 100 percent. If you have a question, go to my Web site, *www.toniturner.com*, and click on "Contact Us." I'll answer as soon as possible. So for now, I wish you the best of everything. Good luck, and keep those trades green!

QUIZ

1. Traders who use the _____, _____ line of thinking stay ahead of the pack.
2. Gold and the dollar have an _____ relationship.
3. The _____ market usually leads the stock market.
4. When bond prices fall, interest rates _____.
5. When oil prices rise, _____ (industry group) stocks may dive lower.
6. True or false? The best time to load up your account with stocks to hold overnight in swing trades is when the market is moving sideways.
7. The Bull/Bear Ratio, the Bullish Consensus, and the Put/Call ratio, when taken as a whole, suggest what theory?
8. Briefly explain the Advance/Decline Line.
9. On the day before the Non-farm Payrolls and Unemployment Rate report is issued, it's a good idea to take some profits off the table. Right?
10. When the underlying company of the stock you own is due to come out with earnings this evening after the market closes, you A) Buy up all the shares you can afford, and some for Aunt Bertha as well. B) Take your profits, sit back, and watch with interest.
11. On options expiration day, what is the correct way to trade?
12. Give one reason why stocks are vulnerable to inflation.
13. Why does keeping a journal contribute so greatly to your trading success?
14. What is the major reason for using level-II order-entry screens?

ANSWERS

1. If, then.
2. Inverse.
3. Treasury bond.
4. Fall.
5. Transportation.
6. Don't you dare say "true"!
7. As contrarian indicators, the Bull/Bear Ratio, Bullish Consensus, and Put/Call ratio suggest that when euphoria reigns, it's time to take profits and hide under the bed. When disgust and pessimism rule the day—cheer up; the silver lining will soon be shining!
8. The A/D Line (NYSE, Amex, and Nasdaq) is a line chart that measures the breadth of a stock market's advance or decline between the number of advancing and declining issues.
9. Absolutely right.
10. B is the correct answer.
11. You don't know the answer, because you have no intentions of placing a trade on options expiration day!
12. Stocks are vulnerable to inflation because rising interest rates means the company spends more money to borrow money, which adds higher costs to debt structure and affects future growth.
13. Keeping a trading journal speeds you on the pathway to success because you can spot winning and not-so-winning behavior quickly, and improve upon it.
14. Level-II order-entry screens give you control over your buy and sell orders.

✦ ✦ ✦

CENTER POINT

The source of all creation is pure consciousness . . . pure potentiality seeking expression from the unmanifest to the manifest.

—DEEPAK CHOPRA

Come Back to Center

Recently, I conversed with David, a top trader, about trading psychology.

"You know what's made me so successful?" He stared at me with his intense blue eyes. "There's a cascading fountain outside in the courtyard. Every morning, I take fifteen minutes to sit and focus on the water. When I feel myself relax, I imagine the trading day. I visualize myself buying and selling trades at the perfect point. I also see trades that go against my plan. I watch as I close the trade with no regret, only satisfaction at taking the right action. It's phenomenal how much these quiet times have increased my trading skills, and my bottom line!"

What a wonderful gift David gave me. He reminded me that for optimal performance, we need to return to our center point, our core essence. Here we can recharge our "energy batteries" from this powerful source that's always available. Taking some time each day to energize ourselves by connecting with our core being offers huge returns in physical, mental, and emotional health.

The process can be a simple one. Find a quiet place offering total solitude. Sit comfortably, arms and legs uncrossed. Close your eyes and concentrate on your breathing, letting all the tension flow out of your body. Now, imagine yourself entering a large, richly paneled elevator. As the doors close, you notice you are on the tenth floor. You push the first-floor button, then observe each button light up as the elevator descends . . . 9, 8, 7, 6, 5, 4, 3, 2, 1.

The doors open, and you step out into a lush garden. The sun shines warmly, and a breeze caresses your face. Brightly flowering trees and plants surround you. (If you prefer, create a tropical beach or mountain retreat—wherever you feel safe and happy.)

A chaise lounge rests in a corner of the garden. Go to it and lay down, sinking into the cushions. Closing your eyes, invite peace to flow through your body and mind. Then, gently visualize yourself going about your day calmly, effectively, purposefully. You give each person you meet a smile, pat on the back, words of encouragement. Or, you can visualize yourself placing trades calmly and with perfect actions, as David did. When you finish your imaginary day or scene, rise from the lounge, enter the elevator, and push the button for the tenth floor. Watch the buttons glow, from one to ten. As the elevator doors slide open, take deep breaths, smile, and welcome the day!

Try this process and note how your days are more productive, more enriched. When you begin from a position of strength, you can give more to your career, your loved ones, and yourself!

✦ ✦ ✦

Glossary of Trading and Financial Terms

Accumulation.

When a stock is being "accumulated," it may indicate that institutional buyers are acquiring stock. It also means buying pressure is increasing. Accumulation is usually evident by increased volume on a stock's chart.

Advance/Decline Line.

The number of declining issues on the NYSE subtracted from the number of advancing issues. The net difference is added to a running total if it's positive, or subtracted from a running total if negative. When the advance/decline line diverges from the Dow Jones Industrial Average or the S&P 500 Index, it gives an early indication of a possible trend change.

Arbitrage.

Arbitrageurs typically buy and sell two different but related financial instruments simultaneously. They profit from the spread created by the divergence. For example, if the S&P 500 Index rises, and the S&P futures fall, they sell short the cash index and buy the futures. *See* Program Trading.

Ascending Triangle.

A sideways consolidation pattern wherein the price range becomes progressively tighter and tighter (between two converging trendlines). The lower line rises while the upper line stays relatively horizontal. This pattern is usually bullish.

Ask.

The price at which a security is offered for sale. Also called "inside ask" or "offer," this is the lowest price for which a broker/dealer (or representative ECN) will sell a stock. It is the lowest price for which the customer can buy it.

Asset Allocation.

The process of designating how an investment portfolio will be divided among various classes of assets, including stocks, bonds, and cash. Risk levels of each asset should be deciding factors as to percentages of weighting (i.e., high-quality bonds are less risky than technology stocks).

Basket Trades.

Large transactions consisting of a number of different securities.

Bear Market.

Generally refers to the overall picture of the stock market when it's in a downtrend, and has fallen 20 percent or more off of its highs. Only short-sellers, and those in cash, experience a bear market without pain.

Beta.

A risk/reward measurement of a portfolio's past price fluctuations as compared to the overall market, or index. The market, or appropriate index, has a beta of 1.0. Therefore, a portfolio (mutual fund, etc.) with a beta of 1.20 would be expected to rise or fall 20 percent when the overall market rises or falls by 10 percent.

Bid.

The best, or lowest, price at which specialists (market makers) will buy a stock. Therefore, the "inside bid" is the best price the seller will receive for a security sold at the "market" price.

Big Board.

Refers to the popular nickname given to the New York Stock Exchange.

Block Trades.

Large transactions of a specific stock, bought or sold in units of 10,000 shares.

Blow-Off Top.

A volcano-like action when a stock explodes to the upside, then suddenly turns and drops back to the downside. May include an exhaustion gap.

Blue Chip Stocks.

The Dow Jones Industrial Average Index stocks are often called "blue chips." The name derives from poker, where the blue chip has the highest value. Blue chip companies typically produce upward growth and dividend payments, and are considered the icons of American industry.

Bond.

A type of loan, or IOU, issued by corporations, organizations, or governments in order to raise capital. The issuer makes regular interest payments and agrees to redeem the face value of the bond at a designated date, called the "maturity date." Bonds can be issued for thirty years or more.

Bracketing.

Sometimes used in the same context as a stock trading in a range. Therefore, the stock moves up and down, "bracketed" between a high and low price.

Breakaway Gap.

A price gap—to the upside or downside—that takes place subsequent to a significant price pattern. This gap may foretell a meaningful price move.

Broker-Dealer.

A securities firm that sells financial instruments to the public, may buy and sell stocks for institutions, and also trades its own accounts.

Buy-and-Hold.

A traditional, long-term investment strategy that focuses on the fundamentals of a company and ignores short-term market fluctuations.

Channel Line.

A straight line drawn parallel to the correlating trendline. In an uptrend, draw the channel line across the peaks of the highs. In a downtrend, draw the channel line connecting the pivot lows. Prices usually find resistance at the upper channel lines, and support on the lower channel lines.

Confirmation.

Occurs when technical signals agree with one another. For instance, when a breakout takes place together with strong volume, volume *confirms* the price rise. When signals move in opposite directions, it's called *divergence*, and the breakout or other assumed price action may fail.

Continuation Pattern.

A price pattern on a chart that indicates the prevailing trend is "resting" or consolidating. The most common continuation patterns are flags, pennants, and triangles. When the stock concludes one of these patterns, it typically resumes the prior trend.

Descending Triangle.

A sideways consolidation in a price pattern considered to be bearish. The upper resistance line declines, while the lower support line remains horizontal—thus forming two sides of a triangle.

Divergence.

This takes place on a chart when an indicator moves in the opposite, or different, direction than the price pattern. For example, the price may make a higher high, while the RSI (Relative Strength Index) or Stochastics hooks to the downside. When a divergence takes place, price reversal may soon occur in the direction of the indicator/oscillator.

Double Top.

This reversal pattern forms with two prominent peaks and resembles an "M." The reversal pattern is complete when it forms the final leg down and penetrates the middle pivot point of the "M." The predictive value is bearish. A double bottom is the reverse of the double top and resembles a "W." The indication is bullish.

Dow Theory.

One of Wall Street's oldest technical theories, the Dow Theory sends a "buy" signal when the Dow Jones Industrial Average and the Dow Transportation Average close above a prior high. Conversely, a "sell" signal is given when the averages, in tandem, close below a prior low.

Downtrend.
A price pattern used in technical analysis in which the stock, index, or market makes a series of lower highs and lower lows. The prevailing downtrend is broken when the price rises above the previous high, making a higher high.

Drawdown.
Loss of value in account equity.

Earnings.
A company's net revenue after deducting all expenses.

Earnings Growth Rate.
A company's average annual rate of earnings during the past five years.

Earnings Per Share.
Derived by dividing a company's earnings by the number of shares outstanding.

Efficient Market Theory.
This theory states that all known information is taken into consideration by the stock market and reflected in stock prices.

Electronic Communication Network (ECN).
Automated systems such as Island (ISLD), Archipelago (ARCA), Bloomberg (BTRD), SelectNet (NASD), Instinet (INCA), and Spear Leeds (REDI) that match orders and allow individual traders to present a price better than the current bid or ask (offer).

Elliot Wave Theory.
Originally introduced by Ralph Nelson Elliot in 1939. Using Fibonacci numbers, this theory holds that price patterns follow a paradigm of five waves up and three waves down (correction waves), forming a complete cycle of eight waves.

Equity Options.
Options traded on shares of a common stock.

Ex-Dividend.
The period of time between the announcement and payment of the next dividend. At the time a stock is trading ex-dividend, the buyer is not entitled to the dividend. Newspapers usually list stocks in ex-dividend with an "x."

Exhaustion Gap.

A price gap, or rising/falling window (candlestick terminology), that takes place at the conclusion of a trend, indicating that the trend is finished. This often happens in stocks that move up steeply during a short period of time.

Expiration Date.

Date on which an option, and the right to exercise it, expires.

Exponential Smoothing.

A moving average employing the same data as a simple moving average, but giving greater weight to recent price closes.

Fade.

To trade against the prevailing trend. For example, a trader who fades a gap up would short the stock. To fade a gap down, he or she would buy.

Failure Swing.

When prices fail to confirm a new low in a downtrend, or a new high in an uptrend.

Federal Open Market Committee (FOMC).

Policy-making arm of the Federal Reserve Board. This committee establishes monetary policy to comply with the Fed's objectives of regulating the money supply and credit. The FOMC's primary actions are the purchase and sale of government securities, which increase or decrease the money supply, respectively. The FOMC also meets every two months in order to regulate key interest rates, such as the discount rate.

Federal Reserve.

Also referred to as "the Fed," the Federal Reserve is the U.S. central bank that sets monetary policy. It oversees money supply, interest rates, and credit. Its objective is to maintain stability in the U.S. currency and economy, with emphasis on deterring inflation. Governed by a seven-member board, the system includes twelve regional Federal Reserve Banks, twenty-five branches, and all national and state banks that act as part of the system.

Fibonacci Numbers.

Originated by the twelfth-century Italian mathematician, Leonardo Fibonacci, these numbers follow a sequence in which each successive number equals the sum of the previous two numbers. The numbers begin: 1, 1, 2, 3, 5, 8, 13, 21, 34, 55, 89, 144, and so forth. Four popular Fibonacci studies are arcs, fans, retracements, and time zones. The lines created by the studies often act as support and resistance.

Fill.

The price at which your order to buy or sell a financial instrument is executed.

Flag.

A continuation price pattern displaying a sideways consolidation that slopes against the prevailing trend. Prices usually break out of this pattern and continue in the direction of the trend.

Fundamental Analysis.

The process of evaluating the financial condition of a company that issues common stock, using financial reports, price/earnings ratios, revenues, market share, etc. A large portion of fundamental analysis is based on supply and demand.

Futures (Futures Contract).

An agreement to purchase or sell a given quantity of a commodity (raw materials or metals), financial instrument, or currency at a specified date in the future.

Gap.

A space left in a price pattern where no trading occurred. A "gap up" takes place when a market/stock opens and continues to trade at higher price levels than the previous day's high. In candlestick terminology, this is referred to as a "rising window" and is bullish. A "gap down" occurs when a market/stock opens lower than the previous day's low and continues to trade lower, which is bearish. Three types of gaps are breakaway, runaway, and exhaustion.

Gross Domestic Product (GDP).

An economic report showing the value of all goods and services produced in the United States in a given time period.

Growth Stocks.

Stocks of companies that have shown brisk growth in sales or earnings. These equities typically offer little or no dividend yields and sell at high prices relative to their book value. Many high-technology stocks fall into this category.

Hard Right Edge.

The farthest right side of a price chart.

Head-and-Shoulders.

A reversal price pattern resembling a human head (the highest peak), with a shoulder on each side (lower peaks). If the price penetrates the horizontal neckline that connects the troughs (support areas), the pattern is complete and suggests the price will plunge lower. When the head-and-shoulders pattern forms upside down, it is called an inverse, or reverse head-and-shoulders.

Hedge.

A strategy used to limit portfolio losses. Usually, this is a transaction that goes opposite to existing positions. For example, a trader holding positions in tech stocks might sell short the QQQ (stock that represents the Nasdaq 100), sell short the same stocks in a different account, or buy puts (options) to reduce market risk.

High Bid.

When an offer appears on the bid that's higher than the previous bid.

In-the-Money.

A call option is in-the-money when the strike price is less than the market price of the underlying security. A put option is in-the-money when the strike price is greater than the market price of the underlying security.

Income.

Earnings from interest on bonds or corporate dividends.

Inflation Risk.

The possible eventuality that cost of living increases will reduce or eradicate investment returns.

Initial Public Offering (IPO).
A company's first, or initial, stock offering to the public.

Inside Day.
Easily noted on a chart, an inside day means the price range of one trading day takes place within the previous day's price range.

Inside Market or **Inside Price.**
Represents the lowest bid and highest ask (offer) price for an equity at a given moment.

Insider.
An officer/director of a corporation, an individual or family owning at least 10 percent of a company's stock, or anyone with access to nonpublic, "inside" information to that company. Insider transactions are regulated by Securities and Exchange Commission (SEC) Rule 144.

Instinet.
An ECN known for dealing with institutional orders.

Intra-day.
This refers to price movement that occurs during the course of a single trading day.

Intrinsic Value.
The dollar amount by which an option is in-the-money.

Island (ISLD).
A popular ECN.

Island Reversal.
A price pattern that begins with an exhaustion gap in one direction, and a breakaway gap in the opposite direction. The time frame between gaps is usually brief. The result is a few candlesticks standing alone on a chart, and may indicate a price reversal.

Key Reversal Day.

When a stock experiences an uptrend, a key reversal occurs when the price opens at a new high (over the prior day's high), then closes below the prior day's low. If a stock is in a downtrend, the stock price opens at a new low, then closes higher than the prior day's close. In candlestick terminology, these are "engulfing" patterns. The wider the range and the higher the volume, the stronger the chance that a trend reversal will occur.

Large Capitalization (Large Cap) Company.

A company that has a capitalization (shares outstanding multiplied by current stock price) of more than $5 billion.

Level I.

Quote information that shows only the current inside bid and ask (offer) prices. Other data displayed may include last trade price, volume, and intra-day high and low prices.

Level II.

Level-II quote screens show real-time, streaming displays of NYSE, Amex, and Nasdaq bids and offers. Typically, a Time and Sales screen accompanies the quotes, exhibiting current trade execution, lot size, and the time they took place.

Level III.

Level-III screens are used by exchange professionals and allow for "refreshing" inside bid and ask, or offer.

Limit Order.

An order to buy or sell stock at a specific price or better. Limit orders may be day orders, or GTC (good-till-canceled).

Liquidity.

When used in referencing stocks, good liquidity refers to a stock that trades with high-average daily volume. When used in reference to investments, most stocks are "liquid," meaning you can turn them into cash quickly. A home is considered an illiquid investment.

Listed Stocks.

Usually refers to stocks listed on the NYSE and Amex.

Long-Term Capital Gain.

A profit, or gain, taken on the sale of a stock or mutual fund that was held for more than one year.

Margin Account.

An account provided by a brokerage house that allows the customer to purchase equities by borrowing a portion (usually 50 percent) of the funds from that broker. Regulation T governs the amount of credit advanced by brokers to customers.

Margin Call.

When a margined account experiences a drawdown of more than a specified amount, the participating broker may issue a margin call to the customer, demanding that the customer immediately deposit funds to cover the call.

Margin Requirement.

The amount of money a trader/investor is required to maintain to cover a margined position. Most accounts are "marked to market" (adjusted to current price) each day, along with margin requirements.

Market Maker.

A broker/dealer who applies to the NASD and must agree to make a market in a particular Nasdaq stock. The market maker must hold the stock in his own account and participate on both the buy and sell side simultaneously.

Market Order.

Order to buy or sell at the best available price.

Market Value.

A company's shares outstanding multiplied by the price per share.

Mark-to-Market.

The process of adjusting equity prices held in an account to the present market value.

Moving Average (MA).

A line indicator used in technical analysis that works best when a market/stock is trending. This lagging indicator many times provides support or resistance for a stock's price pattern. A simple 50-day moving average is calculated by taking the sum of a stock's previous 50 closing prices, then dividing it by 50. As each new day is added, the oldest day is dropped from the calculation. Connecting the averages forms the line indicator. When a short averaging period (for example, 20-day) crosses a longer averaging period (50-day) and moves to the upside, the signal is bullish. When a longer average rolls over a shorter average and heads south, the signal is bearish. Technical analysts use simple, weighted, and exponentially smoothed moving averages.

National Association of Securities Dealers (NASD).

An organization of broker/dealers established to regulate and govern the Nasdaq Stock Market and to protect the investing public from deceptive acts.

Neckline.

The horizontal line that connects the troughs, or support zones, on the head-and-shoulders reversal price pattern. When the neckline is penetrated the head-and-shoulders pattern is complete. The line acts as support or resistance and gives buy and sell signals.

Net Assets.

Total liabilities subtracted from total assets.

Odd Lot.

Order to buy or sell less than 100 shares of stock.

Offer.

Identical to the "ask" price.

Offer Out.

The act of offering to sell a specified stock on "the offer," which if executed will give you a higher price than selling "at the market," or the best bid price.

On-Balance Volume (OBV).

A line indicator that shows if money is flowing into or out of a security by using volume. If the stock closes higher than the prior day's close, the total day's volume counts as up-volume. When the stock closes lower than the previous day's close, the day's total volume registers as down-volume.

Open Interest.

Measures the number of options or futures contracts that remain open (not liquidated) at the close of a trading day. As open interest rises and falls, it indicates money flow into or out of options or futures contracts, thus showing sentiment and liquidity.

Option.

A financial instrument that gives the owner the right to buy or sell shares of stock at a specified price, within a specified period of time.

Oscillator.

Technical analysis indicators that identify when a stock displays an overbought or oversold condition.

Out-of-the-Money.

A call option is out-of-the-money when the strike price is greater than the current market price of the underlying equity. A put option is out-of-the-money when the strike price is less than the current market price of the underlying equity.

Overbought.

Condition of a market/stock indicated by an oscillator. When a stock is overbought, it rises to the oscillator's upper zone and may encounter a sell-off.

Oversold.

Condition of a market/stock indicated by an oscillator. If a stock is oversold, it falls to the oscillator's lower zone, and may soon be ready to bounce.

Pattern Analysis.

The process used by technical analysts to evaluate price formations displayed on a chart, and to predict possible future trends.

Pennant.

A continuation price pattern resembling a flag. A pennant, however, looks like a symmetrical triangle and acts as a price "resting period" before it (usually) resumes its prior trend.

Pivot Point.

A price pattern in which a stock reverses direction. Identifying pivot points was a tactic used by early floor traders to determine support and resistance points without having to consult a chart. A stock may pivot when it encounters previous support or resistance.

Point.

Term used in stock market jargon that equals one dollar. If a share of stock rises "3 points," it's increased in value by $3.

Price/Book Ratio.

The price per share of a stock divided by its assigned book value per share.

Price/Earnings Ratio.

Ratio of an equity's present price to its per-share earnings during the past year. A stock's P/E indicates market expectations for a company's future growth. Therefore, equities referred to as "growth stocks" typically have higher P/E ratios than value stocks.

Program Trading.

Program trading usually defines the trading tactic used by arbitrageurs who trade index futures contracts against the cash indexes when a divergence takes place. *See* Arbitrage.

Put.

An option contract that gives the holder the right to sell an underlying stock at a specified price during a specified period of time.

Put/Call Ratio.

Ratio of volume in put options divided by the volume in call options. This is used as a contrary indicator. When the put/call ratio is high, the market is regarded as oversold, which is bullish. When the put/call ratio is low, the market is considered overbought, which has bearish implications.

Rally Top or **Rally High.**

Pivot point that takes place when a rising price pattern meets with supply and sells off.

Retracement.

When a stock experiences a strong price move to the upside or downside, the price will correct, or retrace, some part of that move before continuing the original trend. The 50-percent retracement is most commonly known. Technical analysts also use Elliot waves and Fibonacci retracements of 38, 50, and 62 percent.

Reversal Gap.

Price formation on a chart that takes place when the current day's low is above the prior day's high, and the current day's close is above the open.

Reversal Pattern.

Formations on a chart used by technical analysts that predict a trend reversal, or change, may soon occur. Common reversal patterns are double and triple tops, head-and-shoulders, and cup-with-handle.

Risk/Reward Ratio.

The process of measuring potential risk, or loss of capital, against potential reward, or gains.

Round Lot.

A unit or lot size usually consisting of 100 shares.

Rounding Bottom or **Saucer.**

Chart price pattern in which the stock gradually halts a downtrend, curves into a sideways movement (on low volume), then climbs back to higher prices—a bullish move. This formation can be seen in the cup portion of cup-with-handle patterns and reversed head-and-shoulders, as well as by itself.

Runaway Gap.

A price gap typically occurring midway in an uptrend or downtrend. Also called a "measuring gap."

Securities and Exchange Commission (SEC).

The government agency that regulates the U.S. stock and bond markets, registered investment advisors, broker/dealers, and mutual fund companies.

SelectNet.

An ECN supported by the NASD that matches orders.

Sentiment Indicator.
A psychological indicator that measures the degree of bullishness or bearishness in the stock market. Sentiment indicators act as contrary signals and work best in extreme overbought or oversold markets.

Share.
A unit of ownership issued to shareholders by a corporation.

Short Interest.
Shares of a financial instrument that have been sold short and not currently repurchased.

Short Sale.
The process of borrowing shares of stock from your broker, then selling them in the market with the intent of buying them back at a later time for a lower price. The spread between the price at which you sell the shares and the price at which you buy them back is your profit.

Short-Term Capital Gain.
The realized profit on the proceeds from the sale of stock or a mutual fund held for one year or less.

Simple Moving Average.
A moving average giving equal weight to each day's data (closing price).

Small Capitalization (Small Cap) Company.
A company that has a market value less than $500 million. Small-cap companies typically use profits for additional development and expansion projects in lieu of paying dividends.

Small Order Execution System (SOES).
Put in use in 1998 by the NASD. Used mainly by individual traders with direct-access accounts, it requires market makers to fulfill certain order requirements.

Specialist.
Assigned to a certain stock or stocks on the floors of NYSE and Amex, the specialist must ensure a fair and orderly market and fill orders out of his or her own account when no matching order exists.

Spread.

The difference between the bid and ask (offer) price.

Stock Index Futures.

Futures contracts traded based on the underlying stock index.

Stop or **Stop-Loss.**

A tactic to limit losses, a trader places a "stop," or "stop-loss" below (or above) his or her entry point in a stock. When that stop-loss is touched, the stock is sold (bought) at the next available price (as a market order).

Stop Order (Buy Stop or **Sell-Stop).**

Order placed to buy a stock at, or above, or sell at or below, the current market price. When the stop order is touched, it turns into a market order.

Support.

A price area where buyers support the stock sufficiently to hold the price up.

Symmetrical Triangle.

A consolidating price pattern that occurs between two trendlines sloping toward each other. The buying and selling pressure is even, but becomes more and more compacted. When the price breaks out, it usually resumes the prior trend and can be quite volatile.

Technical Analysis.

The study of market/stock action that utilizes charts displaying price patterns and volume. These charts and the indicators applied offer predictive price movements and trends.

Tick.

A minimum upward or downward movement in the price of an equity. An "uptick" takes place when the stock trades higher than the previous trade. A "downtick" occurs when a stock trades lower than the prior trade. A "zero-plus tick" means the stock makes an uptick on the prior trade, and then the current trade is executed at the same price.

Tick Index.

A short-term indicator that subtracts the number of stocks currently ticking down from the number of stocks ticking up. A reading above zero indicates bullishness, and a reading below zero indicates bearishness. Each exchange has its own Tick.

Ticker Symbol.

Capital letters that identify a security listed on the exchanges.

Time and Sales.

A ticker that usually runs in a column adjacent to a level-II screen and displays current trades by time, price, and lot size.

Trailing Stop.

A loss-control tactic in which you move your stop-loss up as your stock advances in price. If you've sold short, you move your trailing stop down as your stock falls in price.

Trend.

A price pattern revealing a strong move to the upside, or downside. An uptrend forms from a series of higher lows and higher highs. A downtrend forms from lower highs and lower lows.

Trendline.

A straight line connecting at least two pivot lows in an uptrend, or two highs in a downtrend. The more points connected, the stronger the trendline. When the price "breaks" a trendline, that trend is considered broken; a change in direction may soon take place.

Triangle.

Sideways consolidation pattern in which prices generally move between converging trendlines. Three types of triangles are ascending, descending, and symmetrical.

TRIN.

Originally developed by Richard Arms and sometimes called the Arms Index, the TRIN is an acronym for Traders Index. A short-term indicator often used in conjunction with the Tick, the TRIN is calculated by dividing the number of advancing issues/declining issues by advancing volume/declining volume.

Triple Top.

Price pattern featuring three highs in approximately the same price zone. When the pattern is completed, the indication is bearish. The "triple bottom" is the same pattern, upside down, and is considered bullish.

Volatility.

The measure of price ranges in a financial market or instrument. The wider the price range, the more volatile the market.

Volume.

Equals the number of shares traded for a specified time period. Volume is usually displayed as a histogram at the bottom of a chart. It gives important information to the technical analyst in interpreting price patterns.

Weighted Moving Average.

A moving average utilizing a specific time period, but giving greater weight to recent price data (closing prices).

Whipsaw.

When a trader enters both sides of a stock's price movement—both buying and selling short—and loses money on each trade.

Recommended Reading

Beyond Candlesticks: More Japanese Charting Techniques Revealed by Steve Nison. (John Wiley & Sons, October 1994)

How I Made $2,000,000 in the Stock Market by Nicolas Darvas. (Lyle Stuart, April 1986)

Japanese Candlestick Charting Techniques by Steve Nison. (Prentice-Hall Press, May 1991)

Reminiscences of a Stock Operator by Edwin Lefevre. (John Wiley & Sons, May 1994)

Secrets for Profiting in Bull and Bear Markets by Stan Weinstein. (McGraw-Hill, 1988)

Stock Market Wizards by Jack D. Schwager. (HarperBusiness, January 2001)

Stock Patterns for Day Trading by Barry Rudd. (Traders Press, April 1999)

Technical Analysis from A to Z by Steven B. Achelis. (Irwine Professional Publishing, 1995)

The New Market Wizards by Jack D. Schwager. (HarperBusiness, January 1994)

The Richest Man in Babylon by George S. Clason. (New American Library, reissue August 1997)

Trading for a Living by Dr. Alexander Elder. (John Wiley & Sons, March 1993)

Trading in the Zone by Mark Douglas. (Prentice-Hall Press, January 2001)

Trading to Win by Ari Kiev. (John Wiley & Sons, October 1998)

Index

A

A/D Line. See Advance/decline Line
Abelson, Alan, 50
Acceptance, 156
Accounting irregularities, 109, 204. See also
    Sell signals
Active Trader, 52
Adams, Brian, 133
Advance/decline Line (A/D Line), 240–241
American Stock Exchange, 3
how it works, 7
AMEX. See American Stock Exchange
Amgen, 74, 205
Anderson, Gary, 102
Appel, Gerald, 140
Applied Materials, 175
Appollinaire, Guillaume, 16
Asset allocation plan, 19. See also Capital

B

Bar charts. See also Charting
discussed, 75–76
Barron's, 50, 241
Bears, 9
A Beginner's Guide to Day Trading Online,
    15, 29, 64, 68, 160, 238
Beyond Candlesticks: More Japanese
    Charting Techniques (Nison), 77
Big Charts, 50
BigEasy Investor, 50
BigTrends.com, 50
Biogen, 205
Bloomberg, 49, 50
"Blue chip" stocks, 4–5, 7–8.
Bollinger Bands. See also Oscillators
discussed, 144–146
Bollinger, John, 144
Bonds, 203
Treasury bonds, 238
BOS. See Boston Stock Exchange
Boston Stock Exchange (BOS), 3
Bounce, 97, 135
"Bracketing," 102
Broker. See also Commissions

accounts, direct-access broker, 23–26,
    247–249
choosing
"old-fashioned" way, 21
online, 21–22, 209
"Bucket shops," 2–3
Bull/bear ratio, 244. See also Indicators
Bulls, 9
Business plan, preparing, 17
Buy signals. See also Charting; Indicators;
    Trades
fundamentals and IBD standards, 177
industry sector strength, 177
proper entry point, 187
reversal patterns, 173
Stochastic, 139
trigger list, 178–179
in uptrend, 96–100

C

Cable modem, 20
Candlestick charting. See also Charting
basic patterns, 77–80
doji, 78–79
hammer, 80
hanging man, 80
in general, 76–77
high-wave candlesticks, 87–90
short selling indicators, 210–211
spinning tops, 87–90
three-candlestick patterns, 84–87
evening star, 84
long-legged doji, 86
morning star, 84
two-candlestick patterns, 80–84
bullish piercing pattern, 82
dark cloud cover, 82
harami, 83
harami cross, 83
Capital. See also Cash; Money
allocating for trades, 185
asset allocation plan, 19
conserving, 29
Cash, 240. See also Capital; Money

CBOE. See Chicago Board of Options Exchange
CBOT. See Chicago Board of Trade
CBS Market Watch, 50
CCI. See Consumer Confidence Index
Center, 251
Center Point, 15
Change, 192
Charting
bar charts, 75–76
basics, 73–74, 157
Big Charts, 50
buy signals, 96–100
candlestick charting
basic patterns, 77–80
in general, 76–77
short selling indicators, 210–211
two-candlestick patterns, 80–84
congestion, trading in, 102–108
consolidation, trading in, 102–108
continuation patterns, 158–160
cycles, 55–57
components, 60–63
downtrend, 108–110
downtrend line, 114–115
in general, 26, 55
"averaging down," 59
"basing," 57–58
"break out," 58, 121
"hold up," 58
"nice spring day," 190
"roll over," 58, 102, 109–110
intra-day chart, 232
line charts, 74
range, trading in, 102–108
reactions to stages, 59–60
reversal patterns, 158
discussed, 160–174
sell signals, 110–114
short sell patterns, 204–205
stage analysis, 57–59
support and resistance, 63–69
uptrend, 93–96
buy signals, 96–100
uptrend line, 100–101
Chicago Board of Options Exchange, 3
Equity Put/Call Ratio, 245

Chicago Board of Trade (CBOT), 3
Chopra, Deepak, 198, 235, 251
Churchill, Winston, 43
Cisco Systems, 6, 205
Clarke, Arthur C., 43
Clason, George S., 30
CliffNotes, 240
CNBC, 49, 241
CnetNews.com, 50
CNN, 49
Commissions. See also Broker
discussed, 26–27
Commitment, 32
commodities, 3
Commodity Research Bureau, bonds and, 238
Commodities, 136
Computer, selecting, 20
Congestion. See also Charting
trading in, 102–108
Consolidation. See also Charting
continuation pattern, 159
definition, 104
trading in, 102–108
Consumer Confidence Index, 241
Consumer Price Index (CPI), 241
Continuation patterns. See also Charting
discussed, 158–160
triangle, 159
CPI. See Consumer Price Index
Crash of 1929, 2
discussed, 3–4
Crash of 1987, 4
CRB. See Commodity Research Bureau
Crisis, 194–195
Cycles. See also Charting
components of, 60–63
in general, 55–57

D

da Vinci, Leonardo, 43
DailyStocks.com, 50–51
Dell, 7
Detachment, security and, 235
The Disciplined Trader (Douglas), 33, 41
DJIA. See Dow Jones Industrial Average
Dollar, relation to gold, 238

Douglas, Mark, 33, 41
Dow, Charles, 49
Dow Jones Industrial Average, 5, 175, 216, 239
discussed, 7–8
Dow Jones Transportation Index, 5
Dow Jones Utility Index, 5
Downtrend. See also Charting; Uptrend
definition, 108
discussed, 108–110
downtrend line, 114–115
"molehill," 115
Dreams. See also Goals
goals and, 32
DSL, 20
Dubois, Charles, 218
Durable Goods Orders Report, 241
Dutch Bourse, 1

E

Earnings reports, 241–243
Einstein, Albert, 43
Emerson, Ralph Waldo, 92
Emotions. See also Mindset
greed and fear, 9–11, 13–14, 37, 38, 39, 60
hope, faith, optimism, 39, 187
mastering, 36
overcoming, 200–201
serenity, confidence, detachment, 40
Equity Portfolio Manager (Anderson), 102

F

Fairmark Press, 51
Fear, banishing, 218
Federal Open Market Committee, 238
reports, 243–244
Feelings. See Emotions
Fibonacci retracements, 187. See also
Oscillators
discussed, 146–147
Fibonacci summation sequence, 146
"Flight to safety," 203
FOMC. See Federal Open Market Committee
Forgiveness, 182
Fundamental analysis
in general, 47
vs. technical analysis, 46–47

Fundamentals. See also Trades
checking, 176–177

G

Galileo, 43
Gandhi, Mahatma, 43
Gaps. *See also* Oscillators
discussed, 147–153
breakaway gap, 149
exhaustion gap, 149, 150
runaway gap, 149
GDP. *See* Gross Domestic Product
General Electric, 4, 7, 23, 73
General Motors, 7, 73
GetSmart.com, 22
Giving, receiving and, 198
Goals. *See also* Potential
achieving, 17, 92
determining, 28–29
dreams and, 32
long-term, 29–30
short-term, 29
Gold, 203, 238
Gomez Advisors, 22
Granville, Joe, 141
Great Depression, 3
Greenspan, Alan, 35, 49, 237, 238
Gross Domestic Product (GDP), 241–242

H

Hadady Publications, 244
Harley-Davidson, 13
Hedging, short selling and, 215
Hogs, 9
HOLDRS, 215–216, 220
Homma, Munehisa, 76
Hoover's Online, 51
Housing starts/building permits, 242

I

IBD. *See Investor's Business Daily*
IBM, 7
Indecision, 61
indicators of, 79, 86, 122
Index of Leading Indicators, 242
Indexes

Dow Jones Industrial Average (DJIA), 7–8
Nasdaq 100 Index, 8
Nasdaq Composite Index, 8
NYSE Composite Index, 8
Russell 2000 Index, 9
Standard & Poor's 500 Index, 8
Wilshire Total Market Index, 8
Indicators, 74. *See also* Buy signals;
  Oscillators
  bull/bear ratio, 244
  bullish consensus, 244–245
  CBOE Equity Put/Call Ratio, 245
  common sense and, 178
  Consumer Confidence Index, 241
  Consumer Price Index, 241
  Durable Goods Orders Report, 241
  Gross Domestic Product, 241–242
  housing starts/building permits, 242
  Index of Leading Indicators, 242
  "lagging" indicators, 124
  leading industry selection, 175–176, 177
  moving average, 123–132
  National Association of Purchasing
    Managers Index, 242
  Non-farm payroll/unemployment, 242
  nothing *always* happens, 88–89
  Producer Price Index, 242
  unemployment, 242
  volume, 120–123
Industry sectors, choosing, 175–176, 220
Information. *See* Research
Intel, 6, 7, 175
Intermarket Technical Analysis (Murphy), 34
Internet access
  cable modem, 20
  DSL, 20
  ISDN line, 20
Introspection, 40
Investor's Business Daily, 47, 51, 171, 220
  proprietary corporate ratings, 48–49
Investor's Intelligence, 244
ISDN line, 20

J, L
Japanese Candlestick Charting Techniques
  (Nison), 77, 86

Journal, trading journal, 183, 184, 246
J.P. Morgan, 205
Juniper Networks, 222–232
Lane, Dr. George, 138
Lefevre, Edwin, 2
Level-II platform. *See also* Trades
  is it for you?, 246–249
  placing orders from, 209
Liber abaci (Pisano), 146
Limit orders, discussed, 193
Line charts. discussed, 74
Livermore, Jesse, 1, 2, 17, 33, 45, 55, 73, 93,
  119, 135, 157, 183, 199, 219, 237
Log, for recording trades, 183, 184, 246
Losses, 19, 104, 246

M
MA. *See* Moving average
MACD. *See* Moving average convergence-
  divergence
Magazines. *See also* Research
  for research, 52
"The Magical Work of the Soul," 72
Margin accounts, discussed, 28
Market capitalization (Market cap), 4
Market orders, 193
Micron Technology, 175
Microsoft, 6, 7
Microsoft Money Central, 51
Mindset. *See also* Emotions
  altering, 35
  "if-then" mindset, 238
  for prosperity, 72
  for winning, 37–40
Modem, cable modem, 20
Money. *See also* Capital; Price; Resources
  asset allocation plan, 19
  cash, 240
  characteristics of, 42
  "scared money," 19
  for trading, 18–19
Motley Fool, 51
Moving average (MA). *See also* Indicators
  discussed, 123–132
    200-day MA, 127–128
  short selling and, 208

Moving average convergence-divergence
discussed, 140–141
MACD Histogram, 141
Murphy, John, 34
Murray, W.H., 117

N

NAPM. *See* National Association of
Purchasing Managers Index
NASD. *See* National Association of
Securities Dealers
Nasdaq 100 Index, 8, 216, 239
Nasdaq Composite Index, 8, 175, 239
Nasdaq SmallCap Market, 6
Nasdaq Stock Market, 3
how it works, 6–7
National Association of Purchasing
Managers Index (NAPM), 242
National Association of Securities Dealers
(NASD), 3, 22
*New Concepts in Technical Trading
Systems* (Wilder), 136
New York Stock Exchange (NYSE)
history, 2–3
how it works in general, 4–5
role of trader, 5–6
NYSE Composite Index, 8
Nison, Steve, 77, 87, 151
Non-farm payroll, 242. *See also* Indicators
NYSE Composite Index, 8
NYSE. *See* New York Stock Exchange

O

OBV. *See* On-Balance Volume
Office equipment, selecting, 19–21
Oil, 203, 239
On-Balance Volume. See also Indicators;
Volume
discussed, 141–144
short selling and, 208
O'Neil, William, 47, 171
Oscillators, 74. *See also* Indicators
Bollinger Bands, 144–146
discussed, 135
overbought stock, 135
oversold, 135
Fibonacci retracements, 146–147

gaps, 147–153
Relative Strength Index, 136–138
stochastic oscillator, 138–139

P, Q

Pacific Stock Exchange (PSE), 3
Peoplesoft, 10
Perfection, 156
Philadelphia Stock Exchange, 3
PHLX. *See* Philadelphia Stock Exchange
Pisano, Leonardo, 146
Pogo, 36
Potential. *See also* Goals
achieving, 92
PPI. *See* Producer Price Index
Price. *See also* Charting; Money
relation to choice, 45
Price areas, 67
Producer Price Index (PPI), 242
Profits, goals for obtaining, 29–30
Prosperity mindset. *See also* Mindset
developing, 72
PSE. *See* Pacific Stock Exchange
Quicken.com, 51
Quote.com, 51

R

Ramtha, 54, 133
Range. *See also* Charting
trading in, 102–108
"bracketing," 102
Ratings, IBD SmartSelect ratings, 48–49
Relative Strength Index (RSI)
short selling and, 208
using, 136–138
Reminiscences of a Stock Operator
(Lefevre), 2
Research
fundamental vs. technical analysis, 46–47
magazines for, 52
sources for, 49–50
Web sites for, 50–52
Resistance and support. *See* Support and
resistance
Respect, 41
Responsibility, 41, 156, 182

Reversal patterns, 158. *See also* Charting
  cup-with-handle, 172
  double bottom, 164–166
  double top, 161–164
  in general, 160–161
  head-and-shoulders, 166–168
  intra-day reversal periods, 191–192
  in non-trending markets, 172–173
  reverse head-and-shoulders, 169–171
The Richest Man in Babylon (Clason), 30
"Right" and "wrong," 38
Risk, 19
Risk/reward ratio. *See also* Trades
  calculating, 185–187
RSI. *See* Relative Strength Index
Russell 2000 Index, 9

S

"Scaling in," 97
SEC. *See* Securities and Exchange
  Commission
Securities and Exchange Commission, 3
  Regulation FD, 3
Securities market, history, 2
Security, detachment and, 235
Self-respect, deservedness and, 41–42
Sell order, 193
Sell signals. *See also* Charting
  accounting irregularities, 109, 204
  discussed, 110–114
  "flight to safety," 203
  Stochastic, 139
Sell-stops, 194. *See also* Stop loss order;
  Trades
Sheep, 9
Short selling, 58, 60. *See also* Stop loss order
  chart patterns, 204–205
  in general, 199–200, 202–203
  indicators
    moving average, 208
    on-balance volume, 208
    Relative Strength Index, 208
    volume, 205–208
  mental and emotional blocks, 200–201
  process, 202
  rules, 201

  ticks, 202, 215–216
  Uptick Rule, 201
  short squeeze, 215
  strategy
    candlestick alternative, 210–211
    overextended double top, 211–213
    overextended stock, 209–211
  tips and FAQs, 215–216
  trigger list, 213–215
  what to look for, 203
Silicon Investor, 51
sixer.com, 51
Slippage, 193
  discussed, 27–28
SmartMoney.com, 51
"Spiders," 216
Spinoza, Baruch, 182
Spontaneity, 54
Stage analysis, charting and, 57–59
Standard & Poor's 500 Index, 8, 216, 239
Stochastic oscillator. *See also* Oscillators
  discussed, 138–139
Stock market, 14
  history, 1–3
  market is always right, 35–36
  perceptions about, 33
  price, as ruling factor, 45
  as unstructured entity, 34
Stock options, 243
StockCharts, 51
Stocks. *See also* Trades
  "blue chip," 4–5, 7–8
  "listed stocks," 4
Stocks & Commodities, 52
Stop loss order. *See also* Short selling
  buy stops, 193–194
  in general, 188–189
  placing your order, 208
    level-II platform, 209
    online broker, 209
  sell-stops, 194
  setting, 189, 209
  "trailing stop," 173, 188–189
TheStreet.com, 52
Stuyvesant, Gov. Peter, 1
Sun Microsystems, 23, 74
Supply and demand

discussed, 11–14
relation to greed and fear, 60–62
Support and resistance. *See also* Charting
  discussed, 63–69
    price areas, 67
  in downtrend, 111
  relation to congestion, 104
  in relation to gaps, 151
  relation to moving average, 125
Synchronicity, 117
Systems and Forecasts (Appel), 140

T

Technical analysis, vs. fundamental analysis,
  46–47
Technology stocks, 6. *See also* Stocks
Telephone, Internet access, 20
Thomson Investor Network, 52
Thoreau, Henry David, 32
Thoughts, as things, 133
"Ticker," 2
Ticks, 202
  short selling on downtick, 215–216
  Uptick Rule, 201, 202
Time commitment, considerations, 18
Trades. *See also* Buy signals; Stocks
  big picture dynamics, 174–175, 237
    advance/decline line, 240–241
    broader markets, analysis, 239
    flexibility and adaptability, 245–246
    trading environment assessment, 239–240
  buy stops, 193–194
  checking fundamentals, 176–177
  choosing stocks, 175–176
  crisis affecting, 194–195
  direct-access, 23–26, 247–249
  in general, 220
  how it works, 5–6
  Level-II platform
    is it for you?, 246–249
    placing orders from, 209
  limit orders, 193
  market orders, 193
  planning, 183–188, 190–191
  preparation, 220–222
  resources commitment, 185
  risk/reward ratio, 185–187

sel-stops, 194
TradingMarkets, 52
Transportation, Dow Jones Transportation
  Index, 5
Triangle pattern, 159.

U, V

Unemployment, 242. See also Indicators
Uptick Rule, 201, 202, 215–216
Uptrend. See also Charting; Downtrend
  buy signals, 96–100
  definition, 93
  discussed, 93–96
  trendline tips, 101
  uptrend line, 100–101
Utilities, Dow Jones Utility Index, 5
Volume. See also Indicators
  discussed, 120–123
  On-Balance Volume, 141–144, 208
  as short selling indicator, 205–208

W, Y

Wal-Mart, 73
Wall Street
  as "Animal House," 9
  history, 1–2
Wall Street Journal, 49
"Weekend Review," 220
Wilder, Welles, 136
Williamson, Marianne, 218
Wilshire Total Market Index, 8
Windows. See Gaps
Yahoo! Finance, 52
Young, Margaret, 156

START MAKING MONEY TRADING ONLINE TODAY!

A Beginner's Guide to Day Trading Online contains all the tools, tips, and secrets you'll need to succeed in the highly profitable world of day trading. You don't need to be an expert to get started using these step-by-step techniques, including:

- Setting up your home office with the right equipment
- Choosing an Internet broker
- Weighing the pros and cons of using a day-trading center
- Trading on margin – the right way
- Keeping a trading log
- Spotting easy chart patterns
- Winning Level II tactics

A Beginner's Guide to Day Trading Online is an interactive book, designed to help the reader get the most out of the book as quickly as possible. Each chapter ends with a quiz to reinforce the important topics. This unique book also includes Center Points, short passages inserted between chapters to add a psychological look at what it takes to be a day trader.

"Every new trader should buy *A Beginner's Guide to Day Trading Online*. Toni Turner takes a difficult subject—trading in the stock market—and makes it enjoyable and exciting to learn. I found the book to be highly compelling and a real page-turner. Don't start trading without it!"
–Fernando Gonzalez, co-author of *Strategies for the Online Day Trade*

Price: $15.95 (Canada $24.95)
Trim: 6" x 9 ¼", 288 pages
ISBN: 1-58062-272-0

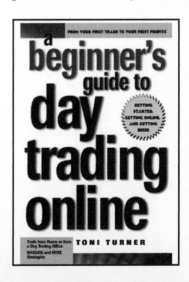

Available wherever books are sold.
For more information, or to order, call
1-800-872-5627 or visit *www.adamsmedia.com*
Adams Media Corporation, 57 Littlefield Street,
Avon, MA 02322